These two important and timely volumes in *Eros & Psyche: Existential Perspectives on Sexuality* are part of a sea change in views about sexuality within professional psychology. For decades, mainstream perspectives were implicitly—and sometimes explicitly— pathologizing of non-normative sexual orientations, desires, and behaviors. As these authors demonstrate, existential scholarship is uniquely positioned to shift the undercurrents of these views and to contribute to new understandings of the full spectrum of human sexuality. In doing so, the authors explore the meanings of human sexuality through all its nuances, ineffabilities, and complexities. At the forefront of a new era, this book will be of great value to practicing clinicians, scholars, and researchers alike.

Sarah Kamens, PhD, Editor-in-Chief, *Journal of Humanistic Psychology*; Editor, *Reconceptualizing Schizophrenia: The Phenomenology of Urhomelessnes*

Eros & Psyche: Existential Perspectives on Sexuality are two volumes that address erotic-sexual experiences through the lens of humanistic-existential psychological theory. These texts span philosophical and clinical issues on sexuality and a plurality of lived experiences of sexual attraction and pleasure, eroticism, gendering, as well as spirituality and religiosity regarding sex and desire—quite a feat, and such a joy, as the works are infused with exemplary scholarship to boot! What I like most of all is the recognition and affirmation of our diverse and embodied sexuality that these volumes inspire and, in doing so, provide an elucidation on a critical aspect of our lives that is often lost within jokes and euphemisms, ignorance, normative taboos, and, at times, covered over with guilt or shame. The works are perfect for undergraduate and graduate courses designed to address contemporary issues regarding the psychological life of human sensuality, attraction, sexuality, and love.

Robert McInerney, PhD, Professor of Psychology, Point Park University

Applying philosophical, spiritual, and clinical perspectives, *Eros and Psyche* explores the powerful, pervasive, collective, experiential, and existential reach of sexuality. The two volumes of *Eros and Psyche* are replete with evocative prompts for contextualizing and advancing the phenomenology of sexuality. The clinical insights offered are derived from serious consideration of the vulnerable subject matter and are generative sources for reflection on practice in the therapy room and in "the bedroom." The influential thinking in *Eros and Psyche* will evoke rich discussion on the intersections of worldview, identity, spirituality, and sexuality for years to come—as such, *Eros and Psyche* is set to be a seminal text on the expansiveness of sexuality for existentialists.

H. Luis Vargas, PhD, Full Professor, Regis University

Eros & Psyche:
Existential Perspectives on Sexuality

Volume 1: Philosophical & Theoretical Perspectives

Edited by
Stephen W. Simpson
Melissa M. Racho
Brent Dean Robbins
Louis Hoffman

University
PROFESSORS PRESS
Colorado Springs, CO
www.universityprofessorspress.com

Copyright © 2023 University Professors Press

Eros & Psyche: Existential Perspectives on Sexuality (Volume 1: Philosophical & Theoretical Perspectives)
Edited by Stephen W. Simpson, Melissa M. Racho, Brent Dean Robbins, & Louis Hoffman

ISBN (Hardcover):   978-1-955737-30-2
ISBN (Paperback):   978-1-955737-28-9
ISBN (Ebook):   978-1-955737-29-6

University Professors Press
Colorado Springs, CO
www.universityprofessorspress.com

Cover Image by Marguerite Laing
Cover Design adapted by Laura Ross

Table of Contents

Acknowledgments

Compiling an edited book is never an easy task; however, it was particularly challenging during COVID. We encountered numerous setbacks from life changes and challenges that happened during the pandemic. And encountered both death and life along the way. We are deeply appreciative that so many of the contributors persevered (and survived!) the challenges that they faced. In addition, we appreciate the patience exhibited by the editors and other contributors during myriad obstacles and delays. In the end, our deepest appreciation goes to the many brilliant and talented contributors who wrote the chapters of *Eros and Psyche*.

We also would like to thank two other people who were, at different times, part of our editorial team. The seeds of this volume began with a conversation between Bob McInerney and two of the editors of the book. Bob was instrumental in helping us construct the initial vision of the book. It is likely that without Bob this book would not have come to fruition. We deeply appreciate his energy and vision that created the initial spark that became *Eros and Psyche*.

We also would like to express our appreciation to Bethany Morris, who joined our editorial team for a period of time before needing to step down to focus on other priorities. Bethany helped advance the vision of *Eros and Psyche* and, for us, is still very much part of this book.

Steve thanks Melissa and Brent for welcoming me, despite my late arrival. I appreciate your patience and thoughtful scholarship throughout the process. I hope to work with each of you again! Thanks so much to our authors for their outstanding contributions, not to mention their enduring patience while these volumes meandered toward publication. Thanks also to my wife, Gently, and my children and stepchildren for love, fun, and remaining my bright source of existential purpose and meaning. And special thanks to Louis Hoffman for his significant contributions to these volumes and even greater contributions to our field.

Melissa has been humbled by the opportunity to aid in the creation of such a unique and rich volume of work under the guidance of three equally edifying and inspiring individuals and co-editors. I want to thank each of you for being mentors in the process of bringing what began as a shadowy idea into this fully developed bright and shiny collection of writings. To Louis Hoffman, my forever supervisor, thank you for your investment in my professional development, and for your steadfast confidence in and commitment to the potential in others. To my couples therapy patients, thank you for reminding me within every session of the magic that can occur when two individuals are committed to being committed to each other. On a personal note, my deepest thanks to past lovers who have taught me in the most experiential and poignant ways the stuff of which much of this volume is comprised. I'm thankful to each of you and the lessons imparted, as well as every moment shared—the glorious and the painful—while our lives were inextricably linked. Last, and with great reverence, thank you to my sons Mateo and Andrei for being such indelible expressions of love and of life. You are each an Adonis, I love you, and I cherish our life together more than I could ever express.

Brent is deeply grateful for the opportunity to collaborate with the co-editors on this volume. Louis, Steve, and Melissa have been a pleasure to work with. Beyond those key figures mentioned above, my friends and colleagues Bob McInerney and Bethany Morris played important roles in the development of this text, and I thank them for their involvement at different stages of the project. I am also grateful for Division 32, the Society for Humanistic Psychology, and the many professional relationships and friendships that have emerged over the years from that organization; it has given fruit to many projects, including this one. I also know that whenever I take on extra scholarly projects, this has a tendency to take time that I might otherwise spend with my family. My contribution here would not be possible without the enormous support of my wonderful wife of 26 years, April Robbins. I also dedicate this book to my two sons, Dean and Dominic. Last but not least, I offer the joys and struggles of this project to God, whose grace alone can transform our flawed strivings into blessings.

Louis, first of all, is appreciative of the co-editors of this volume. I have long believed that collaborating on projects such as this can be a powerful way of deepening relationships. We had to persevere through more changes and challenges with this book than any of the many books I have been part of editing. Steve, Melissa, and Brent—I deeply appreciate all three of you and feel blessed to have been able to work with you on this project. As Yaqui Martínez once noted, writing is always a "we." The more I write, the more I believe this to be true. Ideas are forged through dialogue and relationship, meaning they are never truly ours alone. Therefore, I always feel there are many people to thank. Yet, I will try to be brief in naming several people who were most influential in the ideas I brought to this book and those who have been supportive of me through the journey of this book: Nathaniel Granger, Jr., H. Luis Vargas, Michael Moats, Lisa Xochitl Vallejos, and Francis Kaklauskas. Two of my former teachers and supervisors were very influential in my personal development related to the topics of this book: AnnElise Parkhurst and Jeff Bjork. Last, I want to thank my family, who continue to be my deepest inspiration and support: Heatherlyn, Lakoda, Lukaya, and Lyon. I love you with all that I am.

Introduction

Stephen W. Simpson

Sexuality is a potent existential agitator. It elicits some of the most vulnerable, exciting, and frightening aspects of human experience. Sexuality defines identity in direct and indirect ways. The direct ways are obvious: sexual orientation, gender, attraction, arousal, and sexual behaviors compose a substantial part of selfhood and relationships. Reproduction (usually) requires sex; human life cannot exist without sex. The indirect ways are less obvious, but equally potent. Sexuality influences and collides with politics, law, morality, religious beliefs, cultural norms, family dynamics, fashion, art, and relationships of every variety. An indicator of sexuality's existential importance is the extent to which people remain in denial about sex, just as they remain in denial about death. Like death, sexuality is splattered across popular entertainment and news media but remains a frightening and difficult subject on an individual and relational level. Like death, sex is a part of life in a way that most people prefer not to consider or discuss. In this book, the authors invite readers to stare into a different abyss, one less frightening than death but just as often avoided.

Sexuality is so powerful because its meaning and influence run deep and wide. Sexuality can be a source of pleasure because of its potent physiology. It can be a source of pain because of the shame rooted in everything from self-image to social norms to religious beliefs. To be sexually "different" means being outside a culture's beliefs and practices, which results in isolation and shame. As Sara Bridges and Chandler Batchelor state in Chapter 5 of this volume, titled "Growth through Regret," "Sexual choices can be fraught with judgments, both external and internal. Again and again, Western culture catches people between messages of sex positivity and pleasure and messages of modesty and caution." For example, the impact of sexuality is so pervasive that finding someone sexually attractive, depending on the individual and their context, can be neutral, problematic, or exciting. "The embodiment of sex is an experiential process which fluctuates from moment to moment," says Joel Vos in "Phenomenology in the Bedroom" (Chapter 1 of this volume), "bringing joys and highs, enjoyment and frustrations." Few things are both as personal and public as sexuality. On the personal level, sexuality is "both a reminder of death and source of self-esteem," as McKenzie Lockett and Tom Pyszczynski put it in their chapter on a terror management perspective on sexuality (Volume 2, Chapter 3). On the public level, sexuality impacts everything from religion to pop culture to laws about sexual behavior. Sexuality is in us physically, psychologically, and spiritually, and all around us communally, culturally, legally, and religiously. It is at the center of life, individually and collectively.

Sexuality is far more collective than the norms of Western culture suggest. While sex is often portrayed as a personal issue, individual beliefs and practices result from a collective human experience. The Bible verse 1 Corinthians 6:19 (English Standard Version) is regularly cited to admonish an individual to observe "pure" sexual behavior: "Or do you not know that your body is a temple of the Holy Spirit within you, whom you have from God? You are not your own." However, in the original Greek, the "you" is plural. The Biblical author is saying that "all of your bodies together" are a temple. Sexuality is collective in many ways—from dyadic sexual behavior to the cultural norms of large populations to the laws related to governing those large populations. Many chapters in this book address symbolic interactionism, examining how the language and symbols of everyday life shape both collective and individual sexual experience. Krippner, Cooper, and Speer in Chapter 4 on sexuality and the arts describe sexuality as a creative process influenced by symbolism from a collective human consciousness. Approaching sexuality as a functional, individual phenomenon fails to recognize the symbolic, structural, systemic, and cultural ways that our sexual consciousness is collective. This is one of the reasons that Micah Ingle, in Chapter 6, "Eros and Shame: A theoretical autoethnography on group work and masculinity," encourages group instead of individual therapy for men, saying "group work provides an opportunity for re-formulation of subjectivity in the context of group communal life away from . . . isolated alienation.

This collective, culturally embedded nature of sexuality can function in ways that are both positive and problematic. A collective sense of sexuality can create a sense of community and support for those who follow sexual norms, while resulting in isolation and feelings of alienation for those on the margins. This is evident in the psychological and social struggles of queer and trans persons. In Chapter 2 of this volume, which offers a functionalist approach to gender-addressing tensions between humanistic and queer/trans theories, Levitt, Collins, and Morill examine, among other things, how to combine individual self-exploration for LGBTQIA+ persons with communal and symbolic experiences in response to a history of marginalization. Indeed, LGBTQIA+ persons have little to no communal experience of sexual identity formation until they self-identify ("come out") and seek a shared experience of sexual development that cisgender heterosexuals take for granted. In a chapter about LGBTQIA+ persons in Evangelical Christianity (Volume 2, Chapter 9), I examine the deep cultural influence that religion has on identity development. Queer Evangelicals have part of their identity rooted in a culture that rejects any expression of their sexuality. The process of extricating their identity from the Evangelical community can be difficult, if not impossible. For LGBTIA+ persons, the collective aspect of their sexuality can be cumbersome and confusing in a way that may be difficult for cisgender heterosexual allies, including mental health professionals, to understand.

Individualized medical-model approaches to sexuality and sexual problems fail to account for the complex existential, cultural, and interpersonal dimensions of sexuality. Most Western approaches to sexual disorders focus techniques to reduce distress and improve functioning. While these are worthwhile goals, treatment of sexual disorders often bypasses the meaning associated with sexual problems. The functional/biological emphasis can rob sex of its existential significance by forgetting that sex draws out and upon key aspects of the human experience such as self-image, love, and attachment. As Melissa Racho points out in her chapter about couples treatment, "Romantic love, through an evolutionary lens, is merely a mammalian system that directs mate choice and reproduction . . . to distill and define something as lustrous and inspired as romantic love tends to strip it of heart, and seems in some way heretical" (Volume 2, Chapter 1). Likewise, Joel Vos, in Chapter 1 of this volume, describes how a phenomenological approach addresses meanings associated with sexual problems that a materialistic/functional approach might miss: "The key phenomenological question is to what extent we are aware of the imaginary and symbolic meanings that sex may have for individuals, and to what extent they are able to let go of these meanings and be in the flow of experiencing the present." Susi Ferrarello (Volume 2, Chapter 5,) describes the unique challenges of narcissism to a present, meaningful experience of sexuality and embodiment. This contrasts with Peggy Kleinplatz's description of "extraordinary lovers" in her and Maxine Charest's chapter "Optimal Erotic Intimacy" (Volume 2, Chapter 4). Unlike the narcissistic, shameful, disembodied experience, Kleinplatz says that "extraordinary lovers are so embodied and centered within that they can connect easily during erotic encounters without fears of losing the self in the process." She says that manualized, one-size-fits all treatment for sexual disorders "stops too soon and settles for too little" (Kleinplatz, 2012, p. 108). Sexual behaviors have meanings that can take the client on a journey toward deeper meaning and self-awareness. Avoiding the existential dimensions of sexual problems can result in simplistic, incomplete treatment.

Alienation from the body lies at the root of many sexual problems, from diagnosable sexual disorders to broader forms of body rejection that result in lower self-worth (see May, 1969). Western medical-model approaches often treat the body as a machine, a thing to be wrangled and repaired, rather than part of a full human experience. Both science and religion objectify the body. Even existentialism, with its emphasis on the philosophical, at times can shortchange embodiment for intellectual contemplation. As Vos says in Chapter 1, the "evolutionary goal (telos) seems to be totally explained in materialistic and functionalistic terms and does not seem to do justice to the subjectively lived experience of sex." Many sex therapists and "sexologists" focus on technique to the exclusion of holistic, embodied approaches. "This focus on technique paradoxically culminates in sense of alienation, loneliness, and depersonalization as sex becomes increasingly mechanized," claims Brent Robbins in Chapter 3, "The Erotic in Anesthetic Culture" of this volume. "While the culture remains preoccupied with sex," says Robbins, "the actual experience of the sexual act has suffered from diminished passion." Any existential approach to sexuality cannot fall into the trap of treating the material body as a functional object divorced from a fully embodied human experience.

Religion can also promote a disembodied experience of sexuality. Christianity, in particular, influenced by Greek metaphysical idealism, has a tendency to denigrate "sinful flesh" of the body in pursuit of an incorporeal spiritual telos. As Nisha Gupta points out in Volume 2, Chapter 6, "Finding God in the Bedroom," the Old Testament and Eastern religions, in contrast to Western Christianity, extol a more embodied approach to sexuality as a form of "sacred goodness." Their sacred texts discuss erotic pleasure as bestowed by God or even a pathway to the divine. This provides an existential redemption of sexual pleasure by making it sacred. If this is a challenge for cisgender heterosexual religious persons, it can feel almost impossible for LGBTQIA+ religious persons. Devout religious persons absorb their faith in their identity as part of their culture. Their faith does not consist of freely chosen religious beliefs that they can easily discard. Evangelical LGBTQIA+ persons, for example, risk losing a core aspect of their identity if they leave their faith. Their sexuality must remain hidden or dormant, disembodied and separate from their identity, if they are to remain part of their religious culture. This results in "splitting" the body from the mind and soul, treating non-cisgender and non-heterosexual feelings as something impure and broken. As I (Stephen Simpson) discuss in my Volume 2 chapter on LGBTQIA+ Evangelicals, this spirit/body schism is often too difficult to repair and requires cultural empathy from a therapist. Nwahchi Pressley-Tafari, in a chapter filled with poetry (Volume 2, Chapter 7), chronicles his journey away from being a "Good Black Man" with disembodied sexuality toward an embodied "Radical Ecstasy" by exploring "shadow" experiences such as fetishes and BDSM. He integrates spirituality and sexuality and finds his "ontological soul" through the process of Mythic Inquiry. The traditional, Western paths of "righteousness" inhibited such transformation. Though, as Gupta points out, Jewish tradition and Eastern religions often find the sacred and sexuality, Western Christianity treats sexuality too often as a burden rather than a gift. "Catholic guilt becomes such an ingrained and ever-present voice inside a person's head;" says Ana Wilhem in "Catholic Guilt and Femininity" (Volume 2, Chapter 8), "the moralistic teachings becoming part of the individual's life throughout their formative, exploratory years of puberty and blossoming sexuality." Our authors explore existential approaches to integrating faith and sexuality in ways that remove the burden of shame.

Eros & Psyche follows a long tradition of existential psychology being on the cutting edge of new and progressive perspectives on sexuality. For example, Medard Boss, the existential psychiatrist and founder of the first school of existential psychotherapy known as Daseinsanalysis, was one of the very first European psychiatrists to courageously write and speak publicly in support of a transgender patient's desire to transition. It was only the early 1950s, a full 20 years before Stonewall, that he did so on the basis of his patient's right as an individual to realize his own most authentic being (Erik Craig, personal communication).

This book is divided into three sections across two volumes. The first volume focuses on Philosophical Perspectives, while the second volume encompasses Clinical and Spiritual Perspectives. Readers will notice that many chapters would fit comfortably in multiple sections. This should be no surprise. Sexuality pervades so many aspects of life that any discussion will be relevant across multiple domains. Existential thought, too, emphasizes the interconnection of experience, including the philosophical/theoretical and applied. Yet, the interconnectedness is not without strain. The perpetual tension between the theoretical, clinical, and spiritual is even more pronounced when delving into the existential dimensions of sexuality. Any existential exploration of sexuality will be necessarily wide ranging, and each chapter reflects this. Sexuality shows up everywhere, from the philosophers' study to the therapist's office to houses of worship. It is foundational to existence and warrants investigation across disciplines and every domain of human experience.

References

Kleinplatz, P. (2012). Is that all there is? A new critique of the goals of sex therapy. In P. Kleinplatz (Ed.), *New directions in sex therapy: Innovations and alternatives* (2nd ed.; pp. 101-118). Routledge.

May, R. (1969). *Love and will*. Delta.

Philosophical & Theoretical Perspectives

Chapter 1

Phenomenology in the Bedroom:
How Martin Heidegger and Michel Foucault
Could Reinvigorate Your Sex Life

Joel Vos

Abstract

Phenomenology is the study of how phenomena appear in our consciousness. This chapter examines how sex appears in our awareness. Phenomenology does not tell what sex is or should be for each individual, but it asks a multiplicity of questions to which each individual can give their own answer. Therefore, this chapter will ask ten phenomenological questions about sex. These questions have been derived from Structural Pragmatic Phenomenological Analysis (SPPA), which is based on works of Heidegger, Foucault, and other phenomenological–existential philosophers. How real is a sexual experience, or is it merely imagination and symbols? What meaning does sex have, who is involved, and how do we relate? How do individuals develop their sexuality, and how much freedom do they experience? What is the historical and cultural context of their sex experiences? Why do people have sex? Which impact does sex have on daily life? Each individual will give their own unique answers to these questions. For example, sexual experiences could have physical, hedonistic, self-oriented, social, larger, and existential–philosophical meanings for individuals. People could relate to sex from a traditional or merely functionalistic perspective, or they could be submerged in the flow of experiencing sex in the here-and-now. We can approach our sex partner as a mere sex object (I–It relationship), or as another human being (I–Thou relationship). This phenomenological framework is used to explain a range of variations in sexual experiences, such as the culture of consent, sex work, sex addiction, and BDSM. The chapter will finish with an explanation of how existential therapists may use these ten questions to help clients with sexual problems.

***

Philosophy books and our sex life do not appear to easily go together. Most people do not seem to think about philosophers as humans with a full emotional life that includes sexual desires. Similarly, you may have frowned or giggled about the title of this chapter. You may have experienced an intellectual short-circuit by the mere thought of combining the philosophers Heidegger and Foucault with the experience of sex. Of course, Heidegger has written much about the body, particularly about being-toward-death, and Foucault wrote about the history of sexuality. However, we usually see Heidegger and Foucault from a theoretical perspective and not from the perspective of some of our most personal experiences in life: our personal sexual experiences. This goes precisely to the heart of phenomenology: How do phenomena such as thinkers and sex appear in our consciousness? Whereas we most likely relate to philosophers in a theoretical, reflective way, we may relate to our sex life in an emotional way—a subjectively lived experience that may go beyond any philosophies, theories, or even the words from romantic poets. This chapter aims to examine how sex appears in our awareness, using the phenomenological method from philosophers such as Heidegger and Foucault.

Phenomenology does not tell what sex is or should be for each individual but asks a multiplicity of questions to which each individual can give their own answer (Vos, 2020a, 2020b). For example, the phenomenologist avant-la-lettre Aristotle (2019) proposed a system of four questions, which he asked about a phenomenon: *What* is the matter or material (*hyle*) of the phenomenon; *how* is the form, shape, or appearance (*eidos*); *who* is the individual who created the phenomenon (*kinoun*); and *for what* is the sake for which the phenomenon is what it is (*telos*; Heidegger, 1995; Hankinson, 2001). The philosopher Heidegger (1914) argued that modern scientists, psychologists in particular, seem to have forgotten to ask all four questions about phenomena. Instead, they usually only ask *what* something is and *by whom* is this created, resulting in an obsession with functional efficiency and physical achievement (Vos, 2020a). Aristotle's questions about how and for what a phenomenon exists seem to be answered merely in terms of materialism and efficiency (Visser, 1989). Applied to sex, popular media and magazines seem to focus dominantly on body shapes and sizes and on sexual performance. From a young age onward, people in modern western societies seem to be continuously exposed to eroticized advertisements, images, and symbols in magazines, movies, TV series, and the internet, which implicitly tell us what our sexual looks and behavior should be.

In contrast, the two other Aristotelean questions seem to receive less attention: *how* we relate to the other person and *for which purpose* we have sex. Sex can, for example, be more than working as efficiently as possible toward a goal like orgasm. The full satisfaction (*eudaimonia*) that sex may bring could also reach beyond the mere physical act of an individual; it may involve a relationship or physical–emotional union with another human being who freely shares their body and emotions.

Methodology

In contrast with our modern focus on materialism and efficiency, Heidegger wanted to understand the totality of our subjectively lived experience of phenomena. Toward this end, he asked many questions about each phenomenon, beginning with Aristotle's four questions and extending them with other existential questions. In total, we may at least identify ten possible questions about a phenomenon (Vos, 2020a, 2020b). These questions highlight ten different perspectives from which we can look at a phenomenon, as if casting light at a diamond from different angles. Each different angle will make us see different facets of the diamond; only by combining the lights from multiple angles can we see multiple facets of the phenomenon and develop an understanding of the dynamic and complex totality of a phenomenon. Table 1 provides an overview of the ten questions that we will ask. These questions have been derived from Structural Pragmatic Phenomenological Analysis (SPPA) (Vos, 2020b). This chapter will describe each question, followed by a phenomenological analysis of a variety of sexual examples and will finish with suggestions for existential psychotherapy for clients with sexual problems.

How Real Is a Sexual Experience, or Is It Merely Imagination and Symbols?

What is the ontological status of a sexual experience? That is: Is sex about our immediate experiences of reality, the here-and-now, or is sex merely our imagination, the product of expectations and fantasies? Or does sex symbolize something else for us, such as having power over an individual or distracting ourselves from our boring or challenging daily life? Psychoanalyst Jacques Lacan (2006) noted a difference between Reality and reality, suggesting the latter (reality) is our symbolic and imagined construction of what Reality may look like. In our daily experiences and interactions, we often use symbols and imagination. However, problems may arise when individuals conflate imagination and symbols with Reality, and when individuals lose touch with Reality.

The key phenomenological question involves the extent to which we are aware of the imaginary and symbolic meanings that sex may have for individuals and the extent to which we are able to let go of these meanings and be in the flow of experiencing the present. For example, how much are we in tune with our in-the-moment experiences when we are having sex? Are we present, or are we focused on our fantasies? Is our sexual awareness anchored in our whole body? Formulated with Merleau-Ponty (1982): To what extent are we able to overcome the inauthentic split between our mind and our body, and simply be flesh?

Table 1. Ten Phenomenological Questions (inspired by Vos, 2020b)

Formal name	Applied question	Formal examples
Ontological status	How real is a sexual experience, or is it merely imagination and symbols?	Reality Symbol Imagination
Type of meaning	What meaning does sex have?	Materialistic Hedonistic Self-oriented Social Larger Existential–philosophical
Approach to meaning	How does an individual approach sex?	Traditional Functional Phenomenological (also called critical–intuitive)
Relationship between individual and society	Where in society does an individual experience sex?	Social determinism Social individual interactionism Individual determinism
Development over time (social history)	When in history does an individual experience sex?	Historiography Historiology
Emergence of individual meaning (individual history)	Who develops sexual experiences?	Psychology Pedagogy Anthropology
Sense of freedom	Whose freedom does sex involve?	Symbolic vs realized freedom Negative vs positive freedom Individual vs structural freedom
Existential well-being	Why do individuals have sex?	Existential questions/concerns Realistic sense of freedom and limitations
Impact on daily life	What impact do sexual experiences have on daily life?	Mental health problems Quality of life Life satisfaction

Thus, a full embodied experience of sex does not seem to be merely about an imaginary or symbolic object, theory, goal, or a fixed emotional state: The embodiment of sex is an experiential process that fluctuates from moment to moment, bringing lows and highs, enjoyment, and frustrations. A fully embodied approach to sexuality also implies that we temporarily put aside our expectations about happiness, satisfaction, and other emotions as a possible end goal. We bracket these assumptions. The only goal is to experience whatever reveals itself in the sexual encounter with oneself and/or the other. When we follow our phenomenological intuition, we open ourselves for ourselves and the other person in all our experiences, vulnerabilities, sensitivities, and sensibilities.

What Meanings Can Sex Have?

One hundred and seven research studies involving more than 45,000 participants worldwide have identified that individuals may experience six types of meaning in life (Vos, 2020a, 2017 2016): materialistic, hedonistic, self-oriented, social, larger, and existential-philosophical. This evidence-based sextet seems to be in line with the theoretical models of phenomenologists. For example, in the tradition of Heidegger and Binswanger, Van Deurzen (2014) identifies physical, personal, social, and spiritual worlds, and Laengle (2013) identifies life, world, self and meaning.

What symbolic or imaginary meanings can sex have for individuals? Sex can have a mere physical meaning, for example regarding the physical act, biomedical theories, and the evolutionary drive of reproduction. Hedonism means that individuals enjoy sex for the sake of enjoyment, as it provides them with nice experiences. Research suggests that sex may be one of the most intense emotions that individuals experience and is associated with the release of what has been dubbed "happiness hormones and neurotransmitters" (Hyde, 2005). Sexual experiences may also have self-oriented meanings, such as enjoying one's own body, self-care, feeling validated. and improving one's self-esteem. Sex can also have the social meanings of connecting, caring, helping others, or procreation to bring new life into the social world and look after children. Larger meanings are, for example, about experiencing sex as a self-transcending religious or spiritual experience, like in the Hindu tradition of Tantra. In line with larger types of meaning, sex can also have existential–philosophical meaning for an individual, as a sexual experience could make an individual feel deeply connected with other people, history, and freedom. Thus, a sexual experience could have one or multiple materialistic, hedonistic, self-oriented, social, larger, and existential–philosophical types of meaning, and these meanings could differ by person and by situation. The fundamental phenomenological question is whether individuals are open to experience the broad potentiality of meanings that sex may bring, or whether they rigidly stick to only one type of meaning.

How Do We Approach Sex?

Martin Heidegger (1927) described that we have different ways to be in relationship to a phenomenon such as a sexual experience. Loosely based on his analyses, we may identify three modes-of-being (*Seinsweise*; Vos, 2020a, 2020b): individuals could relate to a phenomenon in traditional-conformist, functional, or phenomenological ways.

Traditional-Conformist Approach

In their approach to sex, individuals may conform to societal norms and values, or follow a religious or philosophical tradition. That is, from the oldest Vedic texts to the most recent YouTube speeches of Christian evangelists, people seem to be calling others to follow their meanings about sex, including their taboos. Anthropologist Marie Douglas (1986, 1996 has, for instance, reports how the female body—particularly during menstruation and childbirth—has been described as 'dirty,' which often meant the social exclusion of women. Some anthropologists have argued that sexual taboos may function to protect vulnerable individuals. For example, the Thora Laws forbid touching menstruating or childbearing women, which may have prevented them from being sexually approached or raped. However, these taboos could also mean exclusion, marginalization, and lack of freedom.

Some cultures and religions seem to have developed intricate systems of sexual dos and don'ts. For example, Christian authors Paul and Augustine forbid sex for mere physical, hedonistic, or self-oriented purposes; sex should always be for the larger meanings of reproduction and serving God. Sex outside this context was deemed sinful. Sex for non-procreational and non-religious purposes was regarded as immoral: We must not follow "the weakness of the flesh." Thus, with few exceptions, sex seems to have become *the* ultimate symbol of immorality and may possibly have also brought the tensions and excitement of transgressing of these moral taboos, as Bataille (1986) describes:

> Eroticism differs from animal sexuality in that human sexuality is limited by taboos and the domain of eroticism is that of the transgression of these taboos. Desire in eroticism is the desire that triumphs over the taboo. It presupposes man in conflict with himself. (p. 45)

The sexual revolution of the 1960s seemed to change the public attitude: Sex was no longer seen as inherently immoral, even outside of procreational and religious purposes. This meant that the conflation of morality and sex started to fade. Morality and sex were less often seen as the opposites of one dimension (immoral sexuality vs. moral asexuality) but more often as two independent dimensions, with the possible combinations of 'immoral sex' and 'moral sex' (cf. Vos, 2015). That is, sexual encounters were no longer regarded as inherently immoral; individuals can have moral or immoral sexual encounters, such as sex with explicit consent of the partner or sex against their will (e.g., rape). This dual attitude toward sexuality also meant that new forms of sexual relationships stopped being taboo, such as LGBTQ, open, and polyamorous relationships. The key questions seem to have become: *How* do you relate morally to the other person? Will you give them the freedom to give consent and do justice to their subjectively lived experiences, or will you deny them this opportunity? For example, during the sexual revolution, BDSM also started to lose its connotations of being "dirty" or "sinful." Not all masochists and sadists are like Marquis de Sade, who violently violated the freedom of vulnerable individuals; in contrast, research indicates that, on average, individuals engaging in BDSM are more mentally healthy, empathic, and intelligent than the rest of the population—like Christian in *Fifty Shades of Grey* (Barker, 2005).

Functionalistic Approach
A functionalistic approach looks at sex from the perspective of its functions, such as a medical explanation about the anatomy of sexual reproduction organs. For example, gynecologists and urologists may look with a "medical gaze" at sexual organs, focusing more on whether the body works as it should and less on the subjective experience of the patient. Similarly, behaviorist sex therapists Masters and Johnson (1980) did experiments with sex in their research laboratory and described sexual activities in relatively mechanical ways. Medical and behaviorist research has helped to understand organic and behaviorist causes of sexual dysfunction and to develop some effective medical and behaviorist–cognitive interventions (Fruhauf et al., 2013).

However, the functionalist approach may lack the phenomenological flow of embodied experiencing. An individual could, for example, have healthy body functions and engage in all the "correct" sexual actions, but still may not be able to get into a phenomenological flow of experiencing sex. Furthermore, medical or psychological research and treatment may have the side effect of increasing a client's functionalistic approach to sex; consequently, clients may find it even more difficult to be in the flesh—that is, to get in the flow of sexual experiencing. Viktor Frankl introduced the two functionalistic terms "hyper-reflection" and "hyper-intention" (Vos, 2017). This means, for example, that individuals think so much about their thinking and are so obsessed with achieving a certain goal, that it becomes self-undermining. For example, to be able to have an orgasm, an individual needs to be in the present moment and not be stuck in theorizing or anxiously trying to perform well or reach a goal.

Phenomenological Approach
Martin Heidegger (1927) differentiated the functionalistic gaze to our body (*Körper* in German) from our phenomenological approach of the body (*Leib*). When we are physically healthy, we usually do not think about sex in medical terms. We do not reduce others to mere sexual objects for our desire. We are not theorizing or trying to achieve any goals. Instead, we are just "flesh," as Merleau-Ponty (1968) calls this. We are submerged in the subjective flow of our physical experiences. Only when our body or mind fails or if our partner challenges us, may we be thrown out of this flow and become conscious of our sexual (dys)functioning.

Why Do We Have Sex?
The standard story that modern schoolbooks give is that, like all animals, people have sex to procreate. In the evolutionary battle of the fittest, species with more offspring are more likely to succeed. The pleasurable emotions associated with sex may have evolved and may have increased the frequency of sex and the

likelihood that partners will stick together and protect their young. Thus, sexual experiences may be explained as purely functional and efficient for the survival of the human species (Bell, 2019).

However, this evolutionary goal *(telos)* seems to be totally explained in materialistic and functionalistic terms and does not seem to do justice to the subjectively lived experiences of sex. There appear to be two ways of experiencing. Functionalistic experiences, which Heidegger (1914) calls *Erfahrung,* are different from our "lived experiences": *Erlebnis.* Heidegger uses the term "lived experiences" to mean that when our phenomenological body experience (*Leib*) is entwined with our experience of our life; our body experience is "lived." The words *Leib* and *Erlebnis* are also etymologically derived from the German word for life, *Leben:* In our daily life, our sexual experiences are part of our general experiences of life.

Sex can make us feel alive. However, while an individual may feel fully embodied and alive during sex, after sex they may feel the opposite, as if life energy is flowing out of them. Sex can thus also remind us of the absence of life: death (Bataille, 1986). In sex, we may be confronted with the fact that our body is not merely a machine that always functions perfectly and achieves its goals; we are limited and mortal beings. The intense positive emotions and ecstasies that we may feel in an orgasm may remind us of our mortality and the lack of enjoyment and excitement during most of our lifetime (contrast effect; Bataille 1986). Therefore, orgasm is also known as "the little death" (*la petite mort*). Research suggests that 40% of the population has experienced such post-coital tristesse, whereas 3–4% frequently experiences this malaise (Maczkowiack & Schweitzer, 2018). Although this sadness could also be explained in terms of neurocognitive functions, such a functionalistic approach seems to lack the "existential perspective on this subjective experience of being limited in time, stretching between birth and death" (Vos, 2020a, p. 319).

In many cultures, sex seems associated with existential anxiety (Douglas, 1966, 1985). Existential anxiety is not about a specific object or situation, such as fear of the immediate symptoms of a sexually transmitted disease but about the fear of losing life. Because, like all animals, human beings want to be alive (Greenberg et al., 2004; Pyszczynski et al., 2015). Anything that reminds people about the end of life can make them anxious, including the feeling that life is flowing out of them after sex, or the reminders of their physicality, vulnerability, and limitations in sex. Subsequently, people may use two ways to cope with this existential anxiety (Greenberg et al., 2004; Pyszczynski et al., 2015). First, individuals may emotionally disconnect from the existential meaning of sex—for example, by having a functionalistic approach or focusing only on the physical aspects of sex (cf. Vos 2017). They may reduce their partner to a mere physical object that functions only for their pleasure to prevent feeling their intense emotions, vulnerability, and intimacy, possibly because they cannot bear the reminder that they will lose their life and love one day. It is this fear of losing life and love that may lead individuals to keep from fully immerse themselves into the subjective flow of feeling alive and loved. Second, instead of emotionally disconnecting from the situation, individuals may also shift their attention toward their worldview, such as conforming to religious rules or sticking to symbolic rituals. Thus, it may be hypothesized that our traditional–conformist and functionalistic approaches and our focus on the physical and hedonistic aspects of sex may function as existential defense mechanisms (cf. Vos, 2021, 2017).

Who is Involved in Sex?

Who do we relate to in a sexual relationship? We can approach our partner(s) as a pleasurable object (Buber, 2012, calls this an 'I–It relationship'), or as a full other human being ('I-Thou-relationship'). Heidegger described different ways that we can relate to another person: We can relate to others as if we are just doing an impersonal activity or service to them (*Besorgen*), or we could take care of the other—for example, by empathizing and following what the other wants. However, we could also go further than an impersonal relationship or just doing what they want: We could authentically care for the other by helping them to open, realize their human potential, and become themselves.

What does "self" mean? Heidegger (1927) uses the word "self" when he writes that we can approach our physical experiences in relationship to our self (*Selbst*). Seen from a mere physical perspective on the self, this could mean that we focus on our own physical desires and self-enjoyment. Seen from an existential perspective, sex can also remind us of who we are and who the other is. It can remind us that although we are embodied beings and we cannot escape our physical facticity, we are also more than mere physical functions.

Heidegger (1927) writes that our self is unique; for example, sex could remind us of the uniqueness of our personal sexual experiences. Even though we are having sex together, I do not know precisely what you are now experiencing; I can only experience my own experiences. I may want to be so connected with you that I could experience the world from your perspective, see it with your eyes, and hear it with your ears, but I cannot. Intimate sexual experiences can confront us with this ultimate boundary between self and other: I am alone in my flow of experiencing, and you are alone in your flow of experiencing. This can feel frustrating and existentially lonely.

Emmanuel Levinas (1979) criticized Heidegger for his solipsism—that is, his persistence on the existential loneliness of the self (although it may be argued that Heidegger's concept of caring for the other comes close to Levinas' own philosophy). Levinas did acknowledge that there is an ontological difference between me and you; there is an otherness in the other that I will never be able to understand or explain. However, Levinas also wrote that whereas I can understand that I have an irreducible and unique totality of embodied lived experiences, I can also understand that the other has a similar irreducible totality. I can come to this conclusion not only via theoretical reflection but also via my flow of experiencing.

To see the otherness of the other, I first need to temporarily put aside (i.e., "phenomenologically bracket") the images and symbols that I have made of the other or of our relationship. I should not see the other as a functionalistic object onto which I could impose the totality of my experiences. Martin Heidegger, Friedrich Nietzsche, and Christian mystic Meister Eckhart used the term *Gelassenheit* (let-it-be-ness) to describe this approach of letting go of self-limiting images and symbols and let ourselves be in the phenomenological flow of our experiencing (Vos, 2015; Visser, 2008). When I am in the phenomenological flow of experiencing our relationship, I may open myself up for meeting the other face-toface—that is, body-to-body, or being-to-being. I may still be unable to experience precisely *what* you experience, but I can understand *that* you experience. We do not connect in our unique what-ness but in our common that-ness.

According to Levinas, this is where morality plays a crucial role, as the question is how I will respond to my understanding of the otherness of the other. I could decide to do justice to your flow of experiencing or I could, for example, merely follow my own desires or engage in sexual activities against your will. Similarly, Heidegger (1927) suggested that when I am authentic in my relationship to myself and the world around me, my conscience may call myself to return to myself; that is, I may understand who I am, where my freedom lies, and where my limitations and responsibilities are. I can answer to this call of my conscience by making the fundamental decision to relate to the other in a mere materialistic–functionalistic way or in an existential way.

Heidegger (1927) described that the ultimate existential opportunity in a relationship is to help the other become themselves or, as Buber (2012) said, an individual may become an "I" through "you" (*Der Mensch wird am Du zum Ich*). Sex may also offer the opportunity for partners to develop their self. However, I may only be able to help the other become themselves when I am myself and do not reduce the other to a mere fulfillment of my desires. Levinas (1979) describes this as "self-enjoyment" that precedes the existential relationship with another. For example, I need to know myself, accept my body and my physical experiences before I can truly care for another being. Formulated in a simplified way, if I do not love myself first, I cannot love another person. Similarly, research suggests that when I feel stuck in my own personal emotional struggles or self-doubt, I may find it more difficult to feel connected with the other and may experience sexual relationships as less satisfying (Atlantis & Sullivan, 2012; Gomes & Nobre, 2011; Laurent & Simons, 2009; West et al., 2004).

Whereas *Gelassenheit* may lead to a mystic union with God in Eckhart's texts, *Gelassenheit* in a sexual relationship may lead to the experience of a spiritual union between partners. This phenomenological experience is more than a mere physical or psychological union; this is an experience of transcendence of the here-and-now and feeling connected with larger space and time, like in Hindu Tantra (Urban, 2016).

Whose Freedom Does Sex Involve?

We have seen that individuals have the existential freedom to either reduce the other to a function of their own sexual drives or to care-for-them by trying to do justice to their subjectively lived experiences. Thus, freedom seems to be the ontological foundation of our sexual relationships (like it seems to be of all relationships: Levinas, 1979). In each situation, the question is whether we will do real justice to this freedom, or whether we will only pretend to give freedom (symbolic or imagined) to the other and to ourselves.

In his famous essay on freedom, Berlin (1959) differentiated negative freedom from positive freedom. Negative freedom is about freedom *from* limitations and suffering. For example, the law limits our freedom by forbidding us to rape another person; this also means that the law protects people's freedom by forbidding rape. Positive freedom is freedom *for* opportunities—for example, by giving the other the freedom to express their feelings and desires, to help them explore themselves and care-for their self-realization. This could imply that individuals temporarily bracket their own desires to give space and time for the other to explore and experiment in the sexual relationship: That is real freedom.

How Do Individuals Develop Their Sexuality?

Sexual experiences can be different in different situations and may change over time. Psychologists have written much about how individuals develop their sexuality, ranging from classical psychoanalytic theories to behaviorist sex experiments in laboratories and research on neurocognitive development (Houlbrook & Cocks, 2005). These texts have given much insight into the development of individual sexual functioning and many clues for treatment of sexual problems.

However, from a phenomenological perspective, it may be more relevant to explore how individuals respond to the specific ways sexuality and the human body are revealed in modern Western culture. That is, how could a young person develop a phenomenological embodied flow of sexual experiencing in our materialistic, hedonistic, and functionalistic era, in which they have been exposed from a young age to eroticized bodies in advertisements, films, and internet porn? What do they imagine sex will be about before their first experience? How do their sexual experiences change their imaginations and their perception of sex symbols in society? How do they learn to let go and be flesh in their sexual experiences? Are they cared-for by their sex partner? Do they care-for them? Each individual will most likely give their own unique answers to these questions.

Where Does Sex Happen?

The answer to the question of where sex happens could be answered quickly: It could, for example, happen in the bedroom, in sex clubs, in a dark alley, or in nature. However, from a phenomenological perspective, the question "where" could be seen as broader. We could, for example, examine how an individual develops their subjective experiences in their unique point in time and space (*epochè*). As in each era, phenomena seem to be revealed in different ways; as we have seen, our era seems to focus on physical looks and physical achievements.

For example, we have already encountered anthropologist Marie Douglas (1986, 1966), who has written extensively on how cultures develop their images of hygiene and dirt, such as blood and germs. People often seem afraid of potential dangers to their health and to the life of their community. These existentially threatening imaginations seem to have resulted in functionalistic rituals such as hygiene laws in the Torah and veils in Islamic cultures—possibly as existential defense mechanisms. According to Douglas, rituals are symbolic ways to prevent personal and social collapse, as they define "who is okay" and "who is not okay," to which group I belong, and who is my enemy. For example, the Spanish Inquisition banned "perverted individuals" from society or burned them at the stake.

There seem to be four general types of responses to these traditional images and functionalistic rituals (Douglas 1986, 1966). Hierarchalists conform to the sexual rules set by religious or legal authorities, even if this goes against their own physical desires. Egalitarians focus on the cohesion within their own group, such as the cohesive gay communities during the HIV pandemic in the 1980s. Egalitarians could also blame outsiders for all problems in society, such as pointing their fingers at "sexual deviants." Individualists seem to determine their own perception and behavior, and fatalists believe that their risks are determined by luck or fate. Thus, different (sub)cultures seem to differ in the imaginary and symbolic meanings that sex may have to them.

When Does Sex Happen?

Philosopher Michel Foucault has written four volumes about the history of sexuality (2016). This is not the history of sexuality as history books usually tell it but of how humans develop in phenomenological–existential ways (historiography versus historiology). He discusses, for example, the role of sex in Greek and Roman antiquity, and how this differs from the approach to sex that emerged from the 17th century onward. He describes how the scientific approach in modern medicine, psychiatry, and psychology has broken the conflation of sexuality with immorality. That is, sex was examined in neutral ways by bracketing connotations of immorality, dirtiness, and perversion. The functionalization of sex meant a break from the traditional moral approach to sex. This led to a trend of increased freedom for people to explore their sexuality without the fear of excommunication or legal prosecution. However, this increase in negative freedom did not automatically imply an increase in positive freedom. Foucault gives the example of the emergence of the new category of "homosexuality" in the 19th century, which replaced labels such as "perverts"; however, these labels enabled a new form of control, such as the psychiatric "treatment" of LGBTQI+ individuals. It took until the 1980s, after Foucault's death, that homosexuality was legalized and no longer regarded as a psychiatric disorder in most Western countries, although many countries still continue to have traditional–conformist taboos and rituals about LGBTQI+.

Furthermore, Foucault (2016) describes how the body is treated in our modern socio-political system as a machine that needs to be controlled. For example, he describes how modern capitalism is based on a functionalistic approach and materialistic, hedonistic, and self-oriented types of meaning (Vos, 2020a). The body is something that needs to be controlled and manipulated, albeit not necessarily via policing by religious or political authorities but by individuals themselves. The external control from the traditional–conformist approach was replaced by internal control—for example, by individuals feeling ashamed or guilty about their body because they do not fulfill the physical ideals and cultural sex symbols. Foucault called this self-governmentality: Individuals developed the mentality of governing themselves.

According to Foucault (2016), self-care (*epimeleia heautou* or *cura sui*, as it was called by ancient philosophers) is not about doing justice to the subjectively lived experiences but involves self-control and the internalization of the imagination and symbols of societal and political powers. However, whereas for Heidegger care for the self seemed to imply an existential transcendence or mystic union, Foucault viewed such existential self-care as impossible; he asserted that individuals cannot escape the increasing powers of our socio-political system ("biopower"). In the words of philosopher Friedrich Nietzsche, who had been a large influence on Foucault's thinking, Apollonic self-care seems to functionalize our Dionysian drives and cannot escape the Will-to-Power (Westfall & Rosenberg, 2018). Thus, Foucault seemed to believe that only traditional–conformist and functionalist approaches are possible and rejected the possibility of a phenomenological approach to sexuality.

However, since the 1970s, when Foucault developed these ideas, society has significantly changed, and researchers have observed a trend toward a meaning-oriented society (Vos, 2020a). This is a society that is characterized by its

> critical-intuitive orientation around a wide' range of meanings, with a dominant focus on social and larger meanings where individuals feel free and responsible towards their life situation while keeping a realistic sense of their limitations. They live a meaningful and satisfying life despite life's challenges and experience positive well-being. (Vos, 2020a, p. 32)

Although this formulation may still be partially an unrealized ideal, economic research confirms this global meaning-oriented trend. For example, consumers are more critical about how and where they buy their products; for example, they may buy bread from their local baker for ecological reasons or because of their social connection with the baker (Vos, 2020a). Thus, the subjective meaning of products and relationships seems to become more important than the mere efficiency or functionality—like buying any random bread in a supermarket. This may be mirrored by a similar trend in sexuality, where functionality and efficiency may be making time and space for phenomenological flow, social and larger meanings (Mosse, 2020; Houlbrook & Cocks, 2005). Furthermore, the COVID-19 pandemic may speed up this meaning-oriented trend (Vos, 2020c), though, more research is needed.

Which Impact Does Sex Have on Our Daily Life?

Research suggests that a satisfying sex life is associated with good mental health, and that sexual problems may lead to psychological worries (Atlantis & Sullivan, 2012; Gomes & Nobre, 2011; Laurent & Simons, 2009l; West et al., 2004). Having fulfilling sexual experiences can be good for our physical and mental health—for example, because as these experiences can temporarily distract us from daily-life problems, release stress, offer physical relaxation, and create an intimate, and possibly even an existential or spiritual, connection with another person (Diamond & Huebner, 2012).

Example: Consent

Consent seems to be the buzzword of the 21st century (Waites, 2005). What is consent, seen from a phenomenological perspective? Consent is not merely imagined (e.g., she said "no," but she meant "yes"). Consent is also not merely a symbol as it is the expression of real boundaries between self and other; therefore, consent may be described as symbolic reality. Consent flows from social and larger meanings in life, such as social connections, altruism, justice, and ethics. Consent is not merely functionalistic—as, for example, giving consent in a mechanical way like a robot is not the same as the free subjectively lived experience of consent. Furthermore, consent is about individuals determining their boundaries, and not, for example, about society, culture, or religion determining sexual relationships.

   Individuals also need to develop their ability to give consent. Children and animals do not seem to have the neurocognitive, psychological, and social abilities to reflect on the implications of sexual encounters and separate themselves from social pressure. For example, the sexual abuse of children and vulnerable individuals in religious institutions, state schools, or orphanages did not do justice to the developmental stage that they were in at that time; they were not treated as others with their own unique subjective experiences but were reduced to mere sexual objects.

   Ultimately, consent is about the real individual positive freedom of individuals; this also means that they do not only experience freedom *from* abuse but also freedom *for* self-development. Self-development is not a black-or-white experience, knowing precisely what one wants and what one does not; instead, self-development seems to involve vulnerabilities, doubts, and uncertainties. Phenomenological care for the other also means giving the freedom, space, and resources to other individuals for their sexual self-development. From a phenomenological perspective, such an authentic connection in the sexual encounter is only possible with two free, fully developed individuals who experience clear boundaries of what they want and what they do not want, and who have a clear understanding of morality (Levinas, 1979).

Some individuals find it difficult to give sufficient time, space, and resources to the other to give consent. They may lack the patience and cognitive or emotional resources to do so. There may also be political reasons. For example, some conservative individuals in the United States have protested the culture of consent as *political correctness*. Another example is individuals who actively act on their pedophilic and exhibitionistic desires; they deny the freedom of the other, objectify them, and impose their desires onto them, and reduce the other to a mere materialistic function of their hedonistic self-oriented desires. From a phenomenological perspective, it is important to differentiate individuals who imagine sexual acts with individuals who are unable to give consent from individuals who actively try to realize their imaginations.

Example: Sex Work
It is a common saying that sex work (called "prostitution" in the past) is the oldest profession in human history, with references in almost all religious and ancient texts. Whereas traditional texts often equate sex work with immorality, in modern times, sex work started to lose some of its immoral connotations. Sex has, in general, begun to lose its conflation with immorality, and it is possible to be an "Ethical Slut" (Dossie & Liszt, 1997). Indeed, several interview studies suggest that both sex workers and sex workers' visitors have moral and authentic experiences of sex work (Sallmann, 2005; Levesque-Lopman, 1988; Holzman & Pines, 1982). Sex work can be both moral and immoral.

From a phenomenological perspective, the key question is whether all stakeholders involved in sex work are free and psychologically able to give explicit consent. This also means that vulnerable individuals should be protected against being forced to give consent, such as pimps controlling immigrant sex workers by keeping their passports. Furthermore, sex worker customers do not live in the solipsistic cocoon of their physical desires, but rather in a world with other people, possibly including their partner with whom they may have agreed to be monogamous. Before an existentialist considers asking a sex worker for their services, they will first listen to the ontological call from the self to the self to do justice to the otherness of others and the subjectively lived experiences of others: the sex worker has their own experiences, as does the partner.

When an individual is with a sex worker, this encounter may actively involve their imagination, like all sexual encounters may. For example, a sex worker may pretend to like or love the customer, or even play a role. Consequently, the relationship may have a more functionalistic approach focused on the materialistic, hedonistic meanings of the customer. Some readers may find such a relationship immoral or undesirable; however, it may be argued that it is the freedom and experiences of the stakeholders, and particularly of the most vulnerable, that should be decisive, as nobody else can determine from the outside how a stakeholder should feel about a situation. We may be paternalistically reducing the otherness of sex workers and sex workers' customers if we impose our morality on them by forbidding sex work or going on a witch hunt. Therefore, the social and political starting point should always be the subjective, lived experiences of sex workers, their needs and wishes, and how society could empower them to live the meaningful and satisfying life that they want: "each individual deserves to live a meaningful life" (Vos, 2020a, p.1).

Example: Sex Addiction
Sex addiction is a controversial diagnosis (Ley, 2012). Seen from a phenomenological perspective, frequent sexual experiences and imaginations do not need to be pathological. However, sex addiction becomes problematic when an individual starts to see others merely as sexual objects and does not give them the opportunity to give or reject consent for sexual encounters. Mental health problems may also emerge when an individual starts to lose connection with reality, as they begin to live merely in an imaginary sexual world and structurally conflate sexual imagination with reality. Frequent sex experiences and imaginations may also become pathological when the individual does not feel the freedom to engage or not engage in these experiences or imaginations, such as in the case of obsessive thoughts or compulsive behavior or when the behaviors contradict their meanings in life. However, paradoxically speaking, creating a taboo by labeling someone's sexual experiences an "addiction" could reinforce their sex addiction, since sexual taboos can increase the eroticization and transgression of the taboos. Therefore, some therapists have recommended an accepting rather than dismissive approach to sexual obsessions or compulsions (Blycker & Potenza, 2018; Coleman, 1987).

Example: BDSM
Kink, or BDSM (Bondage, Dominance, Sadism, Masochism), has long been regarded as a social taboo. BDSM was regarded as inherently immoral and associated with severe violence against vulnerable individuals such as women, children, and animals who were unable to give consent (such as was the case with the Marquis de Sade, whose name gave rise to the term "sadism" (Ortmann & Sprott, 2012).

However, from a phenomenological perspective, this immoral connotation of BDSM seems unfounded, as we have seen in the case of other sexual phenomena. BDSM may not be inherently immoral; individuals could engage in BDSM activities in moral or in immoral ways, like any sexual encounter could be made moral or immoral. For example, many scientific studies have described the BDSM scene as mutually supportive, with social rules and significant attention given to issues of consent and safety (Ortmann & Sprott, 2012; Weiss, 2011; Langdridge & Barker, 2007; Barker, 2005).

From a phenomenological perspective, BDSM experiences are rich in imagination—for example, imagining the complete reduction of individuals to mere sexual functions. One of the most elaborate forms of imaginary objectification is animal play, where individuals dress up and are treated as animals, such as puppy play or pony play. Furthermore, "furnication" means that individuals are treated as inanimate objects like a piece of furniture (Weiss, 2011). An increasingly popular kink is also the furry scene, where individuals dress up in furry suits, usually as an animal, and develop their own personality called "fursona."

Paradoxically, the large imagination does not mean that BDSM denies reality or social and larger types of meaning. On the contrary, a sex master may, for example, do more social justice by treating another person as an object or slave than by not treating them as such. The BDSM experience could be described on two levels: There is the as-if level of the playful relationship, and there is a meta-level where the focus lies on the freedom of all partners, explicit consent, and doing justice to the sexual desires of the other. On a meta-level, the master can be the slave of the person who is the slave on the play level. For example, the master tries to fulfill the desires of the slave and protects their boundaries by giving the sub a safety word. Paradoxically, the BDSM relationship could give the ultimate freedom and I–Thou relationship, as the BDSM partner may do justice to the deepest, and even forbidden, desires of the other. The lack of freedom in a play situation of objectification, bondage, and enslavement could offer the opportunity for an individual to realize their positive freedom by realizing their deepest fantasies.

How do people develop their experiences and imaginations of BDSM? Research seems to suggest that there are generally speaking five ways that individuals come to experience BDSM (Brown et al., 2020; Klement et al., 2017; Pitagora, 2017; Graham et al., 2016; Hebert & Weaver, 2014; Yost & Hunter, 2012). First, there are individuals who like changes and experiments, and trying out something new—for example, in response to the popularity of books and movies such as *Fifty Shades of Grey*.

Second, there are those who may want an intense and extreme experience to forget everyday reality. For example, the I–It relationship between dom/sub may enable the sub to be released in a symbolically and imaginary way from the responsibilities, pressures, and worries of daily life. The *summum bonum* of this is the experience of a "sub-space," the ecstatic experience of a submissive who becomes totally one with their submissive role and who has given total physical and experiential control to the dominant person. The master can experience a sense of total control and responsibility, which they may be lacking in their daily life.

Third, BDSM may offer an integration of physical sensations—for example. via bondage or enclosure in tight clothes—as described by Sensory Integration theories (Smith, 2019). The philosopher Dilthey also described how the experience of intense somatic resistance, such as flagellation, can make us more aware of our body and our self; we no longer relate to our body in a theoretical–reflective way, but the pain and suffering may bring us into the flow of experiencing in the present and becoming our flesh (cf. Vos, 2015).

Fourth, there are those who seem to compensate or act out early life trauma, or who have sexualized early life experiences. For example, in some countries where corporeal punishment (CP) happens in schools, individuals may sexualize CP later in life, re-enacting early experiences by dressing up as schoolmasters and pupils who need to be punished. Individuals may also re-enact or compensate for early sexual abuse or rape by being a rapist in BDSM scenarios. Victims of early life narcissistic abuse may sexualize feelings of submission or objectification; this could be a healthy form of acting out their victimhood in the bedroom instead of in daily life, or it could be an extension of daily life victimhood. Whereas individuals may not have been in control during their traumatic experience, they may create a sense of symbolic or imaginary control via BDSM play; as such, BDSM play in a safe and consensual context may help the recovery of trauma. Individuals may also become sexual sadists in response to early life abuse or trauma—for example, as an overcompensation for having been completely out of control during the trauma or abuse. Narcissists and victims/enablers of narcissists can be pulled toward each other like human magnets due to trauma bonding or being used to the emotional intensity of traumatic/abusive relationships (Rosenberg, 2018). In sum, traumatic and abusive life experiences may be brought into the later sex life of individuals.

Fifth, some individuals have reported intense BDSM desires since early childhood, without any significant traumas, even from ages as early as five years; they describe themselves as "being born a master" or "being born a slave." This may be explained in terms of nurture, such as the sexualization of roles or implicit messages in an abusive family (cf. Rosenberg, 2018). It may also be hypothesized in terms of nature that their BDSM desires may have some genetic foundations, such as the COMT gene ("worrier/warrior gene") is associated with differentiating submissive from dominant psychological patterns (Montag et al., 2012).

Finally, research shows that individuals who frequently engage in BDSM experiences have on average a better mental health than the general population (Brown et al., 2020). This may be attributed to the release of stress in BDSM play, as described above. There may also be a self-selection of individuals in the BDSM scene, as the play/meta-level distinction may require complex psychological skills.

Existential–Phenomenological Sex Therapy

Therapy Aims
Following from the phenomenological analysis in this chapter, we may hypothesize that sexual problems may arise from the lack of phenomenological bracketing of our imaginations and symbols, and thus a denial of our phenomenological flow of experiencing. The illusion that sex may be reified, reduced to a physical object, specific looks, mechanical efficiency, or a goal, could bring a sense of disembodiment, emotional disconnection with oneself, and relational distance from the other. Behavioral therapists have suggested that

many sexual disorders, such as vaginism and erectile dysfunction, are associated with the client's inability to get into the flow of experiencing because of performance stress or self-doubt. Frankl (1975) called these problems of hyper-reflection and hyper-intention (thinking too much and wanting too much) and suggested that existential therapists teach "de-reflection" to help clients deal with sexual problems by facilitating their return to their primary flow of experiencing, being flesh, and phenomenologically bracketing their expectations and assumptions. The following sections derive from previous research on evidence-based existential psychotherapeutic techniques (Vos, 2016, 2017).

Assessment Skills
All sex therapy should start with an examination of possible medical and behavioral causes. For example, several physical conditions have been associated with sexual problems, such as diabetes and high blood pressure. Furthermore, research suggests that mental health problems such as depression, as well as psychiatric drugs, can lead to changes in sexual experiences (Reynaert et al., 2010). A brief functional assessment of behavior may also help in identifying any underlying behavioral problems, such as a lack of knowledge of how to engage in certain sexual activities, wanting to give perfect sexual performance, or having other self-undermining thoughts.

Phenomenological Skills
After any medical or behavioral problems are excluded, it is important to avoid a focus on rationalizations and theories, as such a functionalistic therapeutic approach could make it more difficult for a client to get into the phenomenological flow of experiencing (e.g., during sex a client may only be thinking about perfectly following the instructions of the therapist instead of being in the here-and-now). Phenomenological assessment includes asking the ten questions of this chapter: How real is a sexual experience for the client, or is it merely imagination and symbols? What meanings does sex have, who is involved, and how do they relate? How has the individual developed their sexuality, and how much freedom do they experience and do they give to others? What is the historical and cultural context of their sex experiences? Why do people have sex or want to have sex? Which impact does sex have on daily life?

Key phenomenological skills for the therapist include phenomenological unpeeling of experiences, stimulating acceptance of experiences, helping clients to immerse themselves in the flow of experiencing, phenomenologically exploring hierarchies of meaning in their experiences, using a questioning approach, and asking for examples and specifications (Vos, 2017, p.173). It may help to practice exercises with the client to get in touch with the flow of physical experiences in the present, for example via experiential, non-verbal or mindfulness exercises (see examples in Vos, 2017, pp. 169–175). For example, research suggests that mindfulness training could improve sexual satisfaction (Lazaridou & Kalogianni, 2013). Although the professional focus in the therapy room will lie on non-sexual experiences, clients may generalize their experiential skills to their sexual encounters.

Relational Skills

Therapists should offer a supportive and empathic relationship, which could help clients learn how to share feelings and be in relational depth with another human being. Relational skills include tailoring the therapy to the needs, skills, and wishes of the client, sharing decision making, engaging in meta-communication about the therapy process, deepening the therapeutic relationship, following the client's tempo, offering unconditional positive regard, empathizing with and normalizing the client's struggles, and recognizing the client's meanings (Vos, 2017, p. 144). The therapist should not be a blank screen, but show that they have their own subjective experiences, just like a sexual partner may have.

As in sexual encounters, it is important to explicate relational boundaries, and to ask for explicit consent for the aims and methods of the therapy (sometimes called a "therapy contract"). In sex therapy, there may be a larger likelihood of sexual transference compared to psychotherapy that does not focus on sexual topics. It is important for the therapist not to ignore sexual transference but to work with these feelings. For example, a therapist could explicate that having sexual feelings is normal and may even be a sign of progress, as the aim of the therapy is to get more in touch with one's feelings. The critical question is what the client will do with these feelings, and how psychologically beneficial, meaningful, and moral that response is.

A therapist may prepare a client for an embodied experience but cannot create or control this experience for them. Like a midwife (*maieutika*), professionals may support the client to give birth to their experiences, but the client has to give birth. Even a client may not be able to have functionalistic control over their embodied flow of experiencing as the crux of being flesh is letting go of expectations such as efficiency and performance. Thus paradoxically, to control their flow of sexual experiencing, the client needs to let go of control; Frankl recommended, therefore, the therapeutic technique of "paradoxical intention" (Vos, 2017).

Existential Skills

We have seen how sexual problems may be caused by existential defense mechanisms. Therefore, it may be helpful to explicitly recognize, name, and explore these existential feelings. This may include exploring paradoxical feelings and ambivalences and learning to tolerate difficult existential feelings instead of immediately pushing them away. The client may be stimulated in finding new ways to live a meaningful and satisfying life, despite life's challenges; this may also include learning to experience meaning and satisfaction in sex, despite sexual problems, any organic dysfunctions, or lack of a "perfect" body or "perfect" sexual performance. Thus, the focus should not be on achieving physical goals but on experiencing long-term, deeper meanings in the sexual relationship with oneself and others and to see sex from the broader perspective of life—for example, there are more meaningful experiences in life than sex. Some clients may also benefit from learning self-care and self-compassion as a first step before they are able to care for another human being. Finally, the existential therapist will help the client to take responsibility for living a meaningful life, instead of depending on a therapist or a sex partner and of avoiding life's responsibilities by fleeing into purely materialistic, hedonistic, and functionalistic sexual experiences (Vos, 2018, p. 186).

Discussion

In this chapter, we have seen how ten phenomenological questions can reveal aspects of our sexual experiences that we may not have seen before. Like walking around a diamond, we have started to see more facets and have done more justice to the totality of our subjectively lived experiences than before, possibly because some of these facets may have been taboo in our culture and era. Therefore, it may be helpful to temporarily bracket our cultural–historical assumptions, listen with a critical intuition to what our self is telling us, follow what is existentially meaningful to us, and explore our sex life with an open attitude. Naturally, this chapter has some limitations. It has relied heavily on philosophical–phenomenological texts and less on empirical studies. This may limit the applications of this study, and therefore, practitioners should only use this chapter as an additional source to training in evidence-based psychological therapies. Furthermore, more empirical research into the phenomenology of sex is needed.

Finally, this chapter has shown how asking phenomenological questions can reinvigorate your sex life. Although the texts of Heidegger and Foucault will most likely not directly stimulate sexual fantasies, they may inspire you to have a more fulfilling and satisfying sex life.

> *The body can become a vehicle to that which is beyond body, and sex energy can become a spiritual, existential and social force.* (After: Osho in Urban, 2016, p.103)

References

Atlantis, E., & Sullivan T. (2012). Bidirectional association between depression and sexual dysfunction: A systematic review and meta-analysis. *The Journal of Sexual Medicine, 9*(6), 1497–1507. https://doi.org/10.1111/j.1743-6109.2012.02709.x

Aristotle (2019). *Aristotle's ethics.* Clarendon.

Barker, M. (2005). On tops, bottoms and ethical sluts: The place of BDSM and polyamory in lesbian and gay psychology. *Lesbian and Gay Psychology Review, 6*(2), 124–129.

Bataille, G. (1986). *Erotism.* City Lights Books.

Bell, G. (2019). *The masterpiece of nature: The evolution and genetics of sexuality.* Routledge.

Berlin, I. (1959). *Two concepts of liberty:* An inaugural lecture delivered before the University of Oxford on 31 October 1958. Oxford.

Blycker, G.R., & Potenza, M.N. (2018). A mindful model of sexual health: A review and implications of the model for the treatment of individuals with compulsive sexual behavior disorder. *Journal of Behavioral Addictions, 7*(4), 917–929. https://doi.org/10.1556/2006.7.2018.127

Brown, A., Barker, E.D., & Rahman, Q. (2020). A systematic scoping review of the prevalence, etiological, psychological, and interpersonal factors associated with BDSM. *The Journal of Sex Research, 57*(6), 781–811. https://doi.org/10.1080/00224499.2019.1665619

Buber, M. (2012). *I and Thou*. eBookIt.com.

Coleman, E. (1987). Sexual compulsivity: Definition, etiology, and treatment considerations. *Journal of Chemical Dependency Treatment, 1*(1), 189–204. https://doi.org/10.1300/J034v01n01_11

Diamond, L. M., & Huebner, D. M. (2012). Is good sex good for you? Rethinking sexuality and health. *Social and Personality Psychology Compass, 6*(1), 54–69. https://doi.org/10.1111/j.1751-9004.2011.00408.x

Dossie, E., & Liszt Catherine, A. (1997). *The ethical slut: A guide to infinite sexual possibilities*. Greenery.

Douglas, M. (1966/2013). *Risk and blame*. Routledge.

Douglas, M. (1986/2003). *Purity and danger*. Routledge.

Foucault, M. (2016). *The history of sexuality*. Routledge.

Frankl, V. E. (1975). Paradoxical intention and dereflection. *Psychotherapy: Theory, Research & Practice, 12*(3), 226–237. https://doi.org/10.1037/h0086434

Frühauf, S., Gerger, H., Schmidt, H. M., Munder, T., & Barth, J. (2013). Efficacy of psychological interventions for sexual dysfunction: A systematic review and meta-analysis. *Archives of Sexual Behavior, 42*(6), 915–933. https://doi.org/10.1007/s10508-012-0062-0

Gomes, A.L.Q., & Nobre, P. (2011). Personality traits and psychopathology on male sexual dysfunction: An empirical study. *The Journal of Sexual Medicine, 8*(2), 461–469.

Graham, B. C., Butler, S. E., McGraw, R., Cannes, S. M., & Smith, J. (2016). Member perspectives on the role of BDSM communities. *The Journal of Sex Research, 53*(8), 895–909. https://doi.org/10.1080/00224499.2015.1067758

Greenberg, J., Koole ,S. L., & Pyszczynski, T. A. (2004). *Handbook of experimental existential psychology*. Guilford Press.

Hankinson, R. J. (2001). *Cause and explanation in Ancient Greek thought*. Oxford University.

Hébert, A., & Weaver A. (2014). An examination of personality characteristics associated with BDSM orientations. *The Canadian Journal of Human Sexuality, 23*(2), 106–115. https://doi.org/10.3138/cjhs.2467

Heidegger, M. (1914). *Die ehre vom urteil im psychologismus*. Barth.

Heidegger, M. (1927). *Sein und zeit*. Max Niemeyer.

Heidegger, M. (1995). *Aristotle's metaphysics*. Indiana University.

Holzman, H.R., & Pines, S. (1982). Buying sex: The phenomenology of being a john. *Deviant behavior, 4*(1), 89–116. https://doi.org/10.1080/01639625.1982.9967604

Houlbrook, M., & Cocks, H. (Eds.). (2005). *Palgrave advances in the modern history of sexuality*. Springer.

Hyde, J. S. E. (2005). *Biological substrates of human sexuality*. American Psychological Association.

Klement, K. R., Lee, E. M., Ambler, J. K., & Reid, E. (2017). Extreme rituals in a BDSM context: The physiological and psychological effects of the "dance of souls." *Culture, Health & Sexuality, 19*(4), 453–469. https://doi.org/10.1080/13691058.2016.1234648

Lacan, J. (2006). *Ecrits.* Norton.

Langle, A. (2013). *Lehrbuch zur Existenzanalyse. Grundlagen.* Wien: Facultas.

Langdridge, D., & Barker, M. (2007). *Situating sadomasochism.* Palgrave Macmillan.

Laurent, S. M., & Simons, A. D. (2009). Sexual dysfunction in depression and anxiety: Conceptualizing sexual dysfunction as part of an internalizing dimension. *Clinical Psychology Review, 29*(7), 573–585. https://doi.org/10.1016/j.cpr.2009.06.007

Lazaridou, A., & Kalogianni, C. (2013). Mindfulness and sexuality. *Sexual and Relationship Therapy, 28*(1–2), 29–38. https://doi.org/10.1080/14681994.2013.773398

Levesque-Lopman, L. (1988). *Claiming reality: Phenomenology and women's experience.* Rowman & Littlefield.

Levinas, E. (1979). *Totality and infinity: An essay on exteriority.* Springer.

Ley, D. J. (2012). *The myth of sex addiction.* Rowman & Littlefield.

Maczkowiack, J., & Schweitzer, R. D. (2018). Postcoital dysphoria: Prevalence and correlates among males. *Journal of Sex & Marital Therapy, 45*(2), 128–140. https://doi.org/10.1080/0092623X.2018.1488326

Masters, W. H., & Johnson, V. J. (1980). *Human sexual inadequacy.* Bantam Books.

Merleau-Ponty, M. (1968). *The visible and the invisible: Followed by working notes.* Northwestern University Press.

Merleau-Ponty, M. (1982). *Phenomenology of perception.* Routledge.

Montag, C., Jurkiewicz, M., & Reuter. M. (2012). The role of the catechol-o-methyltransferase (COMT) gene in personality and related psychopathological disorders. *CNS & Neurological Disorders, 11*(3), 236–250. doi: 10.2174/187152712800672382

Mosse, G. L. (2020). *Nationalism and sexuality: Middle-class morality and sexual norms in modern Europe.* University of Wisconsin.

Ortmann, D. M., & Sprott, R. A. (2012). *Sexual outsiders: Understanding BDSM sexualities and communities.* Rowman & Littlefield.

Pitagora, D. (2017). No pain, no gain? Therapeutic and relational benefits of subspace in BDSM contexts. *Journal of Positive Sexuality, 3*(3), 44–54. doi: 10.51681/1.332

Pyszczynski, T., Solomon, S., & Greenberg, J. (2015). Thirty years of terror management theory: From genesis to revelation. *Advances in Experimental Social Psychology, 52,* 1–70. https://doi.org/10.1016/bs.aesp.2015.03.001

Reynaert, C., Zdanowicz, N., Janne, P., & Jacques, D.(2010). Depression and sexuality. *Psychiatria Danubina, 22,* 111–114.

Rosenberg, R.A. (2018). *The human magnet syndrome: The codependent narcissist trap: Surviving narcissistic abuse.* Morgan James Publishing.

Sallmann, J. (2005). *Being in the world of prostitution: An interpretive phenomenological study of women's lived experiences and their relation to service providers.* The University of Wisconsin-Madison.

Smith, M. (2019). *Sensory integration: Theory and practice.* FA Davis.

Urban, H. B. (2016). *Zorba the Buddha: Sex, spirituality, and capitalism in the global Osho Movement.* University of California Press.

Van Deurzen, E. (2014). Structural existential analysis (SEA). *Counselling Psychology Review, 29*(2), 70–83. https://doi.org/10.1007/s10879-014-9282-z

Visser, G. (2008). *Gelatenheid: Gemoed en hart bij Meister Eckhart: Beschouwd in het licht van Aristoteles' leer van het affectieve.* SUN.

Visser, G. (1989). *Nietzsche en Heidegger: Een confrontatie.* Boom.

Vos, J. (2015). Meaning and existential givens in the lives of cancer patients: A philosophical perspective on psycho-oncology. *Palliative & Supportive Care, 13*(4), 885. doi:10.1017/S1478951514000790

Vos, J. (2016). Working with meaning in life in chronic or life-threatening disease: A review of its relevance and the effectiveness of meaning-centred therapies. In S. Schulenberg & P. Russo-Netzer (Eds.), *Clinical perspectives on meaning* (pp. 171-200). Springer.

Vos, J. (2017). *Meaning in life: An evidence-based handbook for practitioners.* Macmillan International Higher Education.

Vos, J. (2020a). *The economics of meaning in life: From capitalist life syndrome to meaning-oriented economy.* University Professors Press.

Vos, J. (2020b). Systematic Pragmatic Phenomenological Analysis (SPPA): Step-wise guidance for mixed methods research. *Journal of Counselling and Psychotherapy Research, 21*(1), 77–97. https://doi.org/10.1002/capr.12366

Vos, J. (2020c). *The psychology of COVID-19: Building resilience for future pandemics.* Sage.

Vos, J. (2021)

Vos, J., Roberts, R., & Davies, J. (2019). *Mental health in crisis.* Sage.

Waites, M. (2005). *The age of consent.* Palgrave Macmillan.

Weiss, M. (2011). *Techniques of pleasure: BDSM and the circuits of sexuality.* Duke University.

West, S. L., Vinikoor, L. C., & Zolnoun, D. (2004). A systematic review of the literature on female sexual dysfunction prevalence and predictors. *Annual Review of Sex Research, 15*(1), 40–172. doi: 10.1080/10532528.2004.10559819

Westfall, J., & Rosenberg, A. (2018). Foucault and Nietzsche: A critical encounter. Bloomsbury.

Yost, M. R., & Hunter, L. E. (2012). BDSM practitioners' understandings of their initial attraction to BDSM sexuality: Essentialist and constructionist narratives. *Psychology & Sexuality, 3*(3), 244–259. doi: 10.1080/19419899.2012.700028

Chapter 2

A Functionalist Approach to Understanding Gender and Sexuality: Reconciling Tensions between Humanistic and Queer/Trans Theories

Heidi Levitt, Kathleen Collins, & Zenobia Morrill

Abstract

This chapter will describe a psychosocial theory that has been developed to articulate the relationship between gender and sexuality by examining its unfolding within LGBTQ+ gender communities (e.g., butch, femme, bear, leather, house/family, transgender, drag). It begins with framing the question around how gender and sexuality are experienced and identifying some historical tensions between humanistic theories and queer/trans theories. It then reviews the theory of gender and its four components while foregrounding aspects that tie into humanistic conceptualizations of development. The four components include a *psychological domain*, which is rooted in a drive toward authenticity; a *cultural domain*, in which gender communities develop healthy social responses within historical contexts that previously did not support their sense of self; an *interpersonal domain*, which reflects the need for symbolization of internal experiences so that people can better relate with others; and a *sexual domain*, in which the symbols of sexuality are transformed into a desirable aesthetic that empowers members of gender communities. Following the description of the theory, we return to the points of tension and consider how the functionalist understanding of gender, understood within these domains, can resolve some areas of conflict between humanistic and queer/trans philosophies.

***

Humanistic and existential psychologists are interested in understanding the lived experience of people and the ways in which diverse groups make sense of their place in the world. Gender identities, gender expressions, and sexual orientations are concepts that help us to make meaning of who we are ourselves and in relation to others. In this chapter, we review a theory of gender that has evolved from a program of research focused on lesbian, gay, bisexual, transgender, queer, and other non-heterosexual (LGBTQ+) gender communities (Levitt, 2019a) and consider it from the perspective of humanistic psychology. This mixed method program has investigated seven distinctive sets of gender identities (i.e., butch, femme, bear, leather, transgender, drag, and house/family genders; see the chapter glossary for a brief description of each) and has been driven by qualitative methods that often included community engagement via authorship, interviews, and/or feedback on findings. The body of work that the theory is based upon includes 17 empirical publications (Hiestand et al., 2008; Hiestand & Levitt, 2005; Horne et al., 2014; Levitt, Wheeler, et al., 2018; Levitt & Bridges, 2007; Levitt & Horne, 2002; Levitt et al., 2003; Levitt & Hiestand, 2004; Levitt et al., 2015; Levitt, Horne, et al., 2017; Levitt & Ippolito, 2014a; Levitt & Ippolito, 2014b; Levitt, Puckett et al., 2012; Manley et al., 2007; Mosher et al., 2006; Panesis et al., 2014 and an earlier theoretical formulation (Levitt, 2006).

The theory was recently the subject of a special section of *Psychology of Women Quarterly* (for discussion of this theory see, Levitt, 2019a; Levitt 2019b; Moradi, 2019; Tebbe, 2019; Watson, 2019) and was described as advancing understandings of gender in psychology in a number of directions. Instead of being focused on heterosexual and cisgender experiences, it is inclusive of LGBTQ+ experience. It explicates the relationship between gender, gender expression, and gender identity in a clear manner. The theory is empirically based in a program of research that has investigated diverse gender communities, often using participatory methods, and spans two decades during a period in which social understandings of gender have been in flux. In this chapter, it links gender to both hegemonic and subversive power as well as humanistic understandings of self-development. This framework has been developed as an analytic tool by others and can be adapted to understand varied genders and identities (see Levitt, 2019b for details on its application).

Humanistic/Existential Theory and Queer/Trans Theory: Commonalities and Tensions

Although theorists have identified a number of commonalities between queer and humanistic/existential philosophies, they have noted points of tension as well (e.g., Goodrich et al., 2016; Plummer, 2005). Shared values between these theoretical approaches include: (1) the preference to understand experience from a holistic perspective. The phenomenological experience of an individual is seen as a meaningful way to unify and examine psychological states, rather than reductionistic categorizations, and is compatible with queer theory's assertion that people's felt sense of sexual and gender identity should not be constrained to fixed, socially mandated categories (Goodrich et al., 2016). Specifically, both humanists and queer theorists argue against pathologizing diagnostic systems (e.g., American Psychiatric Association DSM, 2013) and methods of understanding that focus on decontextualized fragments of experience (e.g., symptoms); (2) they both value self-reflective practices and empathic attunement over the internalization and acceptance of socially dominant ideas of self (e.g., Gendlin, 2003). Learning how to self-reference and direct is a core goal of humanistic and existential psychotherapies and is prized, as this skill assists LGBTQ+ people in accepting gender and sexual identities that are often maligned in their social systems; (3) both humanistic and existential philosophies value qualitative research methods (Levitt, 2019b; Rennie, 2007). These methods support an understanding of psychological experience that is contextualized in interpersonal and systemic dynamics. In addition, these methods can center experiences that, by virtue of being marginalized, can shed light on processes of stigmatization.

Although these converging values provide important common ground, the following are three differences that have been identified between humanistic and queer/trans theories.

The Focus on Cultural Privilege and Oppression
The field of humanistic psychology historically has focused on individual development without consideration of social context, despite some of its founders' specific writings about the importance of culture (e.g., Rogers, 1977). Contemporary humanistic scholars, however, have taken up a call for the genuine examination of the role of culture throughout the field (e.g., Hoffman et al., 2015; Hoffman et al., 2016). In particular, this would involve integrating culture-specific knowledge and consideration of the impact of oppressive systems when conceptualizing the process of individual development. This call has led to a turn in humanistic psychology in which it is becoming more compatible with queer and trans theory approaches that centralize the influence of cultural and oppressive forces. It is exciting to see this evolution underway.

The Role of Autonomy and Self-Determination
A second tension that has been put forward repeatedly is related to the place of self-determination, autonomy, and choice in humanistic and queer theory approaches. Although a normative view of subjectivity tends to view individuals as having freedom in identity, LGBTQ+ people may experience their gender as a core aspect of themselves that was not selected consciously but situated in their bodies (e.g., Cromwell, 2006; Gressgård, 2010). This understanding of identity has been complicated by the need for diagnosis and a biomedical model of gender that grounds gender in the body in order to secure medical treatments that affirm trans people's experiences of their gender (Butler, 2004; Gorton, 2013) and that is often used to argue for the advancement of LGBTQ rights. Although other research focuses more on the fluidity of gender (see Diamond & Rosky, 2016), there is no consensus on the extent to which shifts in sexual and gender identities are willful or self-directed. This understanding can be seen as fitting poorly with a humanistic model of development in which self-determination plays such a central role.

Bodies as Givens and/or Creations

For queer and trans theorists, the discussion of the body is of central importance because it is the focus of their oppression. Trans theorists have been challenging a naturalistic view of bodies and viewing them, instead, as inherently intertwined products of both flesh and techne, crafted via our use of systems and technologies (Sullivan, 2014). From that perspective, the concept of sex may not be seen as based upon a clear biological substrate but on culturally determined ideas—and, indeed, we lack medical consensus today on the set of physical features that should determine sex (e.g., chromosomes, hormones, genitalia, gonads; US Proposal for Defining Gender, 2018). Sex can be seen as a culturally assigned identity that is routinely supported by many forms of deliberate construction (e.g., the use of exercise equipment, tattoos, breast reduction, hair dye, cosmetics, hormone replacement therapy, dieting). In contrast, the creation of body has not received a great deal of attention from humanists. While there may be an understanding of how our psychological experience is unavoidable embodied (e.g., Sundararajan, 2002), bodies tend to be seen as existential givens within humanistic approaches or as functioning in interaction with mind–body systems of stress and healing (Johanson, 2009). They have not held center stage.

Within the next sections, we describe Levitt's (2019a) theory of gender, drawing out ties to the humanistic literature that have not been articulated elsewhere. We then return to consider how this approach can help to reconcile some of the tensions between queer and humanistic theories.

A Functionalist Theory of Gender

This work emerges from within a tradition of queer/trans theorists who accord LGBTQ+ gender the same claim upon the word "gender" as heterosexual genders (e.g., Butler, 2004; Halberstam, 1998). In psychology, our prior authoritative writings have either lacked definitions of gender or have focused on the experience of gender for cisgender and heterosexual men and women (e.g., American Psychological Association, 2007, 2012, 2015). Prior definitions have described gender as culturally grouped traits associated with a person's biological sex or being a man or woman. This understanding does not make sense for transgender and nonbinary people or for LGBTQ+ genders such as butch or femme. As a result, Levitt (2019a) developed an inclusive theory of gender that was based on a series of mixed methods studies on the experiences of people in LGBTQ+ communities to develop an understanding of how gender is experienced from those standpoints. The definition put forward in this theory extends that prior understanding to say that genders *also* can be responses to existing genders, to their social demands, and the stigma related to breaking norms. Furthermore, the theory explicates how gender (i.e., an internal sense of preferred expressions of self and ways of relating to others) and gender expression (i.e., how gender is expressed through appearance and mannerisms) influence the construction and cultural understanding of LGBTQ+ gender identities.

In addition, this approach understands the experience of gender as structured into four domains (i.e., psychological, cultural, interpersonal, and sexual domains) that were found to function in participants' lives across the communities studied (see Levitt, 2019a for descriptions of the primary studies). The theory does not focus on biological contributions to gender, which has been reviewed in other works (Hyde et al., 2019; Polderman et al., 2018). The domains emerged from studying the commonalities across the gender communities within the research program. They encompassed varied forms of gender, including gay masculinities (bears, leathermen, fathers and sons in house/family networks); lesbian femininity (femme lesbians); female masculinities (butch lesbians, trans folk); male femininities (gay male drag, trans folk, mothers and sisters in house/family networks); and nonbinary identities (within trans, drag, and house/family communities). In this section, we describe how the four functions of gender influence people's sense of identity, security, belonging, and social values, all of which are fundamental aspects of being human that hold relevance for humanistic theory (Wong, 2006), as we will describe.

Psychological Domain

Across the communities studied, LGBTQ+ genders were described as emerging to assist people to develop a more authentic sense of self. Many (but not all) were pressured to conform to gender expressions that felt false, embarrassing, and uncomfortable from early ages (e.g., more typically butch women, gay male drag performers, transgender people, mothers and sisters in house/family networks) or were told that their sexual orientations were pathological, unacceptable, and shameful. Many of the participants had struggled through different points in their lifetimes with being hurt and ostracized by others or feeling self-doubt and shame tied to their gender expression and/or sexual orientation. Across the identities explored then, developing an LGBTQ+ gender identity was "a response to the need for the identification and adjustment of gender constructs towards greater authenticity" (Levitt, 2019a, p. 283).

This understanding affirms humanistic theories of development that centralize the quest for authenticity. Carl Rogers (1961) described the fully functioning person as someone who is able to live in the present with an attunement to his, her, or their internal desires, developing congruence between their real and ideal selves. Maslow (1950/1973) described the process of self-actualization as one in which individuals are able to be themselves autonomously, functioning with some independence from societal restrictions or pressures. Gendlin (2003) described the ability to attend to internal experiences and recognize internal needs as a basis for healthy development. In these ways, humanistic theories view self-knowledge and striving for authenticity as essential for optimal human development (Robbins, 2008). In order to live authentically, the LGBTQ+ participants described a process of self-exploration during which they gained insight into the meanings of varied gender constructs and learned what it meant for them to live in accordance with their felt sense of self. In the following subsection, we review how the psychological function of seeking an authentic gender affects people's sense of identity, security, belonging, and social values.

Identity

Across our studies in varied gender communities, experiencing a sense of authenticity through one's gender involved expressing it in a way that was at least mostly consistent with the participants' inner felt sense of their gender (Levitt, 2019a). Developing an LGBTQ+ gender identity often was challenging, as it required self-awareness, tolerance of ambiguity, and courage to transcend the compulsory identities imposed by societies that degrade non-traditional gender identities. This process of self-exploration demonstrated their agentic capacity to develop a complex sense of self that was driven by an internal sense of gender that they tended to understand as either biologically based or as an essential aspect of themselves. Within LGBTQ+ gender communities, they could minimize the incongruence between their internal sense of self and their external experiences. The experience of authenticity has been found to increase life satisfaction, adjustment, and overall well-being (Boyraz et al., 2014), which was in keeping with their reports.

Once identified with an LGBTQ+ gender community, the process of seeking authenticity continued. Participants described learning new language to describe their gender and continually developing an understanding of how their gender positioned them in relation to others in varied contexts. As they learned the stereotypes of their LGBTQ+ gender, some decided to break norms that did not feel authentic (Hutson, 2010; Levitt & Hiestand, 2004). Others discovered alternate gender identities that come to better represent their experience of gender (e.g., some participants shifted from a butch lesbian to a trans man identity; Levitt & Ippolito, 2014a).

Security

LGBTQ+ gender identities can also have the effect of connecting people with communities that provide support to help them reduce or cope with sexual and gender minority stress. These are unique forms of stress that sexual and gender minorities experience, in addition to the stressors that are experienced by everyone, that have been found to influence physical and mental health (e.g., Meyer, 2003; Velez & Moradi, 2016). For example, the house and family networks studied provided support for GBTQ youth of color who often faced rejection from both their family of origin and their religious communities (e.g., Levitt, Horne et al., 2015). Many of these youth struggled with homelessness, poverty, and racism, in addition to heterosexism and transphobia. Within house/family systems, they found an alternate family structure that affirmed their identities and shared strategies to resist the many and intersecting forms of discrimination that they experienced. The communities sometimes offered housing and financial support as well as developmental guidance to help them return to school or become financially independent. In this way, the identification with an LGBTQ+ gender community could be a vitally important buffer in the face of minority stressors. This function may be especially important for communities that experience multiple intersecting minority stressors (e.g., racial, ethnic, or class-related minority stress).

Belonging

In addition to providing support for minority stressors, LGBTQ+ gender communities generated a sense of social acceptance (Levitt, 2019a). Like Rogers' (1981) analogy of a potato in a cellar sending out shoots to reach the light, participants described striving toward social conditions that affirm their sense of self, and these communities were actively sought out. Being authentic in their gender identity within a community made the sense of belonging more meaningful (Vannini & Franzese, 2008); belongingness has been associated with an enhanced sense of meaning in life (Lambert et al., 2013).

Membership in LGBTQ+ gender communities can support the celebration of the aspects of a person's identity that may be marginalized within both heterosexual cisgender society (because of their sexual orientation) and within mainstream LGBTQ communities (because of their genders). For example, gay men who identify as bears (Manley et al., 2007) or leathermen (Mosher et al., 2006) may feel marginalized by a gay community that values youthful thin appearances and middle to upper class values. Similarly, femme sexual minority women may be held as suspect within the queer community, even though they understand their gender expression as a deliberate act of rebellion against conventional femininity (Hoskin, 2019). As such, finding supportive communities in which one's gender is affirmed or shared—such as bears, leatherman, or butch/femme—not only validates one's individual sense of self. These communities provide a sense of acceptance and unconditional positive regard for their gender identity, similar to that recommended by person-centered therapists as especially impactful for marginalized clients (Farber & Doolin, 2011; Knutson & Koch, 2019).

Values

In addition to developing a sense of personal belonging, being part of an LGBTQ+ gender community means that members are surrounded by others who prize that identity and support the internalization of that social valuing (Levitt, 2019a). Stigma about these identities has been found to be associated with a range of harmful consequences, including the need to overcome both external and internal obstacles (dickey et al., 2012; Szymanski et al., 2008). These obstacles can be challenging to overcome in isolation. By subverting traditional gender roles collectively, members of LGBTQ communities engage in an act of resistance that illuminates differences in power within a heterosexist/transphobic society and generates empowerment (Butler, 1999; Goodrich et al., 2016).

Activism and advocacy can increase self-awareness, self-acceptance, and authenticity in the face of discrimination (Levitt, Ovrebo et al., 2009; Szymanski et al., 2017) and many participants described engaging in these efforts either within or external to their communities. For instance, claiming a femme identity can provide the opportunity to subvert notions of femininity, both in relation to sexist beliefs about femininity within a patriarchal society (as femme women tend to be characterized as strong and assertive in contrast to feminine women characterization as passive and meek) and beliefs about the inherent masculinity of sexual minority women (Blair & Hoskin, 2014). Within a gender community, these identities represent an opportunity to subvert notions of heterosexuality and gain community support for the unique constructs of femme and butch genders as distinct from femininity and masculinity (Levitt & Hiestand, 2005). Being part of a community allows for the internalization of emancipatory values tied to an identity to replace stigmatized ones. In this way, it is a collective expression of subversive power that accrues the strength to counter the hegemonic power constituted by dominant societal gender norms.

Cultural Domain

Gender has been understood as collections of characteristics that are associated within a culture with being male or female—a gender binary that constrains the way many people experience their gender. This binary has been found to exact negative psychological and health effects on those who identify otherwise (Goldblum et al., 2012; Grant et al., 2011; Lombardi, 2009). Repeatedly, the studies of LGBTQ+ gender communities demonstrated that these limiting gender constructs restricted participants' interior, authentically felt gender (Levitt, 2019a). The LGBTQ+ gender communities offered alternative gender constructs, supported people to pursue identity congruence and provided a model in which gender might be seen as more of an individual expression. This finding is in concert with the voices of humanistic scholars who have warned against reductive interpretations of the human experience and highlighted the specific ways in which experiences of LGBTQ+ individuals should be understood within cultural contexts and systems (Goodrich et al., 2013; Gupta, 2017). LGBTQ+ cultures have the potential to develop novel gender categories that not only expand the ways that gender is conceptualized but that challenge prior cultural beliefs that have denied or devalued aspects of gender. They do so in four ways that we describe.

Identity

The LGBTQ+ communities developed identities that were in reaction to social messages that portrayed their gender as in conflict with their other identities. For one set of participants (e.g., butch women, gay male drag performers, transgender people, mothers and sisters in house/family networks) their genders were thought to conflict with their sex. They were told that they could not be "real" women, men, or people because their gender expressions did not conform to what was culturally expected of the gender that they were assigned.

For a second set of participants (e.g., femme women, bears, leathermen, fathers and sons in house/family networks), their genders were denied because they were seen as in conflict with dominant cultural stereotypes about their sexual orientation and/or other identities (e.g., racial and class identities). For instance, femme lesbians were taught that lesbians were masculine, and this stereotype made it hard for them to feel comfortable in their sexual identity. Similarly, bear and leathermen described receiving frequent social messaging that being gay meant that they must be feminine. People of color in houses and families were told that being LGBTQ+ meant that they were being White. In each case, it complicated their ability to claim their sexual orientation identity.

In contrast, the development of an LGBTQ+ gender culture facilitated the core need for an identity that reconciled their gender, physical sex, and sexuality. For example, lesbian communities created two new gender identities (i.e., butch and femme). The development of these new identity terms was necessary because butch women could not claim the label of masculinity comfortably because of its tie to conceptions of male physical sex; also, femininity was being contested during the post-war era when these identities emerged (women, especially White women, had just begun working outside the home more often and being more independent) so many femme women of the time did not see themselves as traditionally feminine.

Moreover, the constellation of traits associated with LGBTQ+ gender cultures should be understood as distinctive from cisgender heterosexual masculinities and femininities. For example, butch women at the time were stereotyped as nurturing and prioritizing their partner's sexual needs, and femme women were expected to be assertive and often were the breadwinners in a relationship (because they could pass as heterosexual, they faced less workplace sexual orientation discrimination). This subverts traditional gender roles rather than attempting to mimic them. Even when the same gender descriptor is retained, it might have distinctive meanings in a community. For instance, bear masculinity includes traits of caring, nurturance, and egalitarianism that are not associated with traditional masculinity.

Often within communities, mentor-like relationships developed to assist newcomers in adjusting to the LGBTQ+ culture. Mentors were often those who had faced rejection and marginalization and were seeking to provide support to others within the community (Manley et al., 2007). This was most evident in the house/family cultures where the (teen or young adult) children would take on the surname of their parent (often a gay father or a transgender mother) as well as the extended kinship ties associated with a family (e.g., sisters, uncles, grandparents; Bailey, 2013). The meanings of gender worked to affirm the very constellation of gender traits that had been denied to the members within wider cultural norms. It is important to note that the meanings of gender identities changed alongside continually developing understanding of gender in both mainstream heterosexual and LGBTQ cultures. For example, characteristics associated with butch and femme have not remained static but have dynamically evolved across decades in relation to the types of stigma surrounding them (Levitt, 2019a). In these myriad ways, the forging of new gender labels and expressions allowed for novel forms of identity development that were previously denied by gender labels and assignments.

Security
As new gender cultures were created to assert and value new constellations of traits, they fostered a sense of security for these individuals, whose lives might have felt otherwise threatened. The communities provided the ability to gather in safe spaces such as community centers, private homes, and bars in a spirit of solidarity and support. They offered respite from often intersectional forms of discrimination and social pressures that could be overwhelming.

    To protect themselves, communities sometimes would cohere around social justice activities such as activism and advocacy, which are designed to construct new support, shift cisgenderist and heterosexist structures, and inform policy change toward LGBTQ+ rights (Bassichis et al., 2013; Rawson, 2015. For example, transgender activism has resulted in improvements and increased accessibility in gender-affirming surgical and medical procedures and diagnoses (Dresher, 2015). Furthermore, LGBTQ+ communities have been a source of support to members who seek to physically affirm their gender. In addition to this, however, communities offer a culture of solidarity that can provide security and support to those who confront obstacles, including the stress and discrimination tied to mainstream cultural beliefs that their convergences of identities can or should not exist (Levitt & Ippolito, 2014a).

Belonging
Not only do LGBTQ+ gender communities counter discrimination, they also provide an opportunity to celebrate identity and express pride. For example, conferences and festivals have developed within bear and leather communities to create a sense of national connection and affirm norms that prize devalued aspects of gender (Manley et al., 2007; Mosher et al., 2006). Similarly, houses and gay families provided belonging and deep connection for those who faced rejection from their families of origin and larger communities (Bailey et al., 2013). Many of the family members interviewed reported being in contact daily and having kinship ties that spanned states. The experience of being understood and accepted for all of one's identities was crucial to the experience of belonging. To maintain these connections, research has found that sexual and gender minority youth also may look to online and social media platforms for peer support and solidarity (Steinke et al., 2017), and many of the families in our studies had social media pages that supported their connection.

Values
The forging of these ontological categories of gender allowed LGBTQ+ cultures to resist stigma by reconstructing new gender norms and exercising a subversive social power (Levitt, 2019a). Because LGBTQ+ communities valued sets of traits that were otherwise socially condemned, new members were drawn to them, and communities become more established and visible. For instance, house/family communities hold balls or pageants, competitive dance and fashion shows in which members engage in a wide variety of gender performances (Bailey, 2013; Horne et al., 2014; Levitt, Horne et al., 2015). Houses and family members would travel across the country to attend these events, despite their economic struggles, because the sense of connection, creativity, and engagement was so strong. LGBTQ+ genders led to the creation of cultures that assisted in the internalization of social values that were designed to battle the very sets of traits that were debased elsewhere in their lives.

Interpersonal Domain

In addition to having a psychological and cultural function, gender plays an interpersonal role by communicating information about identities and structuring how people are positioned in relation to each other (Levitt, 2019a). This communication can occur overtly, via claiming a gender identity, or more covertly through the use of symbols, speech, hair, dress, or mannerisms that convey a gender affiliation. These signs affirm personal identity and sense of belonging to a subculture through processes of symbolic interactionism (Hutson, 2010). Just as in therapy, where people may engage images or metaphors as symbolic representations of implicit meanings (Gendlin, 2003), they may engage representations of their gender identity to communicate their LGBTQ+ gender, assert unmet related needs, and establish desired relational positionality to others. This function also has an influence on identity, security, belonging, and social values.

Identity
Following the notion from queer theory that gender is developed through the repetitive performance of sets of characteristics that become associated within a cultural (Butler, 1999), LGBTQ+ gender identities were found to be communicated through varied signifiers (Levitt, 2019a). For instance, butch lesbians' hair might communicate their gender, whereas vocal cadence might be used to suggest a man's drag gender. These aspects of appearance may affirm people's authentic gender identity through symbolic interactions, such that aspects of gender expression facilitate people being regarded or accepted as a member of a particular subculture. They can communicate shared values, meanings, and expectations.

   Therefore, embodying an LGBTQ+ gender identity involves more than tailoring one's appearance; rather, embodiment represents the interaction between one's felt sense of self with the meanings that are read in connection with cues in the environment (Levitt, 2019a). The finding of a bidirectional influence of gender identity on gender expression is consistent with existential theories on embodiment, which posit that the self consists of constant interaction with the environment rather than being contained within a body that is contained within an external environment (Madison, 2010).

Security

Despite the positive effects of communicating one's sexual or gender identity status, it is unsafe to do so in certain contexts. Research has found that being out increases social support but also increases the chances of becoming a target of prejudice or violence (Puckett et al., 2016; Velez & Morado, 2016). LGBTQ+ people still face the threat of violence or loss of personal resources (e.g., jobs, housing, relationships) if their identities are exposed in certain contexts, meaning that being visible as a sexual or gender minority could threaten their safety. However, concealing one's identity can also increase incongruence between one's authentic self and one's external self and result in negative psychological consequences (Boyraz et al., 2014). Covert ways of expressing LGBTQ+ gender allows people to strive for personal authenticity and congruence even when they need to prioritize safety and may allow for subtle shifts in gender expression as it becomes necessary. A method of achieving this balance is illustrated by the hanky code associated with the leather community, in which color-coded handkerchiefs are worn to signal sexual preferences (Mosher et al., 2006). This allows people to stealthily communicate their individual identity as a sexual minority and position themselves in relation to potential partners.

Belonging

In addition to affirming personal identity, the communication of LGBTQ+ gender can allow for a greater sense of connection with a larger community (Levitt, 2019a). This connection accords with the humanistic concept that belonging is a fundamental human need (Baumeister & Leary, 1995) and is supported by the established relationship between level of connectedness to the LGBTQ+ community and psychological well-being in sexual minorities (Frost & Meyer, 2012). The communication of gender could foster a sense of status as well as lowering status. For instance, in the study of gay men who performed drag (Levitt, Wheeler et al., 2018), it was communicated that while they were in drag they tended to be treated as celebrities within the communities. At the same time, when out of drag, they found that they were often marginalized in mainstream gay culture and their status as gay men was questioned. The communication of LGBTQ+ genders, then, could act to either increase or decrease belonging within both heterosexual and LGBTQ+ contexts.

Values

In some cases, the use of culturally sanctioned symbols to express gender identities was used to subvert and challenge norms within both mainstream heterosexual culture and LGBTQ+ culture (Levitt, 2019a). This idea that personal identities and cultures are always interacting and are mutually influential is supported by both existential and queer theorists' writings (Goodrich et al., 2016; Madison, 2010).

For instance, house and family parents could use their gender identities and associated status to set expectations for children in their houses. As part and parcel of a mothers' nurturance, it was accepted that she communicated the need for sexual safety among her young adult children or required them to attend school (Levitt, Horne et al., 2015). Gay drag performers described how they would challenge social norms by exaggerating symbols associated with essentialized notions of masculinity or femininity or by combining traditionally mismatched symbols to highlight the ambiguity of gender or the oppressive nature of traditional gender roles (Levitt, Wheeler et al., 2018). This communication required a shared intersubjective understanding between the performers and audience members about the subversive nature of the performance, so that the enactment can be read in accordance with its intent (Mann, 2011). In these ways, communication of gender within a community could be used deliberately to challenge socially constructed identities or foster social change.

Sexual Domain

Within the communities that were studied, gender was found to function by prompting a new eroticized aesthetic (Levitt, 2019a). This aesthetic replaced the shame that was associated with that gender in mainstream cisgender heterosexual and LGBTQ+ cultures. It acted as a physical manifestation of the reconciliation and valuing of the constellation of gender traits that was devalued previously. Although psychologists have not focused previously on the connection between socially maligned aspects of gender and the development of new protest aesthetics, humanistic writers have argued against the biologizing of sexual functioning and, instead, conceptualized sexual dysfunction as a form of dissent within a culture of sexism and objectification (e.g., Kleinplatz, 1988; Tiefer, 2006). They argue that psychologists should use sex therapy to explore and challenge patriarchal values rather than trying to enforce sexual functioning within them. Again, we review four effects of gender within this domain to explain the process of resistance that unfolds within sexuality.

Identity

The eroticization of gender expression associated with an identity was a powerful affirmation. For instance, butch women entering a butch–femme community reported shifting from having internalized the belief that they were profoundly unattractive because of their gender expression to realizing that they were profoundly attractive to femme women in the community for the same reason (Levitt & Hiestand, 2005). Some described the joy in shifting from feeling pressured to hide or mask their gender to realizing that the more they expressed their gender the more likely they would be to attract a romantic partner. Their gender identity became a source of pride because it was eroticized.

Security

This affirmation was also powerful in countering the internalization of stigma about their gender expression and identity. For instance, bear participants communicated how the aesthetic of being full bodied and hirsute allowed them to overcome the fat-shaming that they had experienced in mainstream gay male culture (Manley et al., 2007). The same signifiers that were read as signs of weakness in one context could be strengths in another. To provide an example, femme women who felt their gender was read as weakness in a heterosexual context might feel empowered within lesbian contexts. Instead of feeling objectified when wearing a short skirt or a low-cut top in a heterosexual bar, their appearance in a lesbian space signaled their agency in directing their sexuality toward butch women, whose sexuality was oriented toward pleasuring femme women rather than treating them as objects for their enjoyment (Levitt, Gerrish et al., 2003).

Belonging

The development of these aesthetics became the foundation for gender play in the community (Levitt, 2019a). Drag performers might creatively combine gender cues to subvert gender stereotypes and expectations (Mann, 2011). Femme women might allow their butch partners to open doors for them to mutually engage in affirmation of each other's gender and to challenge oppressive heterosexual norms (Levitt & Hiestand, 2005). Families and houses at bars might imitate a range of gendered performances (e.g., Wall Street executive, fashion models), claiming gender expressions that are typically barred to them because of their class, age, and race (Bailey, 2013; Levitt, Wheeler et al., 2018). It was because gender signs were read in the same way among community members that play with gender expression could become meaningful and jubilant, as well as increase a sense of belonging to a particular subculture.

Values

The participants described how their gender identities and community affiliations led to increased sexual self-esteem. Their gender communities were instrumental in supporting this internalization of a positive sexuality that challenged the cisgender and heterosexual social norms that limit displays of sexuality to the young and traditionally beautiful and disparage sexuality within other bodies (Whitesel, 2014). The embodiment of affirming values could challenge types of stigma in addition to sexual orientation and gender stigma, including fat stigma and racist beauty ideals. They could replace body shame with feelings of sexual pride. At the same time, some house or family competitions at balls or pageants could be fierce, and although a general esteeming of a new aesthetic might result, individuals might find that the scrutiny of competing within gender performances is challenging (e.g., Bailey, 2013).

Conclusion:
Revisiting Tensions between Humanistic and Queer/Trans Theory

In this section we revisit the three points of tension that were described between humanistic and queer/transgender theories. We examine each in turn.

The Focus on Cultural Privilege and Oppression
As described previously, humanistic scholars have been incorporating the role of culture into their theorizing (e.g., Hoffman et al., 2015; Hoffman et al., 2016). The current theory continues this movement by explicating the processes by which gender shifts into gender identity, with an eye toward two types of power (Levitt, 2019b).

Across each of the domains, heteronormative cisgenderist hegemonic power created the need for LGBTQ+ genders. In short, the participants across the study tended to initially have an internal sense of gender that was denied (across psychological, cultural, interpersonal, and sexual domains), creating a condition in which they were unable to act authentically in accordance with their gender. They then developed a need to seek out other contexts in which they would be supported to act within their preferred social positions and sets of characteristics, finding an LGBTQ+ identity and community.

In this process of seeking and developing new gender constructs and communities, the participants enacted subversive power that allowed them to engage resistance to both oppression and internalized shame. This new culture influenced their gender by resulting in a gender identity that felt more authentic, cultural norms that endorsed qualities that had been marginalized, increased interpersonal status and security, and the eroticization of gender values. This approach holds cultural privilege, oppression, and resistance as central in considerations of gender and gender identity.

The Role of Autonomy and Self-Determination
The functionalist gender theory presented (Levitt, 2019b) and its division into four domains can assist in better understanding how personal agency functions in relation to gender and gender identity development. Across the research on the varied communities, participants reported having a sense of their gender that was essential to their sense of self (often felt as biologically based or as deeply rooted). This sense of self directed their preferred social positioning and the sets of characteristics with which they felt most affiliated. Agency became important when this sense of gender came into conflict with the gendered attributes assigned to them. This will almost invariably occur to some extent because people

tend not to completely fit their gender stereotypes. If the fit is reasonably good, however, the person may elect to veer from social expectations with little repercussion. If the fit is poor, the person may experience heterosexism and transphobia to a strong degree—which was typical for our participants. The distress pushed them to seek out new sexual and gender identities and coalesce communities that better allowed them to express their gender authentically, gain cultural support, have their gender expression prized, and cast it as desirable. In this process, an internal sense of gender was transformed into an LGBTQ+ gender identity. Within this framework, the enactment of agency is not at odds with a strong internal sense of gender but is an outgrowth of its conflict with social expectations.

Bodies as Givens and/or Creations. Humanistic theorists have tended not to take up the debate about the foundation of sex and gender. Tiefer (2006) wrote about how early humanistic approaches to sex therapy have been all but forgotten but invoked a time in which humanists championed views of sex that were relationally based (versus medically based), politically situated (versus apolitical), focused on individual variation (versus standardization), encouraging of self-exploration (versus medical intervention), and focused on empowerment (versus maintaining patriarchal systems). Her account may provide some understanding of the values that humanists can bring to an understanding of the body and may indicate points of similarity with queer and trans theorists—that is, the view of bodies as political, individual ,and social creations.

Within the theory of gender presented in this paper (Levitt, 2019a), the embodied person is central. The communicative function of gender occurred via individuals' agentic decisions to transform their bodies (and general appearances) to resist stigma and maintain safety while also seeking liberation and authenticity. Embodied signifiers of LGBTQ+ gender were developed in response to the specific sociocultural oppression that denied the constellation of gender characteristics that seemed authentic to the members of each community. For instance, leathermen who received messaging that being gay meant that they were feminine crafted hypermasculine bodies. Bears who resisted both gay youth culture and hypermasculinity developed aesthetics that valued body types that were natural for older men. The body became a reflection of participants' sense of self and an affirmation of their identity, culture, and sexuality.

In sum, there is great potential for the convergence of humanistic and critical theories (Levitt, 2019b; Levitt & Whelton, 2019; Levitt, Whelton, et al., 2019). Each perspective brings an invaluable piece to the table when understanding human functioning. Humanistic theories have traditionally focused on the individual, familial, and interpersonal developmental experiences with power that may do harm by leading people to disengage from their own internal experiences. Therapies have focused on the process of learning to connect and utilize individual and interpersonal experiences as a source of knowledge and direction. These approaches have taught people to resist the passive acceptance of external authority or social messages and to reclaim a sense of personal power and direction.

In contrast, multicultural-feminist approaches have focused on people's experiences with systemic and societal power that have distanced people from their own experiences and cultures, as well as leading to social stigma associated with the marginalization. These psychotherapies have focused on helping people value their cultural experiences and on engaging in social justice action to combat social exclusion, economic injustices, oppression, and violence. These two types of experiences do not operate in isolation as both co-occur in our lives and the lives of our clients. Fundamentally, both approaches argue that the development of interpersonal and cultural environments that support congruence with the experiences of self and identities are needed to foster mental health. For this reason, their joint examination is necessary, and it is the authors' intention that this theory, which considers gender in relation to the internal experience of an embodied individual across interpersonal and cultural contexts, will further that integration.

Glossary of Terms

Bears: Communities of gay men who prize a form of masculinity that values a natural mature masculinity, fat positivity, and a hirsute appearance.

Butch Lesbians: Lesbian women who have a gender that is often read as masculine by others, who adopt this identity to signify their gender and sexual orientation and, typically, but not always, their attraction to femme women. "Studs" are similar identities adopted by lesbian women of color.

Cisgender: The characteristic of a person having a gender that corresponds with the constellation of traits associated with the physical sex assigned to them.

Drag: A performance of a gender expression for the purposes of entertaining an audience. It is an enactment of gender assumed to be cross dressing and often functions to subvert and ironize gender norms.

Gender: A set of characteristics that are associated with people's biological sex or that are grouped together in reaction to other genders, the expectations associated with them, and the social stigma that may be invoked when gender norms are broken.

Gender Expression: The way gender is expressed through a person's mannerisms, voice, dress, and socially meaningful symbols.

Gender Identity: The way a person identifies their own gender (e.g., woman, man, butch, nonbinary).

Family Networks: Fictive kinship groups of, typically, GBTQ+ people of color that provide a family structure and support with a focus on children's development.

Femme Lesbians: Lesbian women who have a gender that is often read as feminine by others, who adopt this identity to signify their gender and sexual orientation and, typically but not always, their attraction to butch women or transmen.

House Networks: Fictive kinship groups of typically GBTQ+ people of color that provide a family structure and support, with a focus on competing in community balls or pageants that feature gendered and fashion performances between houses.

Leathermen: Communities of gay men who prize a form of masculinity that values muscular physiques, leather garb, and who tend to incorporate sadomasochistic rituals in their sexuality.

Transgender: An umbrella term that includes identities of people whose gender does not match the gender that was assigned to them by parents and society because of expectations that their body will dictate their gender.

References

American Psychiatric Association. (2013). *Diagnostic and statistical manual of mental disorders* (5th ed.). Author.

American Psychological Association (2007). Guidelines for psychological practice with girls and women. *American Psychologist, 62*, 949–979. https://doi.org/10.1037/0003-066X.62.9.949

American Psychological Association (2012). Guidelines for psychological practice with lesbian, gay, and bisexual clients. *American Psychologist, 67*, 10–42. doi: 10.1037/a0024659

American Psychological Association (2015). Guidelines for psychological practice with transgender and gender nonconforming people. *American Psychologist, 70*, 832–864. https://doi.org/10.1037/a0039906

Bailey, M. M. (2013). *Butch queens up in pumps: Gender, performance, and ballroom culture in Detroit.* University of Michigan Press.

Blair, K. L., & Hoskin, R. A. (2014). Experiences of femme identity: Coming out, invisibility and femmephobia. *Psychology & Sexuality, 6*, 229–244. https://doi.org/10.1080/19419899.2014.921860

Bassichis, M., Lee, A., & Spade, D. (2013). Building an abolitionist trans and queer movement with everything we've got In S. Stryker & S. Whittle (Eds.), *The transgender studies reader* (pp. 653–667). Routledge.

Baumeister, R. F., & Leary, M. R. (1995). The need to belong: Desire for interpersonal attachments as a fundamental human motivation. *Psychological Bulletin, 117*, 497–529. https://doi.org/10.1037/0033-2909.117.3.497

Boyraz, G., Waits, B., & Felix, V. A. (2014). Authenticity, life satisfaction, and distress: A longitudinal analysis. *Journal of Counseling Psychology, 61*, 498-505. https://doi.org/10.1037/cou0000031

Butler, J. (1999). *Gender trouble: Feminism and the subversion of identity*. Routledge.

Butler, J. (2004). *Undoing gender*. Routledge.

Cromwell, J. (2006). Queering the binaries: Transituated identities, bodies and sexualities. In S Stryker & S. Whittle (Eds.), *The transgender studies reader* (pp. 509–520). Routledge.

Diamond, L. M., & Rosky, C. J. (2016). Scrutinizing immutability: Research on sexual orientation and U.S. legal advocacy for sexual minorities. *The Journal of Sex Research, 53,* 363–391. https://doi.org/10.1080/00224499.2016.1139665

dickey, L. M., Burnes, T. R., & Singh, A. A. (2012). Sexual identity development of female-to-male transgender individuals: A grounded theory inquiry. *Journal of LGBT Issues in Counseling, 6,* 118–138. https://doi.org/10.1080/15538605.2012.678184

Drescher, J. (2015). Queer diagnoses revisited: The past and future of homosexuality and gender diagnoses in DSM and ICD. *International Review of Psychiatry, 27,* 386–395. https://doi.org/10.3109/09540261.2015.1053847

Farber, B. A., & Doolin, E. M. (2011). Positive regard. *Psychotherapy, 48,* 58–64. https://doi.org/10.1037/a0022141

Frost, D. M., & Meyer, I. H. (2012). Measuring community connectedness among diverse sexual minority populations. *Journal of Sex Research, 49,* 36–49. https://doi.org/10.1080/00224499.2011.565427

Gendlin, E. T. (2003). *Focusing. How to gain direct access to your body's knowledge.* Rider.

Goldblum, P., Testa, R. J., Pflum, S., Hendricks, M.L., Bradford, J., & Bongar, B. (2012). The relationship between gender-based victimization and suicide attempts in transgender people. *Professional Psychology: Research and Practice, 43,* 468–745. https://doi.org/10.1037/a0029605

Goodrich, K. M., Harper, A. J., Luke, M., & Singh, A. A. (2013). Best practices for professional school counselors working with LGBTQ youth. *Journal of LGBT Issues in Counseling, 7*(4), 307–322. https://doi.org/10.1080/15538605.2013.839331

Goodrich, K. M., Luke, M., & Smith, A. J. (2016). Queer humanism: Toward an epistemology of socially just, culturally responsive change. *Journal of Humanistic Psychology, 56,* 612–623. https://doi.org/10.1177/0022167816652534

Gorton, R. N. (2013). Transgender as mental illness: Nosology, social justice, and the tarnished golden mean. In S. Stryker & A. Z. Aizura (Eds.), *The transgender studies reader 2* (pp. 644–652). Routledge.

Grant, J. M., Mottet, L. A., Tanis, J., Herman, J. L., Harrison, J., & Keisling, M. (2011). *Injustice at every turn: A report of the national transgender discrimination survey.* National Center for Transgender Equality and National Gay and Lesbian Task Force.

Gressgård, R. (2010). When trans translates into tolerance—Or was it monstrous? Transsexual and transgender identity in liberal humanist discourse. *Sexualities, 13,* 539–561. https://doi.org/10.1177/1363460710375569

Gupta, N. (2017). Exploring the schizoid defense of the closet through the existential–phenomenology of RD Laing. *Journal of Humanistic Psychology, 57*(2), 170–189. https://doi.org/10.1177/0022167815597411

Halberstam, J. (1998). *Female masculinity.* Duke University Press.

Hiestand, K., Horne, S. G., & Levitt, H. M. (2008). Effects of gender identity on experiences of healthcare for sexual minority women. *Journal of GLBT Health, 3,* 15–27. https://doi.org/10.1080/15574090802263405

Hiestand, K., & Levitt, H. M. (2005). Butch identity development: The formation of an authentic gender. *Feminism and Psychology, 15,* 61–85. https://doi.org/10.1177/0959353505049709

Hoffman, L., Cleare-Hoffman, H., & Jackson, T. (2015). Humanistic psychology and multiculturalism: History, current status, and advancements. In K. J. Schneider, J. F. Pierson, & J. F. Bugental (Eds.), *The handbook of humanistic psychology: Theory, research, and practice* (2nd ed., pp. 41–55). Sage Publications.

Hoffman, L., Granger, N., Jr., Vallejos, L., & Moats, M. (2016). An existential–humanistic perspective on Black Lives Matter and contemporary protest movements. *Journal of Humanistic Psychology, 56,* 595–611. https://doi.org/10.1177/0022167816652273

Horne, S. G., Levitt, H. M., Sweeney, K. K., Puckett, J. C., & Hampton, M. (2014). African American gay families: An entry point for HIV prevention. *Journal of Sex Research, 3,* 1–14. https://doi.org/10.1080/00224499.2014.901285

Hoskin, R. A. (2019). Femmephobia: The role of anti-femininity and gender policing in LGBTQ+ people's experiences of discrimination. *Sex Roles,* 1–18. https://doi.org/10.1007/s11199-019-01021-3

Hutson, D. J. (2010). Standing out/fitting in: Identity, appearance, and authenticity in gay and lesbian communities. *Symbolic Interaction, 33,* 213–233. https://doi.org/10.1525/si.2010.33.2.213

Hyde, J. S., Bigler, R. S., Joel, D., Tate, C. C., & van Anders, S. M. (2019). The future of sex and gender in psychology: Five challenges to the gender binary. *American Psychologist, 74,* 171–193. https://doi.org/10.1037/amp0000307

Johanson, G. J. (2009). Nonlinear science, mindfulness, and the body in humanistic psychotherapy. *The Humanistic Psychologist, 37,* 159–177. https://doi.org/10.1080/08873260902892121

Kleinplatz, P. J. (1998). Sex therapy for vaginismus: A review, critique, and humanistic alternative. *The Journal of Humanistic Psychology, 38*(2), 41–81. https://doi.org/10.1177/00221678980382004

Knutson, D., & Koch, J. M. (2019). Person-centered therapy as applied to work with transgender and gender diverse clients. *Journal of Humanistic Psychology.* https://doi.org/10.1177/0022167818791082

Lambert, N. M., Stillman, T. F., Hicks, J. A., Kamble, S., Baumeister, R. F., & Fincham, F. D. (2013). To belong is to matter: Sense of belonging enhances meaning in life. *Personality and Social Psychology Bulletin, 39,* 1418–1427. https://doi.org/10.1177/0146167213499186

Levitt, H. M. (2006). Butch, femme, bear and leatherman: A programmatic exploration of gender identities within gay and lesbian subcultures. In K. S. Yip (Ed.), *Psychology of gender identity: An international perspective* (pp. 105–121). Nova Science.

Levitt, H. M. (2019a). A psychosocial genealogy of LGBTQ+ Gender: An empirically based theory of gender and gender identity cultures. *Psychology of Women Quarterly, 43,* 275–297. https://doi.org/10.1177/0361684319834641

Levitt, H. M. (2019b). Applications of a functionalist theory of gender: A response to reflections and a research agenda. *Psychology of Women Quarterly, 43,* 309–316. https://doi.org/10.1177/0361684319851467

Levitt, H. M., & Bridges, S. K. (2007). Gender expression in bisexual women: Therapeutic issues and considerations. In B. Firestein (Ed.), *Becoming visible: Counseling bisexuals across the lifespan* (pp. 297–311). Columbia University Press.

Levitt, H. M., Gerrish, E., & Hiestand, K. (2003). The misunderstood gender: A model of modern femme identity. *Sex Roles, 48,* 99–113. https://doi.org/10.1023/A:1022453304384

Levitt, H. M., & Hiestand, K. (2004). A quest for authenticity: Contemporary butch gender. *Sex Roles, 50,* 605–621. https://doi.org/10.1023/B:SERS.0000027565.59109.80

Levitt, H. M., & Hiestand, K. R. (2005). Gender within lesbian sexuality: Butch and femme perspectives. *Journal of Constructivist Psychology, 18,* 39–51. https://doi.org/10.1080/10720530590523062

Levitt, H. M., & Horne, S. G. (2002). Explorations of lesbian–queer genders. *Journal of Lesbian Studies, 6,* 25–39. https://doi.org/10.1300/J155v06n02_05

Levitt, H. M., Horne, S. G., Freeman-Coppadge, D., & Roberts, T. (2017). HIV prevention in gay family and house networks: Fostering self-determination and sexual safety. *AIDS & Behavior, 10,* 2973–2986. https://doi.org/10.1007/s10461-017-1774-x

Levitt, H. M., Horne, S. G., Puckett, J. C., Sweeney, K. K., & Hampton, M. (2015). Gay families: Challenging racial and sexual/gender minority stressors through social support. *Journal of GLBT Family Studies, 11,* 173–202. doi: 10.1080/1550428X.2014.958266

Levitt, H. M., & Ippolito, M. R. (2014a, August). Being transgender: The experience of transgender identity development. *Journal of Homosexuality, 61,* 1727–1758. https://doi.org/10.1177/0361684313501644

Levitt, H. M., & Ippolito, M. R. (2014b). Being transgender: Navigating minority stressors and developing authentic self-presentation. *Psychology of Women Quarterly, 38,* 46–64. https://doi.org/10.1177/0361684313501644

Levitt, H. M., Ovrebo, E., Anderson-Cleveland, M. B., Leone, C., Jeong, J. Y., Arm, J. R., ... & Vardaman, J. M. (2009). Balancing dangers: GLBT experience in a time of anti-GLBT legislation. *Journal of Counseling Psychology, 56,* 67. https://doi.org/10.1037/a0012988

Levitt, H. M., Puckett, J. A., Ippolito, M. R., & Horne, S. G. (2012). Sexual minority women's gender identity and expression: Challenges and supports. *Journal of Lesbian Studies, 16,* 153–176. doi: 10.1080/10894160.2011.605009

Levitt, H. M., Wheeler, E., Maki, E., Surace, F. I., Alacantra, D., Cadet, M., ... Ngai, C. (2018). Drag gender: Experiences of gender for gay and queer men who perform drag. *Sex Roles, 78,* 367–384. https://doi.org/10.1007/s11199-017-0802-7

Levitt, H. M., & Whelton, W. J. (2019). *Humanistic and feminist multicultural foundations of psychotherapy: Considerations of power and agency.* Unpublished manuscript, University of Massachusetts Boston, Boston.

Levitt, H. M., Whelton, W. J., & Iwakabe, S. (2019). Integrating feminist-multicultural perspectives into emotion-focused therapy. In L. Greenberg & R. Goldman (Eds.), *Clinical Handbook of Emotion-Focused Therapy* (pp. 425–444). American Psychological Association.

Lombardi, E. (2009). Varieties of transgender/transsexual lives and their relationship with transphobia. *Journal of Homosexuality, 56,* 977–992. https://doi.org/10.1080/00918360903275393

Madison, G. (2010). Focusing on existence: Five facets of an experiential-existential model. *Person-Centered & Experiential Psychotherapies, 9,* 189–204. doi: 10.1080/14779757.2010.9689066

Manley, E., Levitt, H. M., & Mosher, C. (2007). Understanding the bear movement in gay male culture: Redefining masculinity. *Journal of Homosexuality, 53,* 89–112. https://doi.org/10.1080/00918360802103365

Mann, S. L. (2011). Drag queens' use of language and the performance of blurred gendered and racial identities. *Journal of Homosexuality, 58,* 793–811. https://doi.org/10.1080/00918369.2011.581923

Maslow, A. H. (1973). Self-actualizing people: A study of psychological health. In R. J. Lowry (Ed.), *Dominance, self-esteem, self-actualization: Germinal papers of A.H. Maslow* (pp. 177–201). Brookes/Cole. (Original work published 1950)

Meyer, I. H. (2003). Prejudice, social stress, and mental health in lesbian, gay, and bisexual populations: Conceptual issues and research evidence. *Psychological Bulletin, 129,* 674–697. https://doi.org/10.1037/0033-2909.129.5.674

Moradi, B. (2019). Naming gender as axis of power and coalition politics. *Psychology of Women Quarterly, 43,* 303–308. https://doi.org/10.1177/0361684319850439

Mosher, C., Levitt, H. M., & Manley, E. (2006). Layers of leather: The identity formation of leathermen as a process of transforming meanings of masculinity. *Journal of Homosexuality, 51,* 93–123. https://doi.org/10.1300/J082v51n03_06

Panesis, C. P., Levitt, H. M., & Bridges, S. K. (2014). *The sexuality within butch and femme sexual minority women* (Honors thesis, University of Massachusetts Boston).

Plummer, K. (2005). Critical humanism and queer theory: Living with the tensions. In N. K. Denzin & Y. S. Lincoln (Eds.), *The landscape of qualitative research* (3rd ed.; pp. 477–499). Sage. https://us.sagepub.com/en-us/nam/home

Polderman, T. J. C., Kreukels, B. P. C., Irwig, M. S., Beach, L., Chan, Y.-M., Derks, E. M., ... Davis, L. K. (2018). The biological contributions to gender identity and gender diversity: Bringing data to the table. *Behavior Genetics, 48,* 95–108. https://doi.org/10.1300/J082v51n03_06

Puckett, J. A., Maroney, M. R., Levitt, H.M., & Horne, S. G. (2016). Relations between gender expression, minority stress, and mental health in cisgender sexual minority women and men. *Psychology of Sexual Orientation and Gender Diversity, 3,* 489–498. https://doi.org/10.1037/sgd0000201

Rawson, K. J. (2015). [Review of the book *Transforming Citizenships: Transgender Articulations of the Law, by Isaac West*]. QED: A Journal in the GLBTQ Worldmaking, 2, 160–162. https://www.muse.jhu.edu/article/602052

Rennie, D. L. (2007). Methodical hermeneutics and humanistic psychology. *The Humanistic Psychologist, 35,* 1–14. https://doi.org/10.1080/08873260709336693

Robbins, B. D. (2008). What is the good life? Positive psychology and the renaissance of humanistic psychology. *The Humanistic Psychologist, 36,* 96–112. https://doi.org/10.1080/08873260802110988

Rogers, C. R. (1961). *On becoming a person.* Constable.

Rogers, C. R. (1977). *On personal power: Inner strength and its revolutionary impact.* Delacourt Press.

Rogers, C. R. (1981). The foundations of the person-centered approach. *Dialectics and Humanism, 8*(1), 5-16. https://doi.org/10.5840/dialecticshumanism19818123

Steinke, J., Root-Bowman, M., Estabrook, S., Levine, D. S., & Kantor, L. M. (2017). Meeting the needs of sexual and gender minority youth: Formative research on potential digital health interventions. *Journal of Adolescent Health, 60,* 541–548. https://doi.org/10.1016/j.jadohealth.2016.11.023

Sullivan, N. (2014). Somatechnics. *Transgender Studies Quarterly, 1,* 187–190. doi: 10.1215/23289252-2399983

Sundarararjan, L. (2002). Humanistic psychotherapy and the scientist-practitioner debate: An "embodied" perspective. *Journal of Humanistic Psychology, 43,* 34–47. https://doi.org/10.1177/0022167802422004

Szymanski, D. M., Kashubeck-West, S., & Meyer, J. (2008). Internalized heterosexism: Measurement, psychosocial correlates, and research directions. *The Counseling Psychologist, 36,* 525–574. https://doi.org/10.1177/0011000007309489

Szymanski, D. M., Mikorski, R., & Carretta, R. F. (2017). Heterosexism and LGB positive identity: Roles of coping and personal growth initiative. *The Counseling Psychologist, 45,* 294–319. https://doi.org/10.1177/0011000017697195

Tebbe, E. (2019). What's past is prologue: Advancing psychological research on LGBTQ+ genders. *Psychology of Women Quarterly, 43*, 271–274. doi:10.1177/0361684319847121

Tiefer, L. (2006). Sex therapy as a humanistic enterprise. *Sexual and Relationship Therapy, 21*, 359–375.

US proposal for defining gender has no basis in science, Editorial (2018, October 30). *Nature.* Retrieved from https://www.nature.com/articles/d41586-018-07238-8

Vannini, P., & Franzese, A. (2008). The authenticity of self: Conceptualization, personal experience, and practice. *Sociology Compass, 2*, 1621–1637. https://doi.org/10.1111/j.1751-9020.2008.00151.x

Velez, B. L., & Moradi, B. (2016). A moderated mediation test of minority stress: The role of collective action. *The Counseling Psychologist, 44,* 1132–1157. https://doi.org/10.1177/0011000016665467

Watson, L. B. (2019). Gender identity and expression in LGBTQ+ communities: Implications for the practice of psychology. *Psychology of Women Quarterly, 43*, 298–302. https://doi.org/10.1177/0361684319846498

Whitesel, J. (2014). *Fat gay men: Girth, mirth, and the politics of stigma.* NYU Press.

Wong, P. T. P. (2006). Existential and humanistic theories. In J. C. Thomas & D. L. Segal (Eds.), *Comprehensive handbook of personality and psychopathology* (Vol. 1, pp. 192–211). John Wiley & Sons.

Chapter 3

The Erotic in Anesthetic Culture: Revisiting Rollo May's Concept of "The New Puritanism"

Brent Dean Robbins

Abstract

Rollo May's *Love and Will*, a classic text in existential psychology, explores three paradoxes in the wake of the sexual revolution: (1) a hyper-focus on sexuality and sexual liberation coupled with diminished feeling and passion in the sexual act, (2) an overemphasis on technique as a means to enhance sexual pleasure, and (3) a "new puritanism" characterized by alienation from the body, the separation of emotion from reason, and the use of the body as a machine. This chapter examines May's cultural critique in light of current empirical evidence and in a larger socio-historical context to assess the ongoing relevance of his theory on the three paradoxes. It also expands and reconceptualizes May's theory in light of the concept of "anesthetic culture." Anesthetic culture reinforces states of anesthetic consciousness, which overlaps conceptually with constructs such as alexithymia and experiential avoidance that are related to various forms of psychopathology and diminished well-being, including sexual problems.

***

In *Love and Will*, Rollo May (1969) offers a diagnosis of the culture that was emerging in the late 1960s. May outlined three paradoxes that he saw emerging at the apex of the sexual revolution. The first paradox he observed was a hyper-focus on sexuality and sexual liberation that was ironically paired with a diminishing experience of feeling and passion in the sexual act. He identified the second paradox as a result of the new emphasis on technique as a means to enhance sexual pleasure. This focus on technique paradoxically culminates in a sense of alienation, loneliness, and depersonalization as sex becomes increasingly mechanized. The third paradox pronounced by May was a "new puritanism" composed of three elements: "First, *a state of alienation from the body*. Second, *the separation of emotion from reason*. And third, *the use of the body as machine*" (p. 45).

It is interesting that May's outline of the three paradoxes and the provocative notion of a "new puritanism" at the height of the sexual revolution has received very little recognition or commentary since the 1969 publication. In this chapter, I take up May's incitement to consider the shadow side of the sexual revolution, and I will aim to situate it within a larger, socio-cultural narrative. This story must include a history of sexual repression rooted in prudish sensibilities, of which Freud's psychoanalysis can be witnessed as both a symptom and cure. This Victorian prudishness, and the shaping of American culture by Calvinist and Puritan influences imported from Europe, are expressions of what May refers to as the "old puritanism," so to speak, to which the structurally aligned but polarized contrary position of the "new puritanism" can be culturally tied and situated. In addition, I will critically review May's observations about sexuality in the modern age by appealing to current evidence from empirical studies in psychology and the social sciences. While his ideas continue to be provocative, I have, generally, found them to be prophetic in that many of his observations predicted cultural trends and subsequent empirical discoveries regarding sex, emotion, and embodiment that were neglected by investigators in his time.

I will expand the scope of May's understanding of the "old" and "new" puritanism by introducing a different but overlapping construct: "anesthetic culture." This construct was the subject of my 2018 book, *The Medicalized Body and Anesthetic Culture: The Cadaver, the Memorial Body, and the Recovery of Lived Experience* (Robbins, 2018). Anesthetic culture is defined as a tendency of Western culture to reinforcement states of anesthetic consciousness, which is characterized by psychic numbing, detached forms of engagement, dissociation from feeling, and diminished empathy. Anesthetic consciousness overlaps conceptually with constructs such as alexithymia and experiential avoidance, which are related to various forms of psychopathology and diminished well-being, including sexual problems. I find the concept of "anesthetic consciousness" and its reinforcement by an "anesthetic culture" to be a more precise and empirically grounded conception of what May attempted to formulate in terms of a "schizoid" character. Finally, my social, cultural, and historical analyses of anesthetic culture has been useful for tracing the roots of these cultural trends much farther back in history than the Puritans. These trends emerged from the influences of Platonic and Neo-Platonic philosophy and a revival of Gnosticism in 14th century Renaissance scholarship, which eventually shaped both the Protestant Reformation, including Calvinism and Puritanism but also the Enlightenment, by which it formed modernity as we know it.

Schizoid Culture and its Consequences

May's (1969) *Love and Will* launches into an indictment of the modern world as a "schizoid world" (p. 13). By "schizoid," he refers to a sense of being "*out of touch; avoiding close relationships; the inability to feel*" (p. 16). For May, the hallmark of this schizoid world is characterized by the misguided pursuit of "technique" that has "lost sight of the salvation we are seeking" (p. 15). He locates this disordered detachment not within the psychopathology of the individual, but as a "general condition" of the culture (p. 16). As a defense against hostility, the schizoid individual retreats from love in fear due to problems of attachment in early development, and as a result, becomes "cold, aloof, superior, detached" (p. 16). While the schizoid individual is expressive of psychopathology rooted in problematic relationships with attachment figures, the cultural expression of a "schizoid world" is the product of our technological age. The schizoid individual, therefore, is expressing at the individual level, as a microcosm, a cultural pathology within the macrocosmic world of the social-cultural system—a system in which detachment has becomes a normative form of disordered character.

May's description of our schizoid world and its symptoms is corroborated by more recent observations in contemporary psychology. Empirical studies have found that schizoid personality is associated with sexual problems and lower levels of sexual functioning (Grauvogl et al., 2018), as well as general disinterest in forming sexual relationships (Collazzoni et al., 2017). On the socio-cultural level, younger generations, since the sexual revolution, have shown a generational pattern of increasingly schizoid-like styles of relating. For example, compared to Generation X, Millennials tend to be generally more permissive in their sexual attitudes, but they have fewer sexual partners while postponing more serious commitment to long-term relationships (Twenge, Sherman, & Wells, 2015). Millennials were also less likely to have sex before the age of 18, whereas Generation X engaged in sex prior to 18 at more than twice the rate of Millennials (Twenge, Sherman, & Wells, 2017). These patterns seem consistent with May's prediction that the sexual permissiveness that emerged during the sexual revolution of the 1960s and 1970s would be paradoxically associated with more detached and less committed relationships. As May (1969) put it, "*The Victorian person sought to have love without falling into sex; the modern person seeks to have sex without falling into love*" (p. 46).

May (1969) also predicted that, as an expression of a schizoid world, society would witness an increase in neuroses, and that the structure of these neuroses would, in turn, mirror the schizoid world that shaped them:

> Our patients are the ones who express and live out the subconscious and unconscious tendencies in the culture. The neurotic or person suffering from what we now call character disorder, is characterized by the fact that the usual defenses of the culture do not work for him—a generally painful situation of which he is more or less aware. The "neurotic" or the person "suffering from character disorders" is one whose problems are so severe that he cannot solve them by living them out in the normal agencies of the culture, such as work, education, and religion. Our patient cannot or will not adjust to the society. (May, 1969, p. 20)

May suggests there are at least two reasons why neurotics do not adjust to society. First, the person may be more sensitive and vulnerable to anxiety, and less able to self-regulate due to past trauma or other developmental challenges. Second, the person who is the creative type, with a strong motivation for originality and innovation, may be frustrated by a culture that blocks creative expression, which therefore results in mental decline.

Empirical evidence strongly supports May's prediction that the modern world would witness an exponential increase in neuroses. For example, a meta-analysis was conducted to track changes in adolescents and young adults on scores of the Minnesota Multiphasic Personality Inventory (MMPI) between 1938 and 2007 (Twenge et al., 2010). While controlling for confounds such as gender, region, and defensive responding, the study concluded that psychopathology has increased with each succeeding generation since the 1930s. Compared to 1938, American college students were 5 to 8 times more likely to score above thresholds on depression. Generational decline in mental health over time was also found in increased scores on the MMPI's F scale (moodiness, restlessness, dissatisfaction, and instability), hypomania, schizophrenia, paranoia, psychopathic deviance, and general symptoms of anxiety.

Twenge and colleagues (2010) suggest that increases in psychopathology across generations correlate with corresponding increases in greater pursuit of extrinsic goals and a decrease in intrinsic goals. In other words, exponential increases in psychopathology may result, at least in part, by giving misguided priority to aims such as material wealth, appearances, and social status rather than striving for more intrinsically satisfactory goals, including competence, affiliation, and autonomy. This suggested explanation is supported by empirical studies that observe an association between extrinsic motivation and psychopathology and lower mental well-being, as compared to those who are more intrinsically motivated—a finding that has been found across cultures (e.g., Chen et al., 2015; Kasser & Ryan, 1993; Sheldon & Kasser, 2001; Dittmar et al., 2014; Van den Broeck et al., 2019).

May's (1969) cultural critique of our schizoid culture views the emergence of apathy as a particular feature of our modern world. He associated apathy with a "state of feelinglessness, the despairing possibility that nothing matters" (p. 27). He also links apathy to a general sense of emptiness by which the individual feels "*powerless* to do anything effective about their lives or the world they live in" (p. 28). He further suggests that this state of feelinglessness and powerlessness operates as a defense against anxiety. The result of apathy as a defensive posture, according to May, entails a diminished capacity for love due to a disordered will. "The interrelation of love and will," writes May (1969),

> inheres in the fact that both terms describe a person in the process of reaching out, moving toward the world, seeking to affect others or the inanimate world, and opening himself to be affected; molding, forming, relating to the world or requiring that it relate to him. (p. 30)

The disordered will of the apathetic person, by contrast, is one that has withdrawn feeling in "a studied practice of being unconcerned and unaffected" (p. 30). May further suggests that the trait of apathy sets up the conditions for violent acting out: "When inward life dries up, when feeling and apathy increases, when one cannot affect or even genuinely *touch* another person, violence flares up as a daimonic necessity for contact, a mad drive forcing touch in the most direct way possible" (pp. 30–31).

Apathy, generally, has been understudied in psychology, with the exception of research on neurological conditions linked to apathy (see, for example, Starkstein & Brockman, 2018). However, recent empirical evidence suggests that subclinical apathy in the general population can be conceptualized as a multidimensional construct (Lafond-Brina & Bonnefond, 2022). Subclinical apathy was empirically verified to have three independent dimensions: cognitive/executive apathy, emotional apathy, and initiative apathy. Cognitive/executive apathy—which is linked to problems with planning novel actions, transitions between tasks, and the capacity to maintain focus on a task—was found among 10–15% of the general population and may be secondary to depression and/or fatigue. Emotional apathy, which may be linked to problems with motivation, clusters around themes of problems with the expression and experience of emotion as well as deficits in empathy and interest. Found among 10% of the sample, emotional apathy was associated with deficiencies in the experience of pleasure in the moment. Finally, initiative apathy was found to cluster around two sub-types: a mixed form with both executive and emotional components and another more purely expressive of problems with the initiation of action. Remarkably, the study found evidence that 40% of respondents exhibited at least one sub-type of apathy, and these traits of apathy led to profound impairments in both academic and daily life (Lafond-Brina & Bonnefond, 2020). While there is a lack of evidence tracking generational trends in apathy, the widespread prevalence of sub-clinical apathy lends some support to May's claim that apathy is a pervasive phenomenon of modern life.

No evidence to date has identified a link between apathy and violence, per se. However, an emerging body of evidence has demonstrated relationships between political violence and deficits in meaning or significance. In one cross-cultural study, researchers examined the relationship between existential motives and intentions to engage in political violence (Adam-Troian et al., 2020). They hypothesized that deficits in significance in life, defined sociologically as *anomie*, would predict willingness to engage in political violence among undergraduate students in Brazil, Turkey, Belgium, and France. Anomia was defined as a "syndrome that includes feelings of meaninglessness, powerlessness, isolation, self-estrangement and normlessness" (p. 217). As hypothesized, self-reported anomia, independent of political ideology, was found to be significantly correlated with the intention to pursue acts of violence for political aims. Similar findings linking anomie to violent extremism have been replicated cross-culturally in other studies (i.e., Mahfud & Adam-Troian, 2019). These findings lend support to May's

(1969) observations that the characteristics of apathy, or existential meaninglessness, powerlessness, and alienation, are linked to tendencies to engage in violent behavior or violent extremism.

May (1969), as noted, also suggested that the link between apathy and violence may result from an effort to overcome a lack of feeling or contact. Lending some support to May's prediction, investigators have found empirical evidence that the relationship between violent extremism and meaning in life is mediated by sensation-seeking motivations (Schumpe et al., 2020).

May's (1969) descriptions of apathy and research on anomie also overlap conceptually with Viktor Frankl's (2004) concept of the "existential vacuum." According to Frankl, as a result of secularization, the modern world has displaced traditional structures for imparting and sustaining frameworks of meaning, such as in religious systems. As a result, a vacuum or absence of meaning has left individuals vulnerable to experiences of anomie. Rather than seeking fulfillment in meaning through significant projects, relationships, or the overcoming of suffering (intrinsic pursuits), individuals become distracted by efforts to acquire pleasure or power (extrinsic goals), which ultimately fail to satisfy the intrinsic desire for meaningful aims. Similarly, Adam-Troian, Tecmen, and Kaya (2021) have suggested that globalization has introduced perceptions of threats to affiliative, economic, and existential motivations, and under these threats, individuals are more willing to promote violent extremism.

Studies have also found associations between the existential vacuum—or deficits in existential fulfillment—and occupational burnout in professions such as nursing and teaching (Alfuqaha et al., 2021; Loonstra et al., 2009). Furthermore, occupational burnout has been found to predict the perpetration of workplace violence (Laeeque et al., 2019; Lozano et al., 2021). Also, parental burnout was found to directly contribute to increased neglect and violence toward children (Mikolajczak et al., 2018). The associations linking the existential vacuum to burnout, and burnout to violence, illustrate the validity of May's (1969) conceptualization of apathy and its links to violent acting out.

But how is all this talk about apathy and burnout relevant to our sexual lives? Let's bring the issue full circle, back to the matter of sexual satisfaction. As we have seen, burnout is a construct that overlaps with apathy, anomie, and the existential vacuum, and it is also a predictor of violent intentions and behavior. As May's (1969) cultural analysis would suggest, burnout is also associated with the quality of one's sexual life. Empirical research has demonstrated a robust association between sexual functioning and burnout, as well as occupational stress (Papaefstathiou et al., 2020). When men self-reported personal burnout, they reported less sexual satisfaction and increased erectile dysfunction. Women, on the other hand, reported problems with lubrication and fewer orgasms linked to job stress. In another study of male nurses who were working in a hospital during the COVID pandemic, the findings demonstrated that working in that environment—under high stress and burnout conditions—increased sexual dysfunction of these nurses compared to control participants (Kumar et al., 2021).

Among a sample of university lecturers, burnout syndrome was also linked to lower satisfaction in romantic relationships (Khohshkar et al., 2020).

Meaning and purpose in life, the very opposite of the existential vacuum, and an antidote to burnout, should, at least theoretically, predict better sexual and relationship satisfaction. An integrative review of the literature found that, indeed, meaning in life was positively and significantly associated not only with the quality of romantic relationships but also with the quality of relations to family and friends (O'Donnell et al., 2014). In an investigation of a daily diary methodology, researchers found that sexual pleasure and intimacy predicted enhanced positive affect and lower negative effect on the day following the reported sexual act (Kashdan et al., 2018). Importantly, however, the association between pleasurable sexual experiences and meaning in life were moderated by reports of relationship closeness. In other words, the intimacy and closeness of the relationship was especially important for the gains in sense of meaning in life following a pleasurable sexual episode. Similarly, in a longitudinal study of midlife women, purpose in life was positively and significantly associated with enjoyment of sex with their partner (Prairie et al., 2011).

Given that religion can be a source of meaning and purpose in life—and an adaptive defense against apathy, burnout, and the existential vacuum—couples who share in religious activities ought to demonstrate greater satisfaction with their sex lives. In fact, a study found that among couples 18–34, the sexual satisfaction of both the husband and wife was enhanced by "marital sanctification," the belief that one's marital relationship is blessed by the presence of the Divine (Dew et al., 2020). In addition, couples who engaged in joint religious activities also reported higher quality sex in their relationship. The association between religion/spirituality and sexual and marital satisfaction (and especially the importance of sexual sanctification) have been replicated in a variety of studies, which have found these associations across cultures, ages, and genders, and even among racial and sexual minorities (Cranney, 2020; Fincham et al., 2011; Hernandez et al., 2011; Leonhardt et al., 2021; Leonhardt et al., 2020; Murray-Swank et al., 2005; Smith & Home, 2008). These findings, taken together, help support May's intuition that sex and existential meaning are mutually enhancing. The findings also support May's suggestion that sexual satisfaction is undermined by detached states of apathy, sexual partnerships that lack intimacy and closeness, and conditions of burnout or existential despair.

In summary, Rollo May (1969) put forth the provocative view that the modern world has taken on schizoid qualities of detachment and apathy. He further suggests that these qualities have increased neuroses, fanned the flames of violence and social unrest, and diminished our capacity for intimacy in our sexual and romantic relationships. As we have seen, copious evidence from the research literature help support May's intuitions.

The Three Paradoxes

As noted previously, Rollo May's diagnosis of our schizoid culture unfolds in the description of three paradoxes that have emerged from the sexual revolution. First, while the culture remains preoccupied with sex, the actual experience of the sexual act has suffered from diminished passion. Second, in an attempt to remedy sexual maladies, the sex industry has tended to prescribe various techniques to improve our sex lives, but the focus on technique at the expense of intimacy and imagination has left us in a state of alienation, isolation, and depersonalization. Finally, the third paradox identified by May is a "new puritanism" operative within the culture, which he characterizes as composed of three elements: Alienation from the body, the divorce of emotion from reason, and the mechanization of the body.

With regard to the first paradox, the overexposure of sex with diminishing returns, May writes, is exasperating, "So much sex and so little meaning or even fun in it!" (p. 40). In contrast to the Victorian who suffered from guilt as a result of sex, the modern person is pressured into guilt if they choose *not* to engage in sex. The pressure to engage in sex is complicated, in turn, by the demands to perform, which leave the participants exposed to feelings of inadequacy and wounded self-esteem. Further, the expansive freedom that is opened up by the range of potential sexual experiences again, paradoxically, leaves the individuals burdened with internal conflict and anxiety at the dizzying variety of options, all with potentially high stakes for personal and social well-being. "What we did not see in our short-sighted liberalism in sex," May contemplates, "was that throwing the individual into an unbounded and empty sea of free choice does not itself give freedom, but is more apt to increase inner conflict" (p. 42).

Are permissive sexual attitudes and casual sex associated with less sexual satisfaction and poorer mental health outcomes? A review of the empirical literature indicates the results are mixed. A systematic review of 71 quantitative studies examined the emotional consequences of casual sexual encounters and experiences (Wesche et al., 2021). The review found that self-reports of satisfaction with casual sexual encounters tended to be more positive than negative. However, after casual sexual encounters, at least in the short term, studies generally found decreases in indices of mental health. Negative mental health consequences were especially linked to alcohol use before the sexual encounter, lack of sexual satisfaction during the encounter, and sex with an unfamiliar partner. Also, in a Brazilian sample, researchers found that women's well-being was negatively impacted by permissive attitudes (Mafra et al., 2021). Other studies have found that while men more frequently engage in casual sex, such encounters were found to be associated with deficits in well-being and greater psychological stress in both men and women (Bersamin et al., 2014).

However, sub-populations of women with more permissive attitudes toward casual sex were found to be more likely to orgasm during casual sex than in committed relationships, in contrast to women with less permissive attitudes, who demonstrated the inverse pattern (Wongsomboon et al., 2020). The issue here may be a matter of congruence or incongruence of sexual behavior with personal values, and the extent to which sexual behavior is motivated by intrinsic rather than extrinsic aims. In line with this observation, individuals who engaged in casual sex were found to demonstrate lower self-esteem, and higher levels of depression, anxiety, and physical symptoms, but primarily when engaged in casual sex for extrinsic, non-autonomous reasons (i.e., external pressure; Vrangalova, 2015; Townshend et al., 2020). When causal sex was engaged in for intrinsic, autonomous reasons, the associations with negative consequences were not evident in the data. With that said, another study found that permissive sexual attitudes were associated with less sexual satisfaction in both genders, which may be a result of increased expectations as a result of a greater variety of sexual experiences (Velten & Margraf, 2017). Negative emotional outcomes of casual sex may be more frequent in women, but are also associated with attempts to use sexual encounters as a way to regulate painful emotions or to enhance positive emotions (McKeen et al., 2022).

While the results on the psychological consequences of casual sex are mixed and complex, May's (1969) observation may be appropriately applied to populations who engage in sexual behavior in order to manage dysregulated emotion, as implied in his description of the apathetic, schizoid type that is characterized by detachment from others and emotional disengagement. Individuals with substance use, for example, are at greater risk of engaging in compulsive sexual behavior as a means to regulate symptoms related to trauma (Brem et al., 2018). The casual sexual encounter in such cases serves as a form of experiential avoidance—that is, it is a strategy to avoid or escape painful emotions, whether because of shame or posttraumatic symptoms. Similarly, among individuals with social anxiety who demonstrated emotional dysregulation and did not accept their emotions, risky sexual behavior, when used as a strategy to regulate emotion, came with a cost of low sexual satisfaction (Rahm-Knigge et al., 2021). In line with these findings, high- and moderate-risk sexual behavior has been linked to lower sexual satisfaction, whereas low-risk sexual behavior predicted higher quality sex (Rudolph et al., 2020).

Also consistent with May's (1969) conjectures, even casual sexual encounters were found to be most satisfying when associated with more familiar partners and more intimate sexual acts (Vrangalova, 2015). A qualitative study found that hookup culture seems to operate in ways that suppress opportunities for intimacy and commitment to partners. Sexual scripts in hookups tend to involve implicit rules, such as hooking up only when using alcohol, inhibiting acts of sexual intimacy (i.e., kissing), being cold to one's partner after the hookup, and refraining from repeated hookups with the same partner (Wade, 2021). These implicit rules may be broken, and when they are, this tends to lead to more long-term, romantic partnerships. However, the emotional consequences of hookups can be negative. Likely for these reasons, casual hookups have been linked to higher depression (Fielder et al., 2014). Consistent with May's observations, causal sex is less problematic for mental health and sexual satisfaction when it is done for intrinsic reasons, when it is congruent with permissive attitudes, and when the sexual encounters allow for intimacy with partners. Causal sex that is a result of external pressures, inconsistent with the individual's personal values, conducted impulsively as a maladaptive strategy to manage dysregulated emotions, engaged in while intoxicated, and/or when lacking in emotional engagement and intimacy has been associated with less satisfaction, greater costs to mental health and well-being, and less sexual satisfaction, for both women and men.

May's (1969) second paradox, which holds that overemphasis on sexual technique results in diminished sexual satisfaction and impaired quality of life, is primarily aimed at psychotherapy or self-help methods that entail a "mechanistic attitude toward love-making" (p. 43). Another problem is the overemphasis on sexual performance rather than a meaningful, erotic encounter with another person as an expression of love, intimacy, and/or tenderness.

Christopher Aanstoos' (2013) phenomenology of sexuality, which draws upon qualitative data as well as phenomenological philosophy, is particularly instructive on these issues. Aanstoos points out that sexuality is necessarily an embodied activity. However, the modern world has been enormously influenced by the mind–body dualism of René Descartes, which presumes an objectivist ontology that reduces the body to a machinal object and the mind to a disincarnate soul. By unreflectively adopting this Cartesian attitude, mechanistic psychology tends toward one of two extremes—on the one hand, reducing the embodied mind to neurology, a form of materialism, or, on the other hand, reducing the body to a representation, which amounts to a form of idealism (p. 53). Yet, the erotic encounter is neither solely a mental event nor a mechanical effect in a chain of material causes. Rather, "Sexual arousal reveals a primordial constituting or flow of meaning coming into existence" (p. 54) through the intertwining of the lived body and lived world.

Phenomenology provides a set of methodological strategies for capturing descriptions of lived experience, which through careful first-person description, are rendered into a structural understanding of the phenomenon as it is given to embodied perception. The erotic encounter operates in the context of a "network of lived relationships, with other people and their world" and constitutes a "bodying forth" of intentionality (p. 56). When taken up from a first-person perspective, the body is not experienced as an object but as an embodied subject, an opening upon a world and an erotic encounter with other embodied subjects. To view the erotic encounter this way requires us to "assert the body's existential character as disclosedness, as openness onto a world," writes Aanstoos (2013, p. 57). Within the sexual relation with a lover, I experience myself caressing my lover, but this caress exhibits a reversibility where the distinction between self and other, touching and touched, break down: My pleasure becomes hers, hers becomes mine. Moreover, sexuality is not restricted to explicit sexual acts but operates as an omnipresent horizon of significance that configures every perception or act.

Like skilled musicians improvising in a blues band, the erotic act of sexual encounter is a dance of call and response. The act "begins with an invitation, a solicitation," by which "the other beckons me, calls me out, arouses me, turns me on" (Aanstoos, 2013 p. 59). The call and response, moreover, takes on an immersive quality by which conjoined bodies erotically merge, and in which neither partner can be entirely certain where their own body ends and the other begins. When fully immersed in this call and response with the sexual partner, each lover achieves a state of ecstasy or self-transcendence—a "going beyond" oneself through the "fulfillment of a complex intermingling of self and other, with variants of reciprocity or mutuality" (p. 63).

The problem with sexual "techniques" is that their deployment in the sexual act tends to disrupt the flow of the immersive call and response between lovers. Rather than merging into a unified bodying forth in sexual union, one is taken out of the immersive experience by focusing on physiological organs in mechanical relation. Sex becomes a performance, a recipe, rather than an improvisational or spontaneous co-joining of embodied subjects. Rather than enhancing the sexual act, we are taken out of it; we become experientially objectified and objectify our partner through a cognitive act of reflexive deliberation focused on a sequence of technical performances.

The overemphasis on technique and performance has been a common critique of the sex industry and conventional sex therapy among existential sex therapists (Barker, 2011). The medical model of sexual dysfunction tends to place too much emphasis on normative views of sex that emphasize sexual functioning and performance over the quality of the experience for the partner and the meaning of the act for the partners (Kleinplatz, 2003). For example, Kleinplatz (2004) has observed that medical treatments for erectile dysfunction measure success in terms of performance, but neglect to examine the context of the sexual relationship. A soft penis may be less an indication of mechanical dysfunction than a signal of a problem in the relationship that may be better resolved by improved communication. To reduce a man's sexual functioning to the performance of the penis amounts to a form of objectification and dehumanization of the man, according to Kleinplatz (2004). Sexual advice found in popular magazines for men and women are more often focused on technical, mechanical, and physical factors of sex than relationship and psychological factors, and they tend to reinforce sex and gender stereotypes and narrow sexual scripts (Menard & Kleinplatz, 2008).

In studies of optimal sexual experiences, or "great sex," by contrast, the technical, mechanical, and physical factors were far less salient than relational factors. In phenomenological interviews with individuals with advanced sexual experience, they were much more likely to describe "great sex" in terms of being fully present in the moment, feeling connected to their partner, feeling cared for and caring for the sexual partner, having exceptional communication and deep empathy, having authenticity and transcendence, having fun, and being safe enough to be vulnerable and surrender to the partner (Kleinplatz et al., 2009).

The third paradox mentioned by May is deemed to result from a "new puritanism" in modern culture. This cultural formation is diagnosed as a cultural pathology that results from three symptoms: the bifurcation of mind and body, the split between emotion and reason, and the adoption of a mechanistic view of the body. This worldview, according to May, "grossly limits feelings, it blocks the infinite variety and richness of the [sexual] act, and it makes for emotional impoverishment" (p. 48). The "new puritanism" can be seen to overlap with the first two paradoxes outlined by May. The diminished satisfaction with sex that results from an overemphasis on the quantity over the quality of sexual encounters, and the sex industry's prioritization of technique and mechanistic interventions rather than relationship factors can be understood as symptomatic of a more general pattern of "schizoid" culture. To better situate May's commentary on the "new puritanism," it is worthwhile to step back and examine the socio-cultural roots of American culture in a "Puritan" ethos. With this understanding, we will be better positioned to examine to what extent the "new puritanism," while in many ways opposed to the Puritanism of the past, is nevertheless structurally tied to the "old puritanism," though in a new form.

Puritanism and Gnosticism

The origin of Puritanism is a contested issue (Hall, 1965; Trinterud, 1951). Nevertheless, the designation of "Puritanism" has become associated with cultural trends in Western culture since the Protestant Reformation and connote an emphasis on moral restrictions on sexual behavior and a strong work ethic (Uhlmann et al., 2011). Some scholars have contested the Puritan stereotype, arguing that Puritans tended to be pro-sex as long as sexual relationships were confined to marital relationships and otherwise conducted within the limits of strict Christian morality (Morgan, 1942). However, there is some historical and theological merit to the characterization of Puritanism. It is a strain of Christianity that has tended to be particularly harsh in its condemnation of behavior considered to reside outside the confines of conventional Christian morality (Smith, 1995).

Puritanism has its roots in Calvinist theology, but in a modified form (Peddle, 1998). Calvinism views the human person as subject to divine predestination, and therefore views human reason and nature as secondary to the Divine will. For the Calvinist, human beings are utterly depraved due to original sin, and only through Divine grace can they become capable of a piety that reconciles rationality and nature. Human reason and will remain passive and dependent upon reconciliation with God, whose grace restrains nature and reason; reason therefore is de-emphasized (Peddle, 1998).

Calvinism culminated in a split between Arminianism and Antinomianism. Arminians rejected Calvin's view that moral behavior is subject to absolute predestination, arguing that "human reason and will" are "prerequisite to the reception of grace" (Peddle, 1998, p. 130). Like the Arminians, the Antinomians (i.e., Anabaptists, Quakers) were also critical of Calvin, but in their view the central problem of Calvinism was its emphasis on the depravity of human nature because it prohibited any assurance of salvation for individuals. In contrast to Calvinism, they asserted that "union with God was immediate and did not require a special act of grace" (Peddle, 1998, p. 130). Puritanism, in effect, can be understood as a synthesis of Arminianism and Antinomianism. In the words of Perry Miller,

> Arminianism was a kind of ethical rationalism that had lost a sense of piety, and Antinomianism was an uncontrolled piety without the indispensable ballast of reason; Puritanism looked at itself as a synthesis of piety and reason, and the...Puritans looked upon the covenant theology as the perfection of that synthesis. (as cited in Peddle, 1998, p. 130)

For the Puritan, the individual person retains a degree of goodness that allows for the acceptance of God's grace. Unlike the passivity of reason and will in Calvinism, the Puritan viewed the individual as taking on an active role in the process of salvation from original sin (Peddle, 1998). Human beings have a capacity for free will that allows for individual rationality and moral behavior as a means to reconcile the individual to God's grace. However, while critical of Calvinism, the Puritan perspective retains certain elements of Calvinist theology. As formulated by Peddle (1998):

> For the Puritan, God is still conceived as sovereign and in Himself unknowable but no longer appears arbitrary or tyrannical in relation to humans. Further, while humanity continues to be seen as fallen and sinful, it is not without rational and moral capacity. And finally, while grace remains a special dispensation, it is thought not to be opposed to human reason but rather to be its elevation. (p. 131)

As a result of Puritan theology, the Church was understood to be constrained only to accept those who were witnessed to have freely accepted God's grace in a public way, and whose sincerity was evaluated in terms of its adherence to "principles of rational charity" (Peddle, 1998, p. 132). Participation in the Church community therefore hinged upon the degree to which the individual visibly adhered to the moral law through visible acts of obedience.

The Puritan worldview was one that sought with great zeal to usher the individual into an authentic conversion from sin through the use of reason applied to the moral law, with the aim of achieving moral and ethical precision (Smith, 1996). A consequence of the Puritan zeal was "a tendency toward moralism, legalism and a conflict over the assurance of salvation" (p. 87). In Smith's (1996) estimation, an error of Puritanism was a "flat" reading of revelation, which entailed a reading of the Old and New Testaments in a way that obscured a reading of scripture as a progressive revelation that culminated in the "climax of Jesus Christ" (p. 89). As a result, Puritans tended to place too much emphasis on interpretations that stressed the unity of the Old and New Testaments, including placing primacy on the moral law as articulated in the Ten Commandments. Consequently, Puritans tended to preach on ethical issues with a "moralistic tone" that was "legalistic in its tendency" (p. 90). The Puritans, in this respect, tended to err on the side of scrupulosity to the extent that they resembled the legalism of the Pharisees and produced faithful who were "preoccupied with moral minutiae while remaining insensitive or impervious to the large issues of the Law: love, faithfulness, justice, and compassion" (p. 94). These tendencies, according to Smith, were further amplified through the Puritans' individualistic and subjectivist reading of scripture. For these reasons, arguably, the reputation of the Puritan as moralistic and harshly punitive may be well-earned.

While the moralistic and legalistic tendencies of Puritanism have been established, the question remains: To what extent do these proclivities of Puritanism lead to the mind–body dualism, a split between emotion and reason, and a mechanistic view of the body that are so central to May's (1969) characterization of the Puritan ethos and "schizoid" modern culture? I believe these paradoxes of puritanism are best understood if Calvinism and Puritanism are properly viewed as expressions of a new variation of a very ancient theological worldview—that of Gnosticism (Robbins, 2018).

In the *Revival of the Gnostic Heresy*, Morris (2008) makes a convincing case that the Christian fundamentalism pervasive in American culture, and rooted in Calvinism and Puritanism, has striking parallels with the ancient spirituality of Gnosticism. Morris points out that Christian fundamentalism and Gnosticism emerged within a similar stage of civilization, during times of radical cultural change that left individuals feeling "rootless, overwhelmed, fearful of losing identity" (p. 92). Harold Bloom also observed, similarly, that "Mormons and Baptists call themselves Christians, but like most Americans, they are closer to ancient Gnostics than to early Christians" (cited in Morris, 2008, p. 93).

While there are clear differences between Gnostic theologies of early Christianity and the Christian fundamentalism of the modern era, the parallels overlap with May's (1969) thematic descriptions of Puritanism and "schizoid culture." They share a dualistic view of spirit and matter, with a tendency to identify the spiritual with moral goodness and to associate matter with qualities of evil and decadence. Similarly, Gnosticism and Christian fundamentalism tend to view human nature as split between spiritual and physical aspects. Also, their respective views of salvation share a stress on individual salvation, based on acquisition of divine knowledge that is found through an inward conversion that tends to neglect a focus on the community.

Further, while Gnostics understand Christ as purely divine rather than human, Christian fundamentalists tend to accept the doctrine that Christ was both human and divine. However, in practice, Morris (2008) contends, "at deeper, more visceral levels, with their near-obsessive need for inerrancy and purity," Christian fundamentalists find it "very difficult…to conceive of the Christ as capable of doubt, fear, despair, sadness, depression or loneliness, or to see him as human, of being compatible with sin...of being sin" (p. 99). In the end, rather than an incarnational Christ, the Christ of Christian fundamentalism is a Christ whose "divinity dominates humanity" (p. 99).

A fourth parallel between Gnostic and fundamentalist Christianity is the absence of intermediaries between the human and Divine. Instead, Divine knowledge is acquired through direct communication with the Divine. This acquisition of Divine knowledge amounts to a kind of mysticism that separates the spiritual elite, the initiates or elect, from those lacking in knowledge of the Divine. "For Gnostics," writes Morris (2008), "this self-knowledge is illuminated by the God within and raises one from the imprisonment of ignorance and incomprehension. For the fundamentalists, it is self-knowledge of guilt and need for repentance, illuminated by the God ('divine spark') within" (p. 101). As a result of the emphasis on mystical acquisition of Divine knowledge, scripture is adopted and interpreted in a highly subjective way, which amounts to a kind of solipsism. As a result, both Gnostics and Christian fundamentalists have had a tendency to retreat from any sort of "hierarchy and organization along vertical lines" (p. 106), leaving the Church increasingly fragmented and dispersed without a central structure, with a corresponding diminution of the sacraments as well as lack of authority to bind it together as a communal unit.

Finally, Gnosticism and fundamentalist Christianity share a propensity for theologies that provide frameworks that support a desire to escape the complexity and tragic dimensions of everyday life within the contingencies of history and community (Morris, 2008). They both emphasize preoccupation with apocalyptic eschatologies that focus on the end of time rather than practicalities of the present moment. Their moralities share a disdain for sexual and other bodily pleasures, and exchange their pursuits for ascent to a purely spiritual plain of existence, freed from the shackles of materiality and bodily desires. Ultimately, as theologies of escape, the Gnostics and fundamentalists reject the world and turn inward as a form of withdrawal both from the world and also from other people. In the end, they amount to "religions of isolation" (Morris, 2008, p. 110).

In short, Christian fundamentalism can be seen to represent parallel developments in Gnosticism, to the extent that Morris (2018) suggests its influence in America amounts to a revival of Gnosticism. However, Rollo May's (1969) theory of schizoid modern culture depends upon forging a link between the "old puritanism" (so to speak), as found in Christian fundamentalism, to the "new puritanism" that is the subject of his cultural critique. Gnosticism provides the connecting thread by which the old and new puritanism are revealed to be structurally coupled even if, at their surface level, they may appear diametrically opposed. While May's cultural critique in *Love and Will* never makes these historical and cultural developments explicit, my scholarship on "anesthetic culture" in the West may serve to fill these gaps in his analysis—or at least, make a start in that direction.

The Origins of Gnosticism in Platonic Philosophy

The early roots of Gnosticism are found in the classical Greek tradition of Plato which became infused into Jewish and Christian mysticism in the 3rd century. In *The Republic*, Plato (2000) used the analogy of the "divided line" to illustrate his philosophy of the psyche. He distinguished between the visible world, which represented the perishable and changing material world, and the intelligible world of abstract ideas, which he took to be eternal and universal truths. He further divided the visible world into realms accessible to the lower cognitive orders of conjecture and belief. In addition, he divided the intelligible world into the higher cognitive orders of thought and understanding.

In Plato's cosmology, the philosopher alone was capable of using reason to ascend from the lower, visible order into the higher realm of intelligibility. By ascending to the realm of ideas, the philosopher became capable of acquiring knowledge of eternal truths that were inaccessible to the lower orders of conjecture and belief, which remained trapped within the changing conditions of material existence. Within the visible order, conjecture and belief remained focused on phenomena that were empirically available to perception but which Plato understood to be ever-changing and therefore incapable of revealing eternal truths accessible only within the intelligible order. As the philosopher became capable of reason and developed the discipline to rule over their passions, they acquired the ability to discern, first, the abstract and universal truths of mathematics, especially geometry, and then, secondarily, was able to ascend to an understanding of the transcendental realm of truth, beauty, and goodness. Ultimately, the ascent of the philosopher terminated, for Plato, in an insight into the emanation of all being from a single source, a kind of Godhead that he deemed the One or the Good. The three transcendentals of truth, beauty, and goodness, in the end, turn out to be attributes of the One or the Good. The idea of the Good, in effect, is revealed to be the summit and source of being, including all existence within the visible and intelligible orders of being.

Plato's theory of knowledge is illustrated in his well-known Analogy of the Cave, which also appears in *The Republic*. In the analogy, prisoners are chained in a cave facing the back wall of the cave. Behind them parades a line of puppeteers who hold cutouts of forms that cast shadows on the wall of the cave as a result of light emanating from behind the puppeteers and prisoners. The prisoners take the shadows on the wall to be reality, and therefore they come to represent the visible realm of concrete perception. When a prisoner is able to break free of his chains, he discovers that, in fact, the shadows are mere reflections. He comes to recognize the forms casting shadows as a higher level of reality than the shadows. This represents an ascent from the visible to the intelligible realm. When the prisoner finds his way out of the cave, he comes to recognize that the source of all light is the sun, which in Plato's analogy represents the One or the Good, which stands for the highest order of intelligibility. When the prisoner returns to the cave, he attempts to inform his fellow prisoners of the reality he has witnessed. To his dismay, however, they mock him and view him as insane rather than taking him at his word. In the end, the freed prisoner illustrates the position of the philosopher who, having made the ascent into the realm of ideas, and who has direct knowledge of the intelligible order, is incapable of bringing these insights to the ignorant, who lack the wisdom to understand his witness to the light.

Plato's theory of knowledge also includes a psychology. In Plato's philosophy of the psyche or soul, the mind has a tripartite structure, composed of reason, a spirited element, and the passions. To be capable of philosophy, the philosopher must have a well-ordered soul, within which reason rules over the passions, with the assistance of the spirited element of the soul. To illustrate this concept, Plato used the analogy of a charioteer. In the analogy, the charioteer represents the aspect of the soul that is capable of reason, propelled by two horses. One horse represents the spirited element, and the other represents the passions. The skilled charioteer is one who has learned to harness the power of these two horses to guide his way, whereas the novice charioteer has not learned to tame his horses. As a result, he is liable to find himself thrown from his chariot as the two horses run wild and lack the coordination to steady the chariot and its rider. Likewise, the philosopher is one who has gained the wisdom to harness the power of his spirited element to tame his passions, and therefore becomes capable of using reason to access the realm of ideas. His reason, in that case, propels him into an ascent from the visible world to the world of ideas, the intelligible order. It is worth noting that Freud's theory of the tripartite structure of the psyche—composed of the ego, id and superego—was inspired by Plato's psychology (Kahn, 1987; Kaplin et al., 2018).

Based upon his psychology of the soul, Plato envisioned a perfectly ordered society that would be ruled by philosopher-kings, who were alone capable of ruling their passions. In his vision of a hierarchically ordered Republic, the warrior classes, who were ruled by the spirited element, would serve the philosopher-kings by keeping social order among the lowest caste, the laborers who remained ruled by their passions. As should be evident here, Plato was not particularly fond of democracy (an understatement, to be sure) and was shamelessly elitist.

In *Phaedo*, Plato also put forward an argument for the immortality of the soul. In his first argument for the immortality of the soul, Plato drew upon an argument also found in his dialogue *Meno*, which posits that knowledge is possible due to anamnesis, a memory of knowledge of the One or Good and the eternal forms, which was acquired upon death and forgotten at birth. In the tradition of Orphic myth, Plato's theory of knowledge as anamnesis depended upon the belief in an immortal and eternal soul that, through a cyclic process of reincarnation, is able to come to know reality within the realm of the intelligible world beyond the visible, material world. Since the soul is capable of innate knowledge, such as through geometry, Plato found this to be a proof of immortality. Plato's second argument for the immortality of the soul relies on evidence that philosophers are capable of arriving at timeless, eternal truths. Since philosophers would be incapable of such knowledge if they did not share in the being of eternal truths, Plato held that the soul, too, must be eternal. Finally, Plato argued that Ideas cannot contradict one another. Since the soul is defined as the life within us, the soul therefore participates in the Idea of life. Further, since death negates the Idea of life and contradicts it, and the soul participates in the Idea of Life, it would amount to a contradiction if the soul were also to participate in the Idea of death. For these reasons, Plato concluded the soul is immortal. As a consequence, he adopted a mind/body dualism, which associated the matter of the body with the perishable visible and material world and the soul with the immaterial aspect of the self that persists beyond death (Pricopi, 2014).

Gnosticism and Neoplatonism represent intellectual and spiritual movements that drew upon Plato's philosophy between the first and 5th centuries AD, and consisted of a Hellenization of Hebraic and early Christian spirituality (Mazur, 2013; Quinney, 2011). Although, they also drew from religious tendencies that derived from the Middle East as well (Malherbe, 1959). Gnosticism and Neoplatonism both expressed cultural tendencies at this time that placed an emphasis on theologies of personal salvation (Quinney, 2011). Gnosticism and Neoplatonism both share a view of the material world that is seen as a degraded state of reality in contrast to the transcendent realm of intelligibility. While the soul is understood to possess a "divine spark" that remains connected to the Divine, in Gnosticism the soul nevertheless remains imprisoned in a material body and a world corrupted by evil forces. While Neoplatonism retains a more optimistic view of the soul and material reality, understood to be emanations of the transcendent reality of the One, the soul is nevertheless also understood to exist in a fallen state, to some degree separated from its home within the intelligible order (Pricopi, 2014). Personal salvation depends upon knowledge, or gnosis, as a means to ascend from the fallen material world into the realm of the intelligible world and ultimately through union with the One or the Good.

The Gnostic and Neoplatonic concept of the soul imprisoned within the body can be traced directly to Plato. For example, in *Cratylus* Plato expressed a negative view of the body, which is viewed as "the tomb of the soul, on the grounds that is entombed in its present life" (as cited in Pricopi, 2014, p. 27). Plato goes on to suggest that this imprisonment of the soul suggests "the soul is being punished for something, and that the body is an enclosure or prison in which the soul is securely kept—as the name soma' itself suggests—until the penalty is paid" (p. 27). Similarly, in *Phaedo* Plato dictates Socrates who also speaks on the imprisonment of the soul in the body. And again, in *Gorgias* Plato states, "Perhaps in reality we're dead. Once I even heard one of the wise men spoken [sic] that we are now dead and that our bodies are our tombs, and that the part of our souls in which are appetites reside is actually the sort of thing to be open to persuasion and to shift back and forth" (p. 27). To the extent that the soul remains housed in a body, Plato regards the soul to exist in a degraded status, cut off from its origin within the intelligible world of truth, beauty, and goodness. It is only through reason and a disciplining of the passions that the philosopher can transcend the soul's imprisonment within the visible order and ascend to the heights of the spiritual and intelligible order.

Within antiquity, Plato's legacy in Gnosticism and Neoplatonism represent many of the themes outlined in Rollo May's three paradoxes of the "puritan" ethos of modernity. With the Platonic traditions, we can certainly identify the origins of an emphasis on the separation of reason from emotion. Whether in the form of Gnostics, Neoplatonists, or Stoics of antiquity, in the Platonists we find a pervasive imperative to use one's capacity for reason in order to dominate and tame the passions. Emotions are seen not as sources of wisdom or insight but as fundamentally corrupt as a result of their corporeal nature. Reason, by contrast, is identified with the immaterial and immortal aspects of the soul. As a result, all of the Platonic traditions discussed thus far share the view that reason and knowledge, especially knowledge of higher forms of intelligibility, necessitate strategies that aim to tame and control the emotions. Furthermore, the distrust of emotions follows mainly from their view that the emotions are identified with the body. From this observation, it follows that the Platonic traditions also entail a profound sense of alienation from the body. Rather than understanding the body as a living organism through which the person enacts their life, the body is perceived as a prison within which the soul is entrapped as a form of punishment.

In short, two of the three aspects of May's critique of Puritanism, the separation of emotion from reason, and alienation of the body, can be traced to Hellenistic influences in Plato, especially as they were expressed through Gnosticism and Neoplatonism. However, May also identifies a third aspect of Puritanism, the mechanization of the body, which is closely linked to the overemphasis on technique in the sexual ethos of the "New Puritanism." However, the mechanization of the body is not found in the Platonic traditions of antiquity. The mechanistic view of the body, as well as all of nature, did not become thematic until the Enlightenment and represents a distinctive feature of modernity. However, as I will argue, the mechanistic view of the Enlightenment represents a unique and distinctive appropriation of Platonism, which can be traced to its origins in Renaissance humanism.

The Mechanistic Worldview

With the Fall of Rome, the Western world after the 4th century was increasingly plunged into illiteracy, and many ancient texts were lost, although many were retained, thankfully, among the Arabs to the East. While early Christianity remained largely influenced by Platonic strains of philosophy such as Augustine's theology, Western thought re-emerged in the High Middle Ages with a particular indebtedness to Plato's student Aristotle. The apex of Neo-Aristotelean philosophy is undoubtably represented in the works of Thomas Aquinas and the Scholastic philosophers who dominated the medieval universities by the 12th and 13th centuries. While Aristotle retained Plato's emphasis on reason and the dialectical method, his rigorous methods in logic and empirical inquiry were decidedly more worldly than Plato and his followers. Aristotle saw emotions less as impediments to reason and virtue and more as integral to and inseparable from reason and judgment (Leighton, 1996). The virtuous person, for Aristotle as well as for Aquinas, was not one anesthetized to their emotions but attuned to their passions in a way that served practical wisdom in daily life. In addition, Aristotle and his followers, including the Scholastics, tended to reject the mind/body dualism of the Platonic tradition. Instead, Aristotle and Aquinas understood the human being as a unity of mind and body. Rather than viewing the soul as a separate entity, distinct from the body, Aristotle and his followers understood the soul to represent the living, animating form of the material body itself (Bos, 2000; DeRobertis, 2011; Garcia-Valdecasas, 2005).

In many respects, the Aristotelian ethos, which dominated the culture of the Middle Ages, was contrary to the Platonic strands of "Puritanism" that May targeted in his cultural critique. Reason and emotion were seen to be unified and integral to each other. The soul and body were viewed holistically and united in their practical engagement with the world. The world and body were not seen as mechanisms but through an organismic sensibility, which viewed the living organism developmentally and teleologically (Bianchi, 2017).

The Platonic tradition, however, would have a resurgence in the 14th century. The Renaissance humanists, as a rule, disdained Aristotelianism and its variations within Scholasticism. The defining moment of Renaissance humanism can perhaps be located in Francesco Petrarca's attack on Scholasticism in his classic text, "On His Own Ignorance and That of Many Others" (1367–1370) (Hankins, 2007). As Aristotle and the Scholastics increasingly lost favor with the "men of letters" of the Renaissance, the resurgence of Plato, Gnosticism, and Neo-Platonism was being fueled by the discovery of many lost texts from antiquity, which were being translated into Latin with the great interest and funding of wealthy merchants such as the Medici family. One major hub of these new translations was the New Plato's Academy in Florence, Italy, which operated under the directorship of Marsilio Ficino. In 1484, in fact, Ficino was the first to complete a translation of Plato's entire works (Robichaud, 2018).

A close affiliate of Ficino who was intimately involved in the translation and dissemination of Platonic works and also engrossed in the re-discovery of ancient geometry and its application, was a man named Paolo dal Pozzo Toscanelli. While Toscanelli is not a well-known figure, as compared to Ficino for example, his impact on the culture has been underestimated, in my opinion. Indeed, Toscanelli was a trained physician who participated in major changes that led to a radically new understanding of the body within medical anatomy. He was part of a small network of physicians that would culminate in Vesalius' major contribution to modern anatomy with the publication of his illustrated text *De Fabrica* (Robbins, 2018).

Toscanelli also had a direct influence on the development of linear perspective technique in art, which revolutionized Renaissance painting. He advised Brunelleschi to apply the new discoveries in geometry to create the illusion of three-dimensional depth on a two-dimensional canvas. This resulted in the first linear perspective painting of the Bapistry in Florence. Leon Battista Alberti studied the technique and formalized it in the book *De Pictura*, which immediately transformed Renaissance aesthetics. This was the technique that led to the celebrated works of Michelangelo, Leonardo da Vinci, and many others. In addition, Toscannelli applied the new geometry in an effort to perfect map making with the hope that improved maps would assist with the discovery of new sea routes to the East. It was at Toscannelli's insistence that Christopher Columbus set sail to discover a new pathway to the East with Toscanelli's map in hand (Robbins, 2018).

It was from the same circle of intellectual elites in northern Italy that Galileo emerged, first in his studies in medicine and then through his pursuits in physics, which led to his proofs of the Copernican theory and his efforts to establish new experimental methods of inquiry that would give birth to modern science. All of these developments provide an essential backdrop to understand how Western culture came to view not only the body but the universe itself as a clock-like mechanism, subject to prediction and control through empirical inquiry (Robbins, 2018).

Within medicine, the Platonizing influences can be seen within a new ethos that placed an emphasis on "detached concern" as a means of coping with death and dying (Robbins, 2018). The education of physicians became defined by a rite of passage that required all medical students to dissect a cadaver as a requirement of their graduation. While dissection of bodies had been conducted as early as the late Middle Ages, the dissection of corpses was conducted primarily for the purpose of medical autopsy to identify the cause of death or as a means to identify physical signs of holiness among prospectus saints, such as in the case of Chiara of Montefalco (Robbins, 2018). In the case of the autopsy of prospective saints, the bodies of the deceased tended to be those who were known and loved; it was understood that they were and needed to be documented and preserved as a saintly relic for the purpose of veneration. In contrast, the cadavers used for medical dissection were typically those of executed criminals, and the public dissection served a dual purpose. In addition to medical education, the cadaver often also served as an extension of the criminal's punishment due to the posthumous humiliation that came with public dissection (Robbins, 2018).

Rather than sanctified, the cadavers of the medical schools were stigmatized bodies. Perhaps for this reason, medical students were more easily trained to suppress empathy or sympathy with the deceased, and students were expected to learn how to view the body primarily as an object, which better lent itself to a mechanistic framework (Robbins, 2018). With the modern anatomy of Vesalius and William Harvey, this mechanistic view of the body came into its own and established the foundations of modern anatomical medicine. This mechanistic view of the body also lent itself to a dualistic conception of the mind–body relationship, which came to fruition in René Descartes' conception of the soul as immaterial, in contrast to an objectified body understood through the metaphor of the machine (Robbins, 2018).

The new technique of linear perspective in art also lent itself to an ethos of detachment and distance from the subject. With the application of geometrical principles to establish an illusion of depth, the artist was required to depict a scene as if viewed through a window from a stationary position and with a single eye—a monocular rather than a binocular style of vision (Robbins, 2018). Whereas medieval art tended to look flat by comparison, it nevertheless depicted its subjects as saturated with symbolism and intrinsic value and invited the viewer to enlist their imagination to enter and walk about the scene, to interact with the subjects and scenery. In contrast, the linear perspective style provides a very different aesthetic, one that positions the viewer as a passive subject and perceiving the object as if at a distance. In that sense, linear perspective painting repeats a theme found among the Platonists and within the new attitude of the Renaissance physicians. In place of a passionate engagement with the image, the reviewer is invited to take on the perspective of detached reason. Rather than engaging with the image in way that one is situated in one's body, linear perspective technique tends to disengage the intellect from the body, which remains fixed in place while the viewer gazes upon the scene within a monocular vision. Finally, the linear perspective style also anticipates a separation of the subject from the object, a style of knowing that would become the hallmark of modern science, with its stress on objectivity and epistemological detachment (Robbins, 2018).

It is finally in Galileo and eventually Newtonian physics that the mechanistic view of the universe, and with it the body, comes into being as a cultural phenomenon (Robbins, 2018). In order to establish physics as a science distinct from theology, Galileo adopted an ontology that understood the material universe to consist only of qualities independent of the observer. He called these qualities "primary qualities," which he understood to consist of properties that lent themselves to mathematical calculation—namely, extension in space and movement. All other qualities, to the extent that they were held to be dependent upon the subject, were deemed "secondary qualities." The perception of color, sound, touch, taste, as well as aesthetic qualities and values, was relegated to properties residing within an immaterial soul. Galileo's distinction between primary and secondary qualities became an essential feature of modern scientific epistemology. To the extent that properties lent themselves to scientific inquiry, they must be calculable and measurable either as units of extension or movement. In effect, this reduced the universe to a mechanistic system propelled by a chain of causal forces. Whereas Aristotle's epistemology required that investigators take account of the structure, materiality, causality, and purpose of a phenomenon, the Galilean epistemology reduced explanation to efficient causality alone. In effect, this rendered the universe into a clock-like mechanism that, with experimental manipulation, could be predicted and controlled (Robbins, 2018). It was through this mechanistic view of the universe that Newtonian mechanics were born and Descartes' soul–body and subject–object dualisms became the central theme of modern ontology and epistemology.

While the traces of Plato in Galileo, Newton, and Descartes may not be obvious, they can be seen on a closer look. The Galilean–Newtonian mechanistic worldview hinges on a separation of subjectivity, or secondary qualities, from the object, understood to be composed of primary qualities. In the tradition of Plato, this subject–object split hinges on a metaphysical presupposition that reality that transcends the visible world amounts to only those qualities that lend themselves to mathematical formulation. As in Plato's philosophy, the visible world given to perception is understood largely to be an illusion, a byproduct of mechanical forces. The key to true knowledge is through a privileging of ideal forms that lend themselves to mathematical calculation. What we see, taste, touch, and value are mere shadows compared to the calculable qualities of extension and movement that alone compose the world beyond the senses.

Plato's dividing line between the visible and intelligible worlds is repeated in a distinctive way within the modern physics of Galileo and Newton. The intelligible forms are not located within an immaterial realm composed of pure ideas. Rather, they are found within the material formation of the physical universe, understood as a mechanism, and denuded of all qualities other than extension and movement. Within this mechanistic framework, the body, too, becomes reduced to a mechanism. The soul is initially rendered by Descartre as an immaterial repository of secondary qualities. However, by the mid-18th century, the physiologists would conceptually reduce these qualities to byproducts of mechanical forces within the brain—essentially, chemical and electrical impulses within the nervous system. With that development, the mechanistic worldview is rendered complete: all is object, all is mechanism. The universe is rendered into an object, as is the body, and, with it, the soul.

By the 20th century, the movements of phenomenology and existentialism came on the scene as a response to this mechanistic worldview. The phenomenological philosophies of Edmund Husserl, Martin Heidegger, and Maurice Merleau-Ponty, for example, attempted to address the cultural crises that emerged as a result of the mechanistic view of the Enlightenment, caught between the errors of idealism and materialistic reductionism. Phenomenology aimed to overcome the subject–object split of Descartes. Husserl's philosophy described consciousness as distinctive in its intentional structure, by which acts of consciousness were inseparable from their correlative objects. Heidegger radicalized Husserl's phenomenology by returning to the existential givens of human existence. The bifurcation of subject and object, for Heidegger, was a byproduct of a disengaged intellect. In everyday engagement with things and other people, Heidegger observed that human being-in-the-world entails a practical comportment to the world in which subject and object are fused, and thinking always entails a moody or affected investment in one's meaningful projects. Merleau-Ponty, in turn, expanded on his phenomenology of the body to demonstrate that consciousness is fundamentally corporeal, but always grounded in a living body rather than the objectified body posited by idealism or materialism. The phenomenologists and existentialists, each in their own way, have attempted to point their way out of the alienated existence of Cartesianism and the mechanistic desert of the Galilean–Newtonian universe.

It is from these developments of phenomenology and existentialism that Rollo May's (1969) *Love and Will* came on the scene. By situating himself in the new perspectives of phenomenology and existential philosophy, May was able to appreciate how the Platonizing tendencies of Western spirituality and science have alienated human beings from their lived, embodied experience. Whether this manifests itself in the "old Puritanism" rooted in Calvinist and Puritan spirituality, or within the "new Puritanism" (reductive materialism, mechanistic metaphysics, and an ethos of detachment), each finds their ground within the traditions of Plato. They each, in their own way, contribute to the severance of emotion and reason, alienation from the body, and instrumental modes of engagement that interrupt the flow of embodied engagement in practical life, including human sexuality. Alfred North Whitehead once said, "All of Western philosophy is but a footnote to Plato." I once thought that was ridiculous hyperbole; not anymore.

Anesthetic Consciousness

While May's (1969) descriptions of schizoid culture paint a vivid picture of alienation from emotion, embodiment, and lived experience, I find the term schizoid to be somewhat limiting and misleading. In considering the problems he identifies—whether the dysregulation of emotion, impaired sexual relationships, tendencies to violence, or estrangement from the body—I have observed that these issues are not restricted to schizoid personalities. In my own work, I prefer the term *anesthetic consciousness* (Robbins, 2018). Anesthetic consciousness, first of all, is a term that points to problems that are not restricted to schizoid traits; rather, it designates problems of consciousness that are transdiagnostic since they can be identified across most, if not all, forms of psychopathology. Moreover, when anesthetic consciousness is situated within a Western socio-cultural context, we can better appreciate how Western culture has contributed to the maintenance of this style of consciousness, a style of living that is found not only among those diagnosed with mental illness but even among those with anesthetic traits that are sub-clinical, normative, or even socially rewarded. This view ultimately accords with May's observation that clinical traits, including schizoid traits, tend to be expressive of the culture that formed the individual's character.

Similarly, Erich Fromm (1990) also stressed that certain character traits can be normative within a culture and yet still express a form of pathology that is pervasive within the culture. When pathological styles of living become normative or socially rewarded in a culture, individuals who express that style of living do not appear deviant to those within the culture. They may even be rewarded for their behavior since it reinforces the maladaptive cultural norm. Anesthetic consciousness is a good example of a cultural pathology that sometimes expresses itself in ways that are recognized as psychopathology but in most cases goes unnoticed since anesthetic styles of living are often viewed as normative within

Western culture and typically rewarded, even though its consequences can be dire.

In my book *The Medicalized Body and Anesthetic Consciousness* (Robbins, 2018), I offer the following definition and description of anesthetic consciousness. It is worth quoting at length.

> As a cultural habit, anesthetic consciousness is characterized by tendencies to objectify self, others, and the natural world. Through an attitude of dispassionate concern, anesthetic consciousness is associated with empathic disengagement and tendencies toward exploitative attitudes toward other people and nature, violence, and expressions that range between the extremes of hedonism and asceticism. As a state of mind, anesthetic consciousness tends to express itself in quasi-dissociative states in which mind and body are experienced as split off from one another, which amounts to a kind of self-objectification. As a perceptual habit and epistemological attitude, it orients itself to the world through ongoing attempts to gain mastery and control, and it seeks to manage risk through the acquisition of power and domination. Beneath ongoing and paradoxically counterproductive attempts at control, lurks the unexamined fear of death and sophisticated and elusive strategies to deny mortality. Cutoff from the embodied, experiential wisdom of the living organism through psychic numbing, the victim of anesthetic consciousness fails to appropriately orient him- or herself toward nourishing and enriching intrinsic needs, instead remaining insatiably geared to extrinsic goals, such as the acquisition of material goods, power, and status, which ultimately fail to satisfy and therefore only amplify desire toward destructive ends. (Robbins, 2018, p. 5)

In the book, I also trace the anesthetic style through the Platonic traditions, and its re-emergence in modernity, as I have already outlined.

Empirically, anesthetic consciousness can be tracked by at least two transdiagnostic personality traits, which have been widely studied: Alexithymia and experiential avoidance. Alexithymia is a term for a personality trait defined by problems with the regulation and processing of emotions (Taylor, 2000). People who score high on measures of alexithymia demonstrate difficulties with identifying emotions; they tend to have difficulties differentiating bodily sensations from feelings during states of high arousal, and they are prone to a more concrete, externally oriented cognitive style. Studies have found that alexithymia is correlated with a wide range of psychopathologies, including depression, anxiety disorders (panic disorder, OCD, PTSD, social phobia, generalized anxiety disorder, autism spectrum disorders, conduct disorder, attention deficit/hyperactivity disorders, somatoform disorders, eating disorders, substance use disorder, personality disorders, psychotic disorders, and sleep disorders (Alimoradi et al., 2022; De Berardis et al., Deborde et al., 2012; De Gucht

& Heiser, 2003; Hamidi et al., 2010; Heshmati et al., 2010; Honkalampi et al., 2000; Kinnaird et al., 2020; Nicolo et al., 2011; Roshani et al., 2017; Westwood et al., 2017) Alexithymia has also been identified as a common factor in the "Dark Triad" traits of narcissism, Machiavellianism, and antisocial personality (Jonason & Krause, 2013).

Experiential avoidance is positively correlated with alexithymia (Cekikbas et al., 2021), and like alexithymia, it has been associated transdiagnostically with a wide variety of psychopathologies (Chawla & Ostafin, 2007). Experiential avoidance involves two interrelated factors: "(a) unwillingness to remain in contact with aversive private experience (including bodily sensations, emotions, thoughts, sensations, and behavioral dispositions), and (b) action taken to alter the aversive experiences or the events that elicit them" (Chawla & Ostafin, 2007, pp. 871–872). In the cases of both alexithymia and experiential avoidance, defensive responding to aversive experiences entails a loss of contact with interoceptive feedback from the body, which results in cognitive inflexibility and problems with regulating emotions (Panayioutou et al., 2021). The habit of evading attention to visceral, bodily feedback leaves the alexithymic with a lack of insight into their own emotions and the emotions of others.

Anesthetic consciousness, particularly alexithymia, has been associated with tendencies to objectify one's own body and the bodies of other people (Ainley & Tsakiris, 2013; Cogoni et al., 2018; Daubenmier, 2005; Peat & Muehlenkamp, 2011; Tiggemann & Williams, 2011; Watson 2012). From the perspective of existential psychology, as informed by Terror Management Theory, the objectification of the body likely serves as a psychological defense against death anxiety (Goldenberg et al., 2000). Individuals who lack self-esteem or a robust worldview are especially vulnerable to stimuli related to death, including thoughts and perceptions of the body, which tend to trigger associations with mortality. Alexithymia and experiential avoidance may represent consequences of terror management defenses against death anxiety. As a result of ineffective anxiety-buffering defenses against mortality, individuals become more vulnerable to develop various forms of psychopathology (Yetzer & Pyszcynski, 2019). The link between anesthetic consciousness and vulnerability to death salience is supported by empirical studies, which have found death anxiety to associated with both alexithymia and experiential avoidance (Asadi et al., 2022; Eyni et al., 2022; Testoni et al., 2020; Testoni et al., 2019).

Individuals who are especially vulnerable to stimuli related to death and who have higher death anxiety tend to objectify their own bodies and the bodies of other people. While this comes at a great psychological cost, the objectification of the body provides an image of the body that takes on an illusion of invulnerability to death (Goldenberg, et al., 2000). After all, objects do not die, while living bodies inevitably do. This tendency to objectify the body typically entails viewing one's body, the body of others, and even the natural world as mechanisms rather than organisms. Thus, the findings in terror management theory suggest that the mechanistic worldview of the Enlightenment may likely have its psychological origins as a sophisticated defense against death anxiety (Robbins, 2018). Furthermore, the distancing from the body entails a psychological defense that puts the subjective person at a distance from their body taken as an object. Here, then, we can begin to understand the possible psychological origins of both mind/body dualism and subject/object dualism. Both styles of relating to self, others, and the world serve to regulate anxieties about death, which are closely linked to feelings of anxiety, disgust, and shame around one's creaturely nature, of which the corporeal self is a constant reminder.

Similarly, the Platonic influences, from Gnosticism to fundamentalist Christianity, share with the Enlightenment a tendency to downplay the importance of the body for one's identity. By placing a distance between the soul and body and positing an eternal soul separate from a perishable corporeal form, the Platonic elements of Western culture provide a robust, cultural worldview to buffer anxiety about death and dying. By giving primacy to reason over the emotions, anesthetic consciousness places the person at a psychological distance from the interoceptive feedback of the body. As a result, through experiential avoidance of one's embodied feelings, one can evade awareness of one's corporeality and its associations with death. Similarly, mind/body dualism conditions anesthetic consciousness by dissociating personal identity from one's corporeal self, allowing the person to retreat into the illusion that the self is bound only to the immaterial aspects of an eternal and immortal soul. Furthermore, the Enlightenment tendency to view bodies and nature as mechanisms serves as a defense against death in that living organisms are reduced to mechanical objects. Since mechanical objects are not viewed as living organisms, the tendencies toward mechanistic metaphysics and epistemologies allow for an additional defense against associations with death and decay. The preoccupation with the world as a mechanism also likely accounts for cultural tendencies to favor solutions that are instrumental in nature—in short, a focus on technical solutions, or techniques, over relational solutions to interpersonal and sexual problems.

Within the Gnostic traditions, and perhaps also in dominant expressions of contemporary fundamentalist Christianity, anesthetic consciousness finds expression in theologies that tend to deny (or downplay) the incarnation of Christ in one way or another. Empirical support for this suggestion can be found in a study by Beck (2008). The study found that Christian participants who had higher death anxiety, and a more rigid religious orientation, were especially vulnerable to repel depictions of Christ as embodied. To suggest that Christ experienced all the indignities and embarrassments of his corporeal self was rejected as demeaning, unrealistic, or unbiblical. As we have explored already, the Platonic strands of Christianity have indeed tended to reject or minimize the incarnation of Christ.

The Christological perspectives of Gnosticism and other strands of Platonized Christianity also provide some insight into ways that the "old puritanism" remains structurally tied to the "new puritanism." In early Christianity, Gnosticism manifested two forms of Christology: Docetic Christology and Hybrid Gnosticism

(Papandrea, 2016). The term "Docetic" derives from the Greek, *dokein*, "to seem" or "to appear." Therefore, Docetic Christology designates a strand of Gnosticism that denied Christ had a body. A consequence of Docetic Christology was an extreme variation of mind/body and nature/spirit dualism. In practice, Docetic Gnostics were extreme ascetics who strove to deny themselves any form of worldly pleasure, since the material world was strongly associated with corruption, decay, and death. They were prone to reject marriage and sexuality, tended to denigrate women, and neglected care for the poor (Robbins, 2018, p. 267). This tendency toward extreme asceticism is mirrored by the "old puritanism" found in its more contemporary form within modern strands of Christianity, including Calvinism, Puritanism, and more generally, fundamentalist Christianity.

Hybrid Christianity took a more moderate form of dualism. While also denying that Christ had a body, it accepted that he at least took on the appearance of having a body. In practice, Hybrid Gnosticism took a position that was the complete contrary of the Docetists. Rather than denying themselves worldly pleasures, they tended toward the most extreme forms of hedonism and sexual libertinism (Behr, 2000). From their perspective, since the body was merely an appearance lacking in substantial ontological weight, there was no harm relishing in even the most extreme forms of sexual pleasure since such pursuits were seen to have little to no moral consequences. Clearly, the worldview of the Hybrid Gnostics mirror the "New Puritanism" denounced by Rollo May (1969). Whether in the form of extreme ascetism or extreme sexual licentiousness, anesthetic consciousness ultimately serves the function of numbing one's senses, distancing the self from the body, and harnessing control over the emotions (Robbins, 2018).

Sex Under Conditions of Anesthetic Consciousness

As the analysis thus far would suggest, anesthetic consciousness is detrimental to sexual well-being. Empirical studies across various age groups and across cultures have found a consistent relationship between alexithymia and diminished sexual satisfaction (Berenguer et al., 2019; Hesse & Floyd, 2011; Humphreys et al., 2009; Lyvers et al., 2022; Scimeca et al., 2013; Sharyati et al., 2010).

One study of undergraduates found that alexithymia was negatively associated with both relationship and sexual satisfaction (Humphreys et al., 2009). In another study of women students at Tabriz University, the negative association between alexithymia and sexual satisfaction, while predicted by the total alexithymia score, was best predicted by the sub-scale measuring difficulty with identifying feelings (Sharyati, et al., 2010). A study by Hesse and Floyd (2011) found that affection was an important mediator that partially accounted for the relationship between sexual satisfaction and alexithymia. In other words, intimacy in sexual encounters tended to help prevent negative consequences of alexithymia on the quality of sexual experiences. Another study found that alexithymia decreased sexual satisfaction, partly as a result of an attitude of sexual detachment, especially among females, and also due to shyness and nervousness about sex in both genders (Scimeca, et al., 2013). The impact of alexithymia on sexual satisfaction was also driven by fear of intimacy and negative affect (Lyvers, et al., 2022). Finally, a study of Portuguese participants found that alexithymia's impact on sexual functioning was closely related to decreased interoceptive awareness (Berenguer et al., 2019). For women, anesthetic consciousness entails problems with arousal, lubrication, achievement of orgasm, pain during sex, and sexual stress, in addition to increased dissatisfaction with the sexual experience. For men, anesthetic consciousness predicted problems with the delay of ejaculation and erectile dysfunction.

Concluding Thoughts

After careful consideration, I am left with the distinct impression that Rollo May's (1969) observations in *Love and Will* have been prophetic. While his insights were driven more by a critique of the culture grounded in existential and phenomenological philosophy, many of his conclusions have been found to be consistent with recent evidence from empirical studies in psychology.

May's cultural critique was also astute in that it offered a counter-cultural perspective that saw potential drawbacks for romantic relationships in the wake of the sexual revolution. While at times May's observations can take on a moralistic tone, I tend to agree with his keen insight that the "New Puritanism" in the 1960s was a new variation on an old theme, which could be traced back to the "old Puritanism," so to speak. With that said, I think May's cultural criticisms remain too restricted to recent history, especially to American culture within the past century. As I have attempted to demonstrate, May's "three paradoxes" have deep cultural roots in Western culture, going back at least to Hellenistic philosophy, especially the strand of philosophy that followed in the wake of Plato. Within the Platonic tradition, we find two of three dimensions of the "New Puritanism," namely alienation from the body, a consequence of Platonic mind/body dualism, and the primacy of reason over the emotions. The third dimension, having to do with the use of the body as a machine, as I have illustrated, is a product distinct to modernity as informed by Enlightenment thought. The new science of Galileo and Newton, however, can also be understood as a peculiar variation of a resurgent Platonism in the Renaissance. The mechanistic view of the Enlightenment ultimately hinged on a mind/body dualism, fully realized in Descartes, which took up the body as a machine interfacing with an incorporeal soul. Moreover, Cartesian mind/body dualism amounted to a solution based on problems that followed from Galileo's subject/object dualism implied in his distinction between primary and secondary qualities. The metaphysical assumptions behind the mechanistic worldview were Platonic primarily for their privileging of mathematical forms as the bedrock of reality, to the exclusion of all other qualities of perception, which were relegated to the interior of the person.

In the final analysis, May's three paradoxes seem to follow from the insight that modernity continues to repeat an ancient theme found among the Gnostics in early Christianity. The Docetic and Hybrid Gnostics shared radical dualistic metaphysics, which aimed to escape the material world through spiritual ascent. Both theologies are grounded in an inauthentic form of experiential avoidance and culminated in an alexithymic numbing of the senses. However, in their expression, one group retreated into an austere aestheticism that remains disgusted by the corruptibility of the human body and its function, including sexuality. The other group coped with their corporeal anxieties by numbing themselves with excessive states of ecstatic and bodily pleasures. In a similar way, Christian fundamentalists of the 20th century have adopted a stance in relation to the body and sexuality that repeats the ascetic sensibilities of the Docetists, while the "New Puritanism" behind the sexual revolution may be seen as adopting the strategy of the Hybrid Gnostics by finding escape through compulsive acts of hedonic pleasure. If the empirical evidence we have reviewed can be taken at face value, neither group has likely found that either the quality of their sexual lives or their relationships have become the better for it.

Some may rightly object that few today would consider themselves Gnostics, and fundamentalist Christianity is generally on the wane. How can I say with a straight face that we remain in many respects Gnostic in our cultural tendencies toward anesthetic states of consciousness? The suggestion may seem especially strained when we consider that those who most enthusiastically embrace the "New Puritanism" of the sexual revolution are less and less religious with each succeeding generation. Let me be clear. I am certainly not suggesting that people today, whether Christian or agnostic, New Age mystic or atheist, are explicitly adopting the identity of Gnostics. The data simply do not support that contention. I suspect the vast majority of modern Americans have never heard of Gnosticism and have little to no interest in adopting a Gnostic identity or practice. Rather, I contend that Platonizing tendencies, including Gnostic tendencies, remain pervasive in the West as a result of a cultural heritage that has been shaped early on by Plato and his followers. As a culture, we are Platonists whether we realize it or not. We are shaped by a Puritan heritage through the implicit adoptions of cultural ideas and practices that have long lost their explicit connection to Puritanism or Gnosticism, or even Plato; but they persist nonetheless in a covert or implicit form through our style of living as an anesthetic culture. Not only do these tendencies shape our sex lives and romantic relationships, they shape many other cultural practices as well.

Moral judgments and behaviors tend to be implicit rather than explicitly adopted through reason. We rarely choose them but are infused with them through cultural conditioning (Uhlmann, et al., 2010). While it is proper to remain incredulous to such a suggestion, I will leave you with a description of an empirical study that suggests I may be right. In a 2011 article, Uhlmann, Poehlman, Tannenbaum, and Bargh set out to test the question of whether Puritan values around sex and work continue to influence American participants as compared to non-Americans. In one study, they primed an experimental group implicitly to engage in deliberation on a task. When Americans were primed to deliberate, they were less likely to express traditional moral beliefs about sexual behavior. In contrast, the control group, which was assigned to a neutral prime or a prime to engage in intuition, comparatively held to traditional values about sexual behavior. British participants were not affected by the experimental manipulation. Whether exposed to a prime to engage in deliberation or intuition, or whether, instead, they were given a neutral prime, the British maintained their culturally liberal attitude toward sexuality. In a second study, Americans and Canadians were given a prime that exposed them to the concept of divine salvation. In the experimental group, only the American participants worked harder on a work task as a result of the prime. The Canadians remains unaffected. A third study illustrated how Americans remain implicit Puritans who tend to link values of work and sex together. When bicultural Asian-Americans were reminded of their American identity and exposed to an implicit prime related to work, they were more likely to also condemn revealing clothing and erotically evocative dancing. Uhlmann and his colleagues (2010) draw the following conclusion:

> As predicted based on prior work on implicit cognition, which indicates that most members of a culture implicitly internalize prevailing attitudes ..., not only devout American Protestants but even non-Protestants and less religious Americans exhibited effects associated with traditional work and sex values. This is consistent with the argument that American's Puritan-Protestant tradition has powerfully shaped the intuitive morality of American culture. According to our theorizing, it is American culture, and not necessarily personal devotion to a particular religion, that underlies these phenomena. (p. 318)

While such a claim based on a limited range of evidence should be accepted only with caution, I find the results quite sobering.

If we are to have better quality sex and relationships, we can draw some lessons from this engagement with Rollo May's (1969) *Love and Will*. First, we must face up to our finitude and accept death with existential courage. By facing death with radical acceptance rather than through defensive experiential avoidance, we are better prepared to find ourselves rooted in our lived body and planted firmly on the soil. To the extent that we become less alienated from our bodies, we are freer to immerse ourselves in meaningful engagement in projects that give our lives meaning. We are also empowered to enjoy sexual relationships without fear of intimacy or bodily shame. By experiencing our encounter with the other through an embodied, passionate engagement, the sexual act can be enjoyed as a spontaneous expression of a loving and intimate encounter rather than a set of techniques on the way to organism. We can also learn to be attuned to the felt sense of our interoceptive feedback and make use of our emotions and moods as sources of experiential wisdom. Sometimes, when it does not feel right and a relationship does not adequately meet our intrinsic needs, it is okay to say "no" to sex. At other times, when our attunement provides feedback that we are ready and willing to surrender ourselves and be vulnerable with a partner, we can happily say "yes" to sex.

All of this is much easier said than done. Most of us cannot simply will an authentic sexual encounter with our partner; erotic intimacy may require ongoing work to heal psychological wounds that keep is habitually severed from our body and emotions as a result of anesthetic consciousness. For healing those wounds, we can be thankful that our age has given us a variety of therapeutic strategies that have been demonstrated to be effective in helping people to overcome anesthetic states of consciousness. I am particularly partial to existential, experiential, interpersonal, and humanistic approaches to psychotherapy. Their strength lies in their refusal to conceptualize treatment in terms of symptom reduction, which always runs the risk of restricting rather than expanding our range of possibilities. Instead, each in their own way aims to help clients in psychotherapy to ground themselves in the present, root themselves in their lived bodies, and attune themselves to the wisdom available in the felt sense of interceptive feedback, given through our moods and emotions. I am also heartened by the increasing popularity of third-wave cognitive–behavioral therapies that have turned toward mindfulness approaches to help ground the person in the present moment, become attune to their bodies, and radically accept what their minds and bodies have to offer them. Interpersonally oriented therapies also offer a safe therapeutic approach to overcome destructive patterns of relating through the corrective emotional experiences with an empathic, caring, and authentic therapist.

Sexual dysfunction is rarely a problem that can be solved in the bedroom, or even by sex therapies that focus primarily on treating mechanical and biological problems. Most often great sex means finding the capacity in ourselves to be fully present in our living bodies with the living bodies of those we love, without flinching. While the Platonists continue to search for truth, beauty, and goodness on a disincarnate spiritual plane, I suggest we may find these transcendentals most fruitfully and directly in loving encounter with another vulnerable human being. Whereas the ancient philosophers were on a quest motivated by the love of wisdom, great sex may come down to the wisdom of love itself, discovered in the face of another.

References

Aanstoos, C. M. (2013). Phenomenology of sexuality. In P.J. Kleinplatz (Ed.), *New directions in sex therapy: Innovations and alternatives* (pp. 69–90). Routledge.

Adam-Troian, J., Bonetto, E., Araujo, M., Baidada, O., Celebi, E., Dono Martin, M., Eadeh, F., Godefroidt, A., Halabi, S., Mahfud, Y., Varet, F., & Yurtbakan, T. (2020). Positive associations between anomie and intentions to engage in political violence: Cross-cultural evidence from four countries. *Peace and Conflict: Journal of Peace Psychology, 26*(2), 217–223. https://doi.org/10.1037/pac0000385

Adam-Troian, J., Tecmen, A., & Kayam A. (2021). Youth extremism as a response to global threats? A threat-regulation perspective on violent extremism among the youth. *European Psychologist, 26*(1), 15–78. https://doi.org/10.1027/1016-9040/a000415

Ainley, V., & Tsakiris, M. (2013). Body conscious? Interoceptive awareness, measured by heartbeat perception, is negatively correlated with self-objectification. *PloS one, 8*(2). https://journals.plos.org/plosone/article?id=10.1371/journal.pone.0055568

Alfuqaha, O. A., Al-olaimat, Y., Abdelfattah, A. S., Jarrar, R. J., Almudallal, B. M., & Abu ajamieh, Z. I. (2021). Existential vacuum and external locus of control as predictors of burnout among nurses. *Nursing Reports, 11*, 558–567. https://doi.org/10.3390/nursrep11030053

Alimoradi, Z., Majd, N.R., Brostrm, A., Tsang, H.W., Singh, P., Obayon, M.M., Chung-Yin, L., & Pakpour, A.H. (2022). Is alexithymia associated with sleep patterns? A systematic review and meta-analysis. *Neuroscience & Biobehavioral Reviews, 133*. https://www.sciencedirect.com/science/article/pii/S0149763421005844

Asadi, N., Esmaeilpour, H., Salmani, F., & Salmani, M. (2022). The relationship between death anxiety and alexithymia in emergency medical technicians. *OMEGA—Journal of Death & Dying, 85*(3), 772-786.

Barker, M. (2011). Existential sex therapy. *Sexual & Relationship Therapy, 26*(1), 33–47. https://doi.org/10.1080/14681991003685879

Behr, J. (2000). *Asceticism and anthropology in Irenaeus and Clement.* University Press.

Berardis, D. D., Campanella, D., Nicola, S., Gianna, S., Alessandro, C., Chiara, C., Valchera, A., Marilde, C., Salerno, R.M., & Ferro, F.M. (2008). Impact of alexithymia on anxiety disorders: A review of the literature. *Current Psychiatry Reviews, 4*(2), 80-86. https://doi.org/10.2174/157340008784529287

Berenguer, C., Rebolo, C., & Costa, R.M. (2019). Interoceptive awareness, alexithymia, and sexual function. *Journal of Sex & Marital Therapy, 45*(8), 729-738. https://doi.org/10.1080/0092623X.2019.1610128

Bersamin, M. M., Zamboanga, B. L., Schwartz S. J., Donnellan, M.B., Hudson, M., Weisskirch, R.S., Kim, S.Y., Agocha, V.B., Whitbourne, S. K., & Caraway, S. J. (2014). Risky business: Is there an association between casual sex and mental health among emerging adults? *The Journal of Sex Research, 51*(1), 43–51. https://doi.org/10.1080/00224499.2013.772088

Bianchi, E. (2017). Aristotle organism, and ours. In A.J. Greenstine & R.J. Johnson (Eds.), *Contemporary encounters with ancient metaphysics* (pp. 138-157). Edinburgh University Press.

Bos, A. P. (2000). Why the soul needs an instrumental body according to Aristotle (Anim. I, 3, 407B13-26). *Hermes, 128*, 20–31. https://www.jstor.org/stable/4477343

Brem, M. J., Shovey, R. C., Anderson, S., & Stuart, G. L. (2018). Does experiential avoidance explain the relationship between shame, PTSD symptoms, and compulsive sexual behavior among women in substance abuse treatment? *Clinical Psychology & Psychotherapy, 25*(5), 692–700. https://doi.org/10.1002/cpp.2300

Chawla, N., & Ostafin, B. (2007). Experiential avoidance as a functional dimensional approach to psychopathology: An empirical review. *Journal of Clinical Psychology, 63*(9), 871-890. https://doi.org/10.1002/jclp.20400

Celikbas, Z., Batmaz, S., Yavuz, K.F., Akpinar Aslan, E., Yesilyaprak, N., Kocakoya, H., Demir, M.O., Songur, E., & Yildiz, M. (2021). How are experiential avoidance and cognitive fusion associated with alexithymia? *Journal of Rational-Emotive Cognitive-Behavior Therapy, 39*, 86-100. https://doi.org/10.1007/s10942-020-00359-y

Chen, B., Van Ascche, J., Vansteenkiste, M., Soenens, B., & Beyers, W. (2015). Does psychological need satisfaction matter when environmental or financial safety are at risk? *Journal of Happiness Studies, 16*, 745–766. https://doi.org/10.1007/s10902-014-9532-5

Collazzoni, A., Ciocca, G., Limoncin, E., Marucci, C., Mollaioli, D., Di Sante, S., Di Lorenzo, G., Niolu, C., Siracusano, A., Maggi, M., Castellini, G., Rossi, A., & Jannini, E.A. (2017). Mating strategies and sexual functioning in personality disorders: A comprehensive review of literature. *Sexual Medicine Reviews, 5*(4), 414–428. https://doi.org/10.1016/j.sxmr.2017.03.009

Cogoni, C., Carnaghi, A., & Silani, G. (2018). Reduced empathic response for sexually objectified women: An fMRI investigation. *Cortex, 99*, 258-272. https://doi.org/10.1016/j.cortex.2017.11.020

Cranney, S. (2020). The influence of religiosity/spirituality on sex life satisfaction and sexual frequency: Insights from the Baylor Religion Survey. *Review of Religious Research, 62*, 289–314. https://doi.org/10.1007/s13644-019-00395-w

Daubenmier, J.J. (2005). The relationship of yoga, body awareness, and body responsiveness to self-objectification and disordered eating. *Psychology of Women Quarterly, 29*(2), 207-219. https://doi.org/10.1111/j.1471-6402.2005.00183.x

Deborde, A.S., Miljkovitch, R., Roy, C., Dugre-Le Bigre, C., Pham-Slottez, A., Speranza, M., & Corcos, M. (2012). Alexithymia as a mediator between attachment and the development of borderline personality disorder in adolescence. *Journal of Personality Disorders, 26*(5), 676-688. https://doi.org/10.1521/pedi.2012.26.5.676

De Gucht, V., & Heiser, W. (2003). Alexithymia and somatization: A quantitative review of the literature. *Journal of Psychosomatic Research, 54*(5), 425-434. https://doi.org/10.1016/S0022-3999(02)00467-1

DeRobertis, E. M. (2011). Aquinas's philosophical-anthropology as a viable underpinning for a holistic psychology: A dialogue with existential-phenomenology. *Janus Head, 12*(1), 62–91.

Dew, J. P, Uecker, J. E., & Willoughby, B. J. (2020). Joint religiosity and married couples' sexual satisfaction. *Psychology of Religion & Spirituality, 12*(2), 201–212. https://doi.org/10.1037/rel0000243

Dittmar, H., Bond, R., Hurst, M., & Kasser, T. (2014). The relationship between materialism and personal well-being: A meta-analysis. *Journal of Personality & Social Psychology, 107*, 879–924. https://doi.org/10.1037/a0037409

Eyni, S., Hashemi, Z., & Ebadi, M. (2022). Relationship between cognitive emotion regulation strategies and experiential avoidance with death anxiety veterans with post-traumatic stress disorder: The mediating role of coping self-efficacy. *Iranian Journal of War & Public Health, 14*(2), 147-155.

Fiedler, R. L., Walsh, J. L., Carey, K. B., & Carey, M. P. (2014). Sexual hookup and adverse health outcomes: A longitudinal study of first year college women. *The Journal of Sex Research, 51*(2), 131–144. https://doi.org/10.1080/00224499.2013.848255

Fincham, F. D., Ajayi, C., & Beach, S. R. H. (2011). Spirituality and marital satisfaction in African American couples. *Psychology of Religion & Spirituality, 3*(4), 259-268. https://doi.org/10.1037/a0023909

Frankl, V. E. (2004). *Man's search for meaning: An introduction to logotherapy.* Random House/Rider.

Fromm, E. (1990). *The sane society.* Holt.

Garcia-Valdecasas, M. (2005). Psychology and mind in Aquinas. *History of Psychiatry, 16*(3), 291–310. https://doi.org/10.1177/0957154X05051920

Goldenberg, J.L., & Pyszczynksi, T., Greenberg, J., & Solomon, S. (2000). Fleeing the body: A terror management perspective on the problem of corporeality. *Personality & Social Psychology Review, 4*(3), 200-218. https://doi.org/10.1207/S15327957PSPR0403_1

Grauvogl, A., Pelzer, B., Radder, V., & van Lankveld, J. (2018). Associations between personality disorder characteristics, psychological symptoms, and sexual functioning in young women. *The Journal of Sexual Medicine, 15*(2), 192–200. https://doi.org/10.1016/j.jsxm.2017.11.222

Hall, B. (1965). Puritanism: The problem of definition. *Studies in Church History, Volume 2: Papers read at the second winter and summer meetings of the Ecclesiastical History Society* (pp. 283–296).: Cambridge University Press.

Hamidi, S., Rostami, R., Farhoodi, F., & Abdolmanafi, A. (2010). A study and comparison of alexithymia among patients with substance use disorder and normal people. *Procedia—Social & Behavioral Sciences, 5*, 1367-1370. https://doi.org/10.1016/j.sbspro.2010.07.289

Hankins, J. (2007). Humanism, Scholasticism, and Renaissance philosophy. In J. Hankins (Ed.), *The Cambridge companion to Renaissance philosophy* (pp. 30-48). Cambridge University Press.

Hernandez, K. M., Mahoney, A., & Pargament, K. I. (2011). Sanctification of sexuality: Implications for newlywed's marital and sexual quality. *Journal of Family Psychology, 25*(5), 775–780. https://doi.org/10.1037/a0025103

Heshmati, R., Jafari, E., Hoseinifar, J., & Ahmadi, M. (2010). Comparative study of alexithymia in patients with schizophrenia spectrum disorders, non-psychotic disorders, and normal people. *Procedia—Social & Behavioral Sciences, 5*, 1084-1089. https://doi.org/10.1016/j.sbspro.2010.07.240

Hesse, C., & Floyd, K. (2011). Affection mediates the impact of alexithymia on relationships. *Personality & Individual Differences, 50*(4), 451-456. https://doi.org/10.1016/j.paid.2010.11.004

Honkalampi, K., Hintikka, J., Tanskanen, A., Lehtonen, J., & Viinamaki, H. (2000). Depression is strongly associated with alexithymia in the general population. *Journal of Psychosomatic Research, 48*(1), 99-104. https://doi.org/10.1016/S0022-3999(99)00083-5

Humphreys, T. P., Wood, L. M., & Parker, J. D. (2009). Alexithymia and satisfaction in intimate relationships. *Personality & Individual Differences, 46*(1), 43-47. https://doi.org/10.1016/j.paid.2008.09.002

Jonason, P. K. & Krause, L. (2013). The emotional deficits associated with the Dark Triad traits: Cognitive empathy, affective empathy, and alexithymia. *Personality & Individual Differences, 55*(5), 532–527. http://dx.doi.org/10.1016/j.paid.2013.04.027

Kahn, C. H. (1987). Plato's theory of desire. *The Review of Metaphysics, 41*(1), 77–103. https://www.jstor.org/stable/20128559

Kaplin, D., Giannone, D. A., Flavin, A., Hussein, L., Kanthan, S., & Young, S. H. A. (2018). The religious and philosophical foundation of Freud's tripartite theory of personality. *Janus Head, 16*(1), 227–264.

Kashdan, T. B., Goodman, F. R., Stiksma, M., Milius, C. R., & McKnight, P. E. (2018). Sexuality leads to boosts in moods and meaning in life with no evidence for the reverse direction A daily diary investigation. *Emotion, 18*(4), 563–576. https://doi.org/10.1037/emo0000324

Kasser, T., & Ryan, R. M. (1993). A dark side of the American dream: Correlates of financial success on a central life aspiration. *Journal of Personality & Social Psychology, 65*(2), 410–422. https://doi.org/10.1037/0022-3514.65.2.410

Khoshkar, P. G., Farmanesh, P., & Nweke, G. (2020). Assessing the impact of burnout syndrome on romantic relationship satisfaction: The dark side of workplace bullying. *South East European Journal of Economics & Business, 15*(1), 44–55.

Kinnaird, E., Stewart, C., & Tehanturia, K. (2020). Interoception in anorexia nervosa: Exploring associations with alexithymia and autistic traits. *Frontiers in Psychiatry, 11*. https://psycnet.apa.org/record/2020-17659-001

Kleinplatz, P. J. (2003). What's new in sex therapy? From stagnation to fragmentation. *Sex & Relationship Therapy, 18*, 95–106. https://doi.org/10.1080/1468199031000061290

Kleinplatz, P. J. (2004). Beyond sexual mechanics and hydraulics: Humanizing the discourse surrounding erectile dysfunction. *Journal of Humanistic Psychology, 44*(2), 215–242. https://doi.org/10.1177/0022167804263130

Kleinplatz, P. J., Menard, A. D., Paquet, M. P., Paradis, N., Campbell, M., Zuccarino, D., & Mehak, L. (2009). The components of optimal sexuality: A portrait of "great sex." *The Canadian Journal of Human Sexuality, 18*(1–2), 1–13.

Kumar, M., Mohindra, R., Sharma, K., Soni, R.K., Rana, K., & Singh, S. M. (2021). The impact of working in a COVID hospital on sexual functioning in male nurses: A study from North India. *Indian Psychiatry, 30*(1), 18–190. https://doi.org/10.1038/s41443-019-0170-7

Laeeque, S. H., Bilal, A, Hafeez, A., & Khan, Z. (2019). Violence breeds violence: Burnout as a mediator between patient violence and nurse violence. *International Journal of Occupational Safety & Ergonomics, 25*(4), 604-613. https://doi.org/10.1080/10803548.2018.1429079

Lafond-Brina, G. & Bonnefond, A. (2022). The stability of multidimensional subclinical apathy during a pandemic and its relations to psycho-behavioral factors. *Scientific Reports, 12*, 2931. https://doi.org/10.1038/s41598-022-06777-5

Leighton, S. R. (1996). Aristotle and the emotions. In A. Rorty (Ed.), *Essays on Aristotle's Rhetoric* (pp. 206–237). University of California Press.

Leonhardt, N. D., Busby, D. M., Hanna-Walker, V. R., & Leavitt, C. E. (2021). Sanctification or inhibition? Religious dualities and sexual satisfaction. *Journal of Family Psychology, 35*(4), 433–444. https://doi.org/10.1037/fam0000796

Leonhardt, N. D., Busby, D. M., & Willoughby, B. J. (2020). Sex guilt or sanctification? The indirect role of religiosity on sexual satisfaction. *Psychology of Religion & Spirituality, 12*(2), 213–222. https://doi.org/10.1037/rel0000245

Loonstra, B., Brouwers, A., & Tomic, W. (2009). Feelings of existential fulfilment and burnout among secondary school teachers. *Teaching and Teacher Education, 25*(5), 752-757. https://doi.org/10.1016/j.tate.2009.01.002

Lozano, J. M.G ., Raman, J. P. M., & Rodriguez, F. M. M. (2021). Doctors and nurses: A systematic review of the risk and protective factors in workplace violence and burnout. *International Journal of Environmental Research & Public Health, 18*(6), 3280. https://doi.org/10.3390/ijerph18063280

Lyvers, M., Pickett, L., Needham, K., & Thorberg, F.A. (2022). Alexithymia, fear of intimacy, and relationship satisfaction. *Journal of Family Issues, 43*(4), 1068-1089. https://doi.org/10.1177/0192513X211010206

Mafra, A. L., Defelipe, R. P., Varella, M. A. C., Townshead, J. M., & Valentova, J. V. (2021). Mate value, intrasexual competition and sociosexual desire drive Brazilian women's well-being. *Evolutionary Human Sciences 3*, e25. https://doi.org/10.1017/ehs.2021.18

Malherbe, A .J. (1959). Gnosis and primitive Christianity: A survey. *Restoration Quarterly, 3*(3), 99–107.

Maufud, Y. & Adam-Troian, J. (2019). "Macron demission!": Loss of significance generates violent extremism for the Yellow Vests through feelings of anomie. *Group Processes & Intergroup Relations, 24I*(1), 108–124. https://doi.org/10.1177/1368430219880954

Mazur, Z. (2013). The Platonizing Sethian Gnostic interpretation of Plato's Sophist. In A. DeConick, G. Shaw, & J.D. Turner (Eds.), *Practicing Gnosis: ritual magic, theurgy and liturgy in Nag Hammadi, Manichaean and other ancient literature* (pp. 409–493). Brill.

May, R. (1969). *Love and will.* W.W. Norton & Company.

McKeen, B. E., Anderson, R.C., & Mitchell, D.A. (2022). Was it good for you? Gender differences in motives and emotional outcomes following casual sex. *Sexuality & Culture, 26*, 1339–1359. https://doi.org/10.1007/s12119-022-09946-w

Menard, A. D. & Kleinplatz, P. J. (2008). Twenty-one moves guaranteed to make his thighs go up in flames: Depictions of "great sex" in popular magazines. *Sexuality & Culture, 12*, 1–20. https://doi.org/10.1007/s12119-007-9013-7

Mikolajczak, M., Brianda, M. E., Avalosse, A., & Roskam, I. (2018). Consequences of parental burnout: Its specific effect on child neglect and violence. *Child Abuse & Neglect, 80*, 134–145. https://doi.org/10.1016/j.chiabu.2018.03.025

Morgan, E. S. (1942). The Puritans and sex. *The New England Quarterly, 15*(4), 591–607. https://doi.org/10.2307/361501

Morris, J.E. (2008). *Revival of the Gnostic heresy: Fundamentalism.* Palgrave Macmillan.

Murray-Swank, N. A., Pargament, K. I., & Mahoney, A. (2005). At the crossroads of sexuality and spirituality: The sanctification of sex by college students. *The International Journal for the Psychology of Religion, 15*(3), 199–219. https://doi.org/10.1207/s15327582ijpr1503_2

Nicolo, G., Semerari, A., Lysaker, P.H., Dimaggio, G., Conti, L., D'Angerio, S., Procacci, M., Popolo, R., & Carcione, A. (2011). Alexithymia in personality disorders: Correlations with symptoms and interpersonal functioning. *Psychiatry Research, 190*(1), 37-42. https://doi.org/10.1016/j.psychres.2010.07.046

O'Donnell, M. B., Bentele, C. N., Grossman, H.B ., Le, Y., Jang, H, & Steer, M. R. (2014). You, me, and meaning: An integrative review of connections between relationships and meaning in life. *Journal of Psychology in Africa, 1*, 44–50.

Panayiotou, G., Pantell, M., & Vlemincx, E. (2021). Adaptive and maladaptive emotion processing and regulation, and the case of alexithymia. *Cognition & Emotion, 35*(3), 488-499. https://doi.org/10.1080/02699931.2019.1671322

Papaefstathiou, E., Apostolopoulou, A., Papaefstathious, E., Moysidis, K., Hatzimouratidis, K., & Sarafis, P. (2020). The impact of burnout and occupational stress on sexual function in both male and female individuals: A cross-sectional study. *International Journal of Impotence Research, 32*(5) 510-519. https://doi.org/10.1038/s41443-019-0170-7

Papandrea, J. L. (2016). *The earliest Christologies: Five images of Christ in the postapostolic age.* InterVarsity Press.

Peat, C.M., & Muehlenkamp, J.J. (2011). Self-objectification, disordered eating, and depression: A test of mediational pathways. *Psychology of Women Quarterly, 35*(3), 441-450. https://doi.org/10.1177/0361684311400389

Peddle, D. (1998). Puritanism, Enlightenment, and the U.S. Constitution. *Animus, 3*, 43–58.

Plato (2000). *The Republic*. (G.R.F. Ferrari, Ed., & T. Griffith, Trans.). Cambridge University Press.

Prairie, B. A., Scheier, M. F., Matthews, K. A., Chang, C. C. H., & Hess, R. (2011). A higher sense of purpose in life is associated with sexual enjoyment in midlife women. *Menopause, 18*(8), 839–844. DOI: 10.1097/gme.0b013e31820befca

Pricopi, V. A. (2014). Platonists and Gnostics on negative theology and true inner self. *Agathos, 5*, 21–30.

Quinney, L. (2011). Romanticism, Gnosticism, and Neoplatonism. In C. Mahoney (Ed.), *A companion to Romantic poetry* (pp. 412–423). Blackwell.

Rahm-Knigge, R., Prince, M.A., & Conner, B.T. (2021). More likely to have risky sex but less sexually satisfied: A profile of high social interaction anxiety, urgency, and emotion dysregulation. *Journal of Psychopathology & Behavioral Assessment, 43*, 890–903. https://doi.org/10.1007/s10862-021-09889-w

Robischaud, D. J. J. (2018). *Plato's persona: Marsilio Ficino, Renaissance humanism, and Platonic traditions*. University of Pennsylvania Press.

Robbins, B.D. (2018). *The medicalized body and anesthetic culture: The cadaver, the memorial body, and the recovery of lived experience*. Palgrave Macmillan.

Roshani, F., Najafi, M., Naqshbandi, S., & Malekzade, P. (2017). Comparison of alexithymia in individuals with and without attention deficit/hyperactivity disorder. *Journal of Clinical Psychology, 9*(2), 73-82. doi 10.22075/JCP.2017.11204.1109

Rudolph, K., Littleton, H., & Schoemann, A. (2020). Patterns of sexual risk behaviors among college women: A latent profile analysis. *Journal of Sex & Marital Therapy, 46*(5), 403–418. https://doi.org/10.1080/0092623X.2020.1748777

Schumpe, B. M., Belonger, J. J., Moyano, M., & Nisa, C. F. (2020). The role of sensation seeking in political violence: An extension of the Significance Quest Theory. *Journal of Personality & Social Psychology, 118*(4), 743–761. https://doi.org/10.1037/pspp0000223

Scimeca, G., Bruno, A., Pandolfo, G., Mico, U., Romeo, V.M., Abenavoli, E., Schimmenti, A., Zoccali, R., & Muscatello, M.R.A. (2013). Alexithymia, negative emotions, and sexual behaviors in heterosexual university students from Italy. *Archives of Sexual Behavior, 42*, 117-127. https://doi.org/10.1007/s10508-012-0006-8

Sharyati, M., Ghamarani, A., Solati Dehkandi, S.K., & Abbasi Molid, H. (2010). The study of relationship between alexithymia and sexual satisfaction among female married students in Tabriz University. *Journal of Family Research, 6*(1), 59-70.

Sheldon, K. M. & Kasser, T. (2001). Goals, congruence, and positive well-being: New empirical support for humanistic theories. *Journal of Humanistic Psychology, 41*(1), 30–50. https://doi.org/10.1177/0022167801411004

Smith, B. L., & Home, S. G. (2008). What's faith got to do with it? The role of spirituality and religion in lesbian and bisexual women's sexual satisfaction. *Women & Therapy, 31*(1), 73–87. https://doi.org/10.1300/02703140802145243

Smith, T. N. (1995). The perils of Puritanism. *Reformation & Revival, 5*(2), 83–99.

Starkstein, S. E. & Brockman, S. (2018). The neuroimaging basis of apathy: Empirical findings and conceptual challenges. *Neuropsychologia, 118, Part B*, 48–53. https://doi.org/10.1016/j.neuropsychologia.2018.01.042

Taylor, G. J. (2000. Recent developments in alexithymia theory and research. *Canadian Journal of Psychiatry, 45*, 134–142. https://doi.org/10.1177/070674370004500

Testoni, I., Ronconi, L., Cupit, I.N., Nodari, E., Bormolini, G., Ghinassi, A., Messeri, D., Cordioli, G., & Zamberini, A. (2019). The effect of death education on fear of death amongst Italian adolescents: A nonrandomized controlled study. *Death Studies,* *44*(3), 179-188. https://doi.org/10.1080/07481187.2018.1528056

Testoni, I., Tronca, E., Biancalani, G., Ronconi, L., & Calapai, G. (2020). Beyond the wall: Death education at Middle School as suicide prevention. *International Journal of Environmental Research & Public Health, 17*(7), 2398. https://pubmed.ncbi.nlm.nih.gov/32244681/

Tiggemann, M., & Williams, E. (2012). The role of self-objectification in disordered eating, depressed mood, and sexual functioning among women: A comprehensive test of objectification theory. *Psychology of Women Quarterly, 36*(1), 66-75. https://doi.org/10.1177/0361684311420250

Townshend, J.M., Jonason, P.K., & Wasserman, J.H. (2020). Associations between motives for casual sex, depression, self-esteem, and sexual victimization. *Archives of Sexual Behavior, 49,* 1189–1167. https://doi.org/10.1007/s10508-019-01482-3

Trinterud, L.J. (1951). The origins of Puritanism. *Church History, 20*(1), 37–57. https://doi.org/10.2307/3162047

Twenge, J. M., Gentile, B., DeWall, C.N., Ma, D., Lacefield, K., & Schurtz, D. R. (2010). Birth cohort increases in psychopathology among young Americans, 1938–2007: A cross-temporal meta-analysis of the MMPI. *Clinical Psychological Review, 30*(2), 145–154. https://doi.org/10.1016/j.cpr.2009.10.005

Twenge, J. M., Sherman, R.A., & Wells, B.E. (2015). Changes in American adults' sexual behavior and attitudes, 1972–2012. *Archives of Sexual Behavior, 44,* 2273–2285. https://doi.org/10.1007/s10508-015-0540-2

Twenge, J. M., Sherman, R. A., & Wells, B. E. (2017). Sexual inactivity during young adulthood is more common among US Millennials and iGen: Age, period and cohort effects on having no sexual partners after age 18. *Archives of Sexual Behavior, 46,* 433–440. https://doi.org/10.1007/s10508-016-0798-z

Uhlmann, E.L., Poehlman, T.A., Tannenbaum, D., & Bough, J.A. (2011). Implicit Puritanism in American moral cognition. *Journal of Experimental Social Psychology, 47,* 312–320. https://doi.org/10.1016/j.jesp.2010.10.013

Van Den Broeck, A., Schreurs, B., Proost, K., Vanderstukken, A., & Vansteenkiste, M. (2019). I want to be a millionaire: How do extrinsic and intrinsic values influence youngsters' well-being? *The ANNALS of the American Academic of Political & Social Science, 682*(1), 204–219. https://doi.org/10.1177/0002716219831658

Velten, J. & Margraf, J. (–2017). Satisfaction guaranteed? How individual, partner, and relationship factors impact sexual satisfaction with partnerships. *PLoS ONE, 12*(2), e0172855. https://doi.org/10.1371/journal.pone.0172855

Vrangalova, Z. (2015). Hooking up and psychological well-being in college students: Short-term prospective links across different hook up definitions. *The Journal of Sex Research, 52*(5), 485–498. https://doi.org/10.1080/00224499.2014.910745

Wade, L. (2021). Doing casual sex: A sexual fields approach to the emotional force of hook up culture. *Social Problems, 68*(1), 185–201. https://doi.org/10.1093/socpro/spz054

Watson, L.B. (2012). *The relationships among childhood sexual abuse, self-objectification, and sexual risk behaviors in undergraduate women.* Dissertation, Georgia State University. https://scholarworks.gsu.edu/cps_diss/59/

Wesche, R., Claxton, S.E. & Waterman, E.A. (2021). Emotional outcomes of casual sexual relationships and experiences: A systematic review. *The Journal of Sex Research, 58*(8), 1069–1084. https://doi.org/10.1080/00224499.2020.1821163

Westwood, H., Kerr-Gaffney, J., Stahl, D., & Tchanturia, K. (017). Alexithymia in eating disorders: Systematic review and meta-analyses of studies using the Toronto Alexithymia Scale. *Journal of Psychosomatic Research, 99*, 66-81. https://doi.org/10.1016/j.jpsychores.2017.06.007

Wongsomboon, V., Burleson, M.H. & Webster, G.D. (2020). Women's orgasm and sexual satisfaction in committed sexed casual sex: Relationship between sociosexuality and sexual outcomes in different sexual contexts. *The Journal of Sex Research, 57*(3), 285–295. https://doi.org/10.1080/00224499.2019.1672036

Yetzer, A.M., & Pyszczynski, T. (2019). Terror management theory and psychological disorder: Ineffective anxiety-buffer functioning as a transdiagnostic vulnerability factor for psychopathology. In. C. Routledge & M. Vess (Eds.), *Handbook of terror management theory* (pp. 417-447). Academic Press.

Chapter 4

Sexuality and the Arts:
Implications for Existential Psychologists

Stanley Krippner, Callum E. Cooper, & Steve Speer[1]

Abstract

Psychologists, including existential psychologists, have always taken an interest in sexuality and the arts, but rarely on the connection between them. This chapter identifies many of those psychologists who have explored this connection, as well as a few writers from the humanities who have shared this interest. It includes, in its purview, the study of aesthetics, especially what Darwin called "aesthetic selection," which compliments natural selection in human evolution. The study of sexuality and the arts within the scope of existential psychology offers several paths of further exploration and mapping beyond the history outlined within this chapter. These routes of inquiry can include aesthetics, phenomenology, and intentionality, as potential ways forward for the current and next generation of researchers.

***

Psychologists have always been fascinated by sexuality, the ability to derive pleasure from any form of sexual activity or behavior (VandenBos, 2007), or simply being or doing something sexual (Spinelli, 2013). Sexuality itself can be understood as "how individuals view and understand themselves as sexual beings" (Brandon-Friedman, 2021, p. 657). The scope of psychology's interest in this area is broad, given that sexuality is argued to be formed of "psychological variables, cultural and societal factors, and biological and evolutionary influences" (Lehmiller, 2014, p. 2). Psychologists have also shown an interest in the arts, especially aesthetics, which is defined as the study of how sensory stimuli acquire hedonic value and become connected with feelings of pleasure. Aesthetics is a

[1] The authors acknowledge the support of the AUM Center in Baltimore, MD for its support of the preparation of this chapter. They also thank Peggy Kleinplatz, existential psychologist, for editorial suggestions and advice on an early draft of this chapter, likewise, Jon Nestor for his input on Jungian Analysis. Finally, thanks to Steve Hart, for assisting with the final draft.

fundamental topic for psychology because it leads to concrete empirical questions such as how perceptual information comes to engage value signals in the brain's reward circuit or why different psychological (and neurobiological) factors elicit different appreciation events for identical sensory objects (Skov & Nadal, 2020). This perceptual information sometimes comes from sexual stimulation, providing a connection between sexuality and aesthetics. Psychologists also study how hedonic values are integrated into decision making and behavioral regulation and how they may differ from one setting to another.

Aesthetics differs from the study of art, the human-made products (objects, environments, and experiences) that elicit aesthetic pleasure and the processes (both inner and outer) that evoke that product (citation). Visual arts, performing arts, and various forms of literature all result from creative processes and produce offerings that are novel and either useful or hedonic, or both, for an individual or for a society. Ruth Richards (1990) has differentiated between "everyday creativity" and "eminent creativity," but both exemplify the creative process.

In searching for a link between sexuality and the arts, one will find that scant attention has been paid to the connection between sexuality and aesthetics, even though sexuality and the arts have been widely discussed (e.g., Mahon, 2005). Nonetheless, this chapter surveys some of the writers who have discussed the connection between sexuality and the arts, focusing on those who are of major interest to existential psychologists, as well as to their humanistic psychologist siblings. This chapter will have a Western bias, as the pertinent literature comes from Western Europe and the United States.

Sigmund Freud and the Neo-Freudians

Psychoanalysts, in general, did not address the study of aesthetics, but they frequently wrote about sex and the arts (e.g., Freud, 1910, 1966). Sigmund Freud linked them in several of his publications, notably *Leonardo da Vinci and a Memory of His Childhood*. Leonardo had written about an early memory, namely being attacked by a bird as an infant. Freud thought this was a wish-fulfilling infantile fantasy rather than a memory, a fantasy reflecting a desire to suck his mother's nipple. Da Vinci's painting "Adoration of the Virgin and Child with St. Anne" and similar paintings of the two women have also been given a psychoanalytic interpretation—namely, that Freud associated them with da Vinci's birth mother and his adoptive mother.

Freud took a pathological view of aspects of the creative process, proposing that unhappy people experience vivid daydreams and fantasies, which are integral parts of the creative process (Arieti, 1976). For Freud, unsatisfied wishes are the driving power behind fantasies; every separate fantasy contains the fulfillment of a wish and improves an unsatisfactory reality (Taylor, 2009). However, "sublimation" of one's sexual drives can divert libidinal fantasies to more socially acceptable endeavors such as the arts. In sublimation of sexual drives, from the unconscious diversion of sexual energy ("primary processes") to more socially acceptable endeavors such as the arts ("secondary processes"), sublimation serves as a mature, healthy defense mechanism (Freud, 1930/1952). However, Freud (1927/2010) admitted that the concept of sublimation cannot fully elucidate the nature of artistic gifts; nor can it explain the choice of artistic technique.

Members of Freud's inner circle, such as Carl Gustav Jung, Otto Rank, and Alfred Adler, developed their own theories of creativity. Otto Rank (1932/1989) wrote about the need for the creative person to establish a "safe container" that permits an artist to step outside of their everyday experience to allow for a fresh way of looking at the world. Based firmly on Rank's knowledge of psychology and psychoanalysis, his writings range widely through anthropology and cultural history, reaching beyond psychology to a broad understanding of human nature. Without this balance, the artist is prone to become too self-critical or too inclined to self-idealization. Not only must artists step outside the frame of their culture but outside of their own ideological mindset and framework.

Alfred Adler championed a "compensatory theory of creativity"—that human beings produce art, science, and other aspects of culture to compensate for their own inadequacies (see Ansbacher & Ansbacher, 1964). An analogy would be the oyster producing a pearl to cover up the grain of sand intruding into its shell. In like fashion, Beethoven's deafness, Van Gogh's psychosis, and Virginia Woolf's depression all compensated for some defect or "organ inferiority." Both Rank and Adler extended their theories to society at large, resulting in adaptations and applications of their work by social organizations, corporations, and action researchers.

Other psychoanalytic thinkers of the Freudian school have built further on Freud's premise that individuals use creativity to seek pleasure and avoid pain. Ernst Kris (1952) maintained that the use of "primary processes" in creativity is "a regression in service of the ego." He held that the dynamics occur in the preconscious, an area not momentarily in consciousness but easily accessible. However, Lawrence Kubie (1958) noted that neurotic distortion can occur when the conscious mind inhibits the creative process by overly rigid use of symbolic functions. Kubie adds that the unconscious can hinder creativity with an even more rigid anchorage in unreality.

Several Neo-Freudians have addressed the source and motive of the creative act, noting that the link between primary processes (primarily sexuality) and creativity is important. They suggest that there is an energy that can be sublimated into higher psychological processes when one's primary gratification urges are inhibited (Taylor, 2009). Philip Weissman (1968) hypothesized that the groundwork for these creative capacities may be the infant learning to visualize the mother's breast independently of oral needs; later in life this endowment is preserved and transferred into the creative act. Phyllis Greenacre (1958) speculated that the future artist learns to disassociate with real objects and falls in love with an imaginary world, a dynamic dating back to breast-feeding. She presented in depth studies of Jonathan Swift (author of *Gulliver's Travels)* and

Lewis Carroll (author of *Alice's Adventures in Wonderland*), claiming that Swift's protagonist, Lemuel Gulliver, was afflicted with coprophilia (fascination with feces) and distortions of body image. Carroll's condition, on the other hand, was more serious as he purportedly was on the brink of psychosis, defending against it with his literary endeavors.

Freud's concept of sublimation found its way into artistic portrayal in the 1956 film *Written on the Wind*. Dorothy Malone plays the role of Marylee Hadkey, the irresponsible nymphomaniac daughter of a Texas oil baron. When her father dies and her brother leaves Texas, Marylee takes over the company. The last scene shows her in a business suit, stroking a miniature oil well as if it were a penis. In *Little Children*, a 2006 movie, Jackie Earle Haley depicts Ronnie McGarvey, a child molester whose collection of porcelain children's images seems to have served to sublimate desires that are abhorrent to both him and his neighbors. Ronnie fails but Marylee succeeds; Ronnie had been receiving psychotherapy, Marylee had not. Both actors won awards for their portrayals.

Carl Gustav Jung

Jung developed his own school of therapy based on what he termed "analytical psychology," an approach that contains a number of existential themes (Krippner & Easton, 1970). Jung used Freud's term "sublimation" differently than Freud, linking it to alchemy, the medieval attempt to transmute common metals into gold. Jung used the term as a metaphor for internal processes in which potentially harmful unconscious material can be transformed into growth-enhancing development. He provided several examples, many from the field of the arts. The French psychoanalyst Jacques Lacan (1992) used the term to denote a vacuum in one's functioning that is filled through creative activity. An experimental approach to sublimation found support for the concept, but noted it was largely culture dependent (Kim et al., 2013).

Jung (2016) divided artistic creativity into two categories: psychological art and visionary art. Psychological art appears to be generated by primary processes. Visionary art, on the other hand, reflects deeper unconscious processes, especially those from what Jung termed the "collective unconscious," images and concepts that reflect the entire history of humankind. Jung's own illustrations can be found in *The Red Book,* a journal he kept following his split with Freud but not published until 2009. In commenting on his illustrations, Jung recalled, "While I was writing [down my visions] once I said to myself, 'What is this I am doing, it certainly is not science, but what is it?' Then a voice said in me, 'That is art'" (Jung, 1925/1989, p. 45).

Jung agreed that there is a link between primary processes (specifically sexuality), and creativity. Like Freud, Jung held that these processes can be sublimated into higher psychological processes when primary gratifications are inhibited. This phenomenon—creativity—is equally operative as both a biological and psychological function. However, Jung felt that interpreting creativity solely as sublimated sexual energy and libidinal curiosity was reductionistic and could not explain its entire dimension. This is especially true of visionary art, which reflects the deep unconscious, specifically the archetypes, those inherited components of the "collective unconscious" that derive from humankind's accumulated experiences over the millennia (VandenBos, 2007, p. 69). The collective unconscious is the deepest and least accessible component of the unconscious (p. 195). Two of the most influential archetypes are the *anima*, the unconscious feminine aspects of the male psyche, and the *animus*, the unconscious masculine aspects of the female psyche. Once these archetypes are brought into conscious awareness then fusion is achieved, and an individual is capable of enhanced creative functioning. Jung used the term "syzygy" to describe this process.

Jung (1992) proposed that the collective unconscious is present in everyone, consisting of images that represent the libido, images that are available for analytic interpretation. He termed this analytic method "amplification," using historical, cultural, and mythological material to deepen one's understanding of images, especially those found in dreams (a counterpart to Freud's "condensation"). Jung (1971) wrote that sexuality and the other "great problems of life" were related to the primordial images of the collective unconscious. Hence, sexuality and the arts interact at a deep, unconscious level. There are multiple layers of sexuality, including its spiritual aspects. The goal of Jungian analysis is to maximize an individual's growth in consciousness. Each successive level of increased consciousness is enabled by the appearance of a new Transcendent Function. In turn, each new Transcendent Function appears after a dialogue between ego consciousness and the unconscious and represents a new balance between the ego's demand for reason and the chaos of the unconscious at each successive level of increased consciousness (see also Jung, 1966a, 1966b; Stein, 2013).

The work of the Dutch artist Marcel Duchamp serves as an example of syzygy, his conscious integration of the *anima* into artistic endeavors. Duchamp named this female *alter ego* "Rrose Sélavy" (in French pronounced *Eros c'est la vie*), which translates into English as "Eros, such is life." It has also been interpreted to read as *arroser la vie* ("to make a toast to life"). Sélavy emerged in 1921 in a series of photographs by the surrealist Man Ray, portraying Duchamp as identifying as a woman. Through the 1920s, Man Ray and Duchamp collaborated on more photos of Sélavy. Duchamp later used the name as the byline on written material and occasionally credited the creation of art works to his *alter ego*, signing them "Rrose Sélavy." Duchamp, a prominent painter, and sculptor who reveled in psychological twists (see Bouchard, 2017), was a close contemporary of Wilhelm Reich, a psychoanalyst who was an amateur painter and sculptor.

Wilhelm Reich

Wilhelm Reich was a European physician who became a member of the "second generation" of psychoanalysts, following Freud (Thompson, 2014). But where

Freud had advocated sublimation and adaptation, Reich's credo was action-oriented and revolutionary. Reich proposed that blocking sexual expression was the basis of neurosis and that one's "orgiastic potential" determined mental health status and served as the basis for human creativity. For Reich, the creative act is akin to the sexual act as it is a release of energies from oneself to the outside world. For him, creativity is a cathartic act designed to propel consciousness beyond itself to where one, from an outside perspective, can become aware of oneself as a creator. An amateur painter himself, Reich's writings are attempts to articulate his point of view on sexuality and creativity. Reich discovered late in his career that art, expressed through his own creative impulse offered a different point of view on the issues of sexuality and creativity with which he had been struggling. In his diary entry of February 8, 1951, he wrote, "I am painting one picture after another. I discovered a new way of expression. A good way, a way of seeing" (Reich, 2012, p. 85).

However, the creative act of orgasm must be totally satisfying rather than a simple discharge if one's "orgiastic potential" was to be fulfilled. Reich's approach was not simplistic; his method of "character analysis" was the first to deal systematically with a patient's resistances. He observed his patients' ways of moving, sitting, and standing to determine the type of "body armor" they were using as psychological defenses. Reich's work on emotional and muscular "armoring" and "character analysis" made a lasting impact on psychotherapy, most directly with such therapists as his former student Alexander Lowen, who with John Pierrakos founded the Institute of Bioenergetic Analysis, which has dozens of training centers around the world. Reich's ideas also influenced Arthur Janov's "primal scream" therapy and F.C. Perls' "Gestalt therapy." The latter approach is generally considered a "humanistic psychotherapy," as are several body-based interventions that date back to Reich's ideas.

Reich's post-war cry for greater sexual and thereby greater creative freedom resonated strongly through the *avant garde* community. It resonated in accord with the postulates of Marcel Duchamp, who maintained that art was a literal ejaculation of innovation into the mundane and the sacred into the profane—or vice versa, depending on which side of the cultural wars one stood. Reich's work influenced the post-World War II "beat movement" as well as such writers as Allen Ginsberg, William Burroughs, Jack Kerouac, J. D. Salinger, Paul Goodman, and Norman Mailer. His perspectives on sexuality had a major impact on the French philosopher Michel Foucault. Kenneth Noland (1971), whose work resides in the collections of the Tate Museum in London and the Museum of Modern Art in New York, attributed his greatest creative impulses to his Reichian therapy sessions, stating in a 1971 interview that the sessions "had a great deal of significance on my life, on my work ... opening me up personally. I mean opening up a lot of my perceptions and a lot of my feelings, and as a consequence, what I do" (p.19).

In many ways a revolutionary, Reich violated the social and academic norms of his time and sought to instill a greater measure of sexual health to humanity, based on the unfettered release of energy in orgasm (cf. Reich, 1951; Krippner,

2004). His writings on social psychology influenced Herbert Marcuse, Eric Fromm, and Erik Erickson, the latter maintaining that intimacy, including sexual intimacy, served to confirm one's ego identity (e.g., Reich, 2012).

Reich eventually settled in the United States, developing the "orgone energy accumulator," a device that purportedly stores the energy that was the basis for unfettered sexuality and creativity. The writer and Nobel Laureate Saul Bellow bought an accumulator in the early 1950s and sat in it daily for "irradiations." Accumulators have also been used by Academy Award-winning actor Sean Connery and William Steg, the author of *Shrek* and the illustrator of Reich's 1948 booklet, *Listen, Little Man!*. The British educator A.S. Neill based his experimental school, Summerhill, on many of Reich's principles, most notably his advocacy of teenage sexual expression. Neill and Reich carried out an extensive correspondence, much of it regarding the necessity of removing children from adult control so that they could discover and develop their own interests (Turner, 2011).

The actor and director Orson Bean (1978/2000) was instrumental in bringing Reich's work to a wider audience with his book *Me and the Orgone: One man's sexual revolution,"* in which he describes his own sexual transformation through Reichian therapy. To his credit, Bean does not neglect what he calls Reich's "descent into madness" at the end of his life. But Reich will be remembered for taking the position that "armoring" stifled innovation both sexually and creatively, and that the yearning for re-connecting with one's origins "is at the root of man's great intellectual and artistic achievements" (Reich, 1949/1973, p. 121).

A specific application of Reichian techniques in the modern art world was the work of multi-media artist Carolee Schneemann. It was in the early 1960s that Schneemann, acknowledged as a "first-generation feminist artist," discovered the writings of Wilhelm Reich and subsequently moved from painting to performance. In 1964 Duchamp, after witnessing Schneemann's "Meat Joy" in Paris, declared it "the messiest work of art France has ever witnessed." "Meat Joy" featured nude women and men writhing among dead fish and chicken carcasses in an atmosphere of "orgiastic potency" and sexual liberation. While these artistic practices might be thought of as a Gestalt therapy, "acting out," Schneemann's intentions were more aligned with Reichian principles. Schneeman viewed her cathartic performances as bringing forth "Just about everything that had been denied and ignored that was part of human experience and which the theories of Reich could put forward" (as cited in Schwarz, 2019).

Using her body as the canvas, employing postural contortions, Schneeman sought to free herself of the emotional armoring that Reich found so debilitating, and that he found expressed in "muscular body armor." The creative act, which might result in an authentic work of art, required that the artist, in Reich's words, "discharge completely the dammed up sexual excitation through involuntary, pleasurable convulsions of the body" (Reich, 1927/1942a, p. 90). Schneemann remained a Reichian until the end of her life stating, "The history of male obsession with blood and female sexuality—Freud and Jung, and, of course, Wilhelm Reich and Simone de Beauvoir—these have all been guidelines to try to see better what I'm looking at" (as cited in Schwarz, 2019).

Reich's accumulators were denounced by the U.S. Food and Drug Administration, which banned their import across state lines. When Reich violated this order, he was arrested, convicted, and given a two-year sentence in a federal prison in Pennsylvania. He died there in 1957 while applying for parole. An estimated six tons of his books and literature were burned on government orders in one of the most flagrant examples of U.S. censorship. Why did officials overreact in this way? Perhaps they were aware of Reich's earlier attempts to combine Marxism and psychoanalysis and suspected him of subversive behavior. However, Reich objected to Stalin's invasion of Finland and was expelled from the Communist party. Perhaps his advocacy of what appeared to be "free love" was seen as a threat to conventional values (Reich, 1942). In any event, the enterprise cost the U.S. Department of Justice an estimated three million dollars.

Marcel Duchamp

The goal of Marcel Duchamp's artistic and sexual processes was the alchemical impulse towards androgyny (the presence of male and female characteristics in one individual (Grew, 2007)). This blending of art and sex in the act of self-creation and transformation is reminiscent of Jean-Paul Sartre's statement (1847/2000), "Man is nothing else but what he makes of himself. Such is the first principle of existentialism.... For we mean that man first exists, that is, that man first of all is the being who hurls himself toward a future and who is conscious of imagining himself as being in the future..." (p. 456). It could also serve as an example of Jung's concept of "individuation," the integration of all elements of the psyche. And again, Duchamp found himself in league with Reich, who expressed this utopian hope for a transformed being in his *Children of the Future* (Reich, 1984).

While Duchamp did not explicitly describe the process of his work, he often alluded to it: "If I have ever practiced alchemy, it was in the only way it can be done now, that is to say, without knowing it?" Using his found objects or "readymades" as examples, Duchamp asked, "For what else is the transmutation of transforming discarded and leaden readymades into high art more precious than gold but alchemy?" (as cited in Lebel, 1959, p. 98). Upon viewing Duchamp's "Nude Descending a Staircase," Jung (1925/1989) was compelled to state that the painting "might be said to present a double dissolution of the object" (p. 54). In Jung's alchemical worldview, this dissolution or shutting down could be the precursor to a greater and further integration, according to the maxim *solve et coagula*, dissolve and then coagulate. This painting, controversial at the time, is now regarded as a modernist classic.

Duchamp reveled in dissonance and often expressed this clash in sexual terms. Whether he was transforming the Mona Lisa by adding a mustache, cross dressing as Rrose Sélavy in photos by Man Ray, or having a "bride stripped bare by her bachelors" in a 9-foot-tall glass sculpture, Duchamp amplified erotic juxtaposition in his art (Mahon, 2005, p, 104). Along with Reich, Duchamp felt that the sexual energies of one's being were a wellspring of creative energy (or "orgiastic potency"), and that the creative use of these energies could engender a more fulfilling way of life (Tompkins, 1996). Duchamp expressed both syzygy and double dissolution in his final masterpiece, "Étant donnés," created in secrecy between 1946 and 1966 when many thought he had retired from art to play chess. A multimedia construction, this sexually charged work can be viewed properly only from a pair of peepholes through which one can investigate the box containing the tableaux that lies hidden behind the museum walls. The artist Jasper Johns, on the website of the Philadelphia Museum of Modern Art, described it as "the strangest work of art in any museum." An examination of the construction of Étant donnés reveals Duchamp's final trick, a most astounding "double dissolution," in which there are two shutdowns, "The Waterfall" and "The Illuminating Gas," both involving an image of a nude woman. The woman seems to be a fusion of one of Duchamp's lovers and of Rrose Sélavy.

Serkan Özkaya, a Turkish artist, studied Duchamp's creation and came to the realization that Étant donnés, when viewed through its two peepholes, functioned as a camera obscura. When the hall outside the box is shuttered into total darkness, an image is projected through the peepholes and onto the facing wall. Upon inspection, this image is said to be recognizable as Duchamp's feminine *alter ego*, Rrose Sélavy. Duchamp had, in a profound alchemical turn, projected his muse and alter ego into the future as a being of light (Bouchard, 2017). It is worth noting the sexual connotations of Reich's orgone energy accumulator "box" and the "box" in which Duchamp's Étant donnés resides at Philadelphia's Museum of Modern Art. Duchamp's "Nude Descending a Staircase" is located in the same museum, allowing viewers to view two iconic works of a remarkable career (Tompkins, 1996).

Duchamp was not the only artist who linked sexuality and the arts. The Roman poet Ovid claimed that he could never write unless he was in love. A later Roman poet, Dante, met Beatrice when he was nine and never knew her well; yet she became indispensable for his writing and for his life itself. The Bohemian–Austrian writer Rainer Maria Rilke noted, "Artistic experience lies so incredibly close to that of sex, to its pain and its ecstasy, that the two manifestations are indeed but different forms of one and the same yearning and delight" (Mood & Rilke, 1994, p. 43). Pablo Picasso made no secret about how his paintings were fueled by his sexuality. "Nude, Green Leaves, and Bust," "Minotaur Caressing a Sleeping Woman," and "The Kiss" are blatantly erotic. The English poet Philip Larkin noted, "The vision required of the artist has something to do with sex. I do not know what, and I don't particularly want to know. It's not surprising because obviously two creative voices would be in alliance" (Schultz, 2008).

Anaïs Nin (1978), the French diarist, entered a long-term love affair with Otto Rank while her husband was in analysis with him. She was pleased when he showed an interest in reading her diaries. Another writer, Henry Miller, discouraged Nin's diary writing but shared her fascination with Rank, especially Rank's proposed "birth trauma" and his concept of "body memories," which provided a somatic component to his speculations about creativity. In *Death of Venus,* Nin (1978) compared her erotic writings with those of Miller (e.g., 1934/1971), which she found to be more explicit and less ambiguous, more humorous but less poetic.

Colin Wilson

Colin Wilson was a writer and existential philosopher; his best known book, *The Outsider,* was published in 1956 and has never gone out of print. In it, he identified various rebels who had an artistic, political, or spiritual innovation that transformed society. *The Misfits: A Study of Sexual Outsiders* was published in 1961 and discussed the unconventional ideas of such writers as Lord Byron and their social impact. *The Quest for Wilhelm Reich: A Critical Biography,* published in 1981, holds that despite his personality flaws, Reich established the healing powers of sexual expression.

Intentionality, the act of being deliberate is a key concept in existential philosophy, and Wilson applies it to sexual outsiders. Wilson saw intentionality as the essential element of consciousness. Imagination was seen as *applied* intentionality, an immense untapped source of power for the human spirit. The most dramatic and powerful form of imagination for contemporary humans seems to be demonstrated in sexuality, providing its link with the arts. Wilson maintained that, fundamentally, sex is a much more a mental, imaginative process than a physical one. Its central function is to trigger an intensification of consciousness and to promote its evolution. This evolutionary impulse is the most basic human drive, contrary to Freud's assertion that the sexual impulse was the basic human drive. Both Freud and Jung used the term "instinct" to refer to a powerful drive or urge. But biologists use the term to denote an inborn pattern of behavior that characterizes a species, salmon spawning being an example. Wilson added that because there is no "sexual instinct," humans can be conditioned to respond sexually to almost anything.

In Wilson's view, sex is subjective; there is no necessary relation between sexual energy and an external object. Specific sexual behaviors are responses to *symbols.* Except for human consciousness, the response would not happen at all. In addition to taking issue with Freud, Wilson also disagreed with the behaviorists, noting that when all the elements of the universe "out there" have been mapped and compressed into formulae, the key factor will still be missing, for the key is "in here." It is an inner purpose that imposes responses on the outside world.

In his autobiography, Wilson recalled that Julian Huxley had asked him to consider the role that art had played in human evolution (see Wilson, 2004, p. 326). Later, Wilson elucidated this thesis in several of his books, most notably *Origins of the Sexual Impulse* (Wilson, 1963). Those who suspect that Wilson exaggerated the role that sexuality plays in human life only need to read evolutionary psychologist David Buss' (2003) seminal book *The Evolution of Desire*. After surveying sexual behavior in other species and dozens of contemporary societies, Buss concluded that human mating strategies permeate every human behavior. Sexual conflict, competition, and manipulation, as well as love, shape the expression of one's genetic potential.

Wilson's biographer Colin Stanley (2009) felt that *Origins of the Sexual Impulse* and *The Misfits: A Study of Sexual Outsiders* took him one step further into his existential study of the role and function of sex. These books emphasize Wilson's overall thesis: the intentionality of consciousness and its role in the evolutionary purposiveness of life. Indeed, for Wilson the aim of life is the increase of consciousness and the development of methods for extending consciousness into the realms of intentionality.

Wilson applied his thesis to the impact made by the publication of the first modern novel, *Pamela; Or, Virtue Rewarded*, written in 1740 by a middle-aged printer named Samuel Richardson who had decided to tell the story of a servant girl named Pamela in the form of letters. Pamela's master makes every possible attempt to seduce or rape her before capitulating to her virtue and leading her to the altar. In one sequence, he leaps out of a cupboard on Pamela as she is undressing. In another, he places her in charge of a procuress who holds Pamela's hands while he tries to ravish her. For readers of the 18th century, accustomed only to picaresque novels like *Don Quixote* and *Robinson Crusoe*, the impact of this sexual realism must have been stunning. Until 1740, sermons had been the most popular form of reading, probably because of their inclusion of colorful Biblical stories (Wilson, 1988, Chapter 4). Nothing like *Pamela* had ever occurred in Europe, a moral tale that read somewhat like pornography. The book became a best seller. Clergymen praised it from the pulpit because of its moral lesson. By the second half of the 19th century, imagination—which had seemed so harmless in *Pamela*—was revealing its darker and more disquieting aspects.

The impact of the novel was not limited to England. In his 1774 book, *Sorrows of Young Werther*, the 24-year-old Johann Wolfgang von Goethe succeeded in repeating the success of *Pamela*. Its hero, a young painter, falls in love at first sight with an attractive country girl, Charlotte, and his love takes on the character of a fever, an obsession so intense that when she marries someone else, he commits suicide. The novel triggered a wave of suicides; in the three decades since *Pamela*, readers had learned to sympathize with ecstasies of love and transports of misery. The Romantic Age had arrived; men and women were no longer ashamed to burst into tears, and novels of unhappy love affairs poured from the presses. Poets, novelists, painters, and musicians gave free expression to their emotions, the hallmark of Romanticism.

George Gordon Byron, simply known as Lord Byron (an inherited title), became one of the most important figures of the Romanic Age. According to Wilson, Byron not only invented the swashbuckling hero but lived out the role. Byron had decided at an early age that the best way of achieving permanent contact with the forbidden was to become identified with it, to see himself as his own mixture of hero and villain. By identifying himself with his heroes and heroines such as Childe Harold, Lara, and Manfred, Byron was, in effect, engaging in playacting. This is why the Byronic hero dominated literature in the first half of the 19th century; he expressed the very essence of Romanticism: Humans are capable of challenging God, of demanding to know why human life seems so chaotic and meaningless. Byron wanted to know why he was in the world and what he was supposed to do now that he was here. In that sense, Wilson claims that Byron deserves to be called the father of existentialism, antedating Kierkegaard by several decades. Wilson (1988) concluded that no one before Byron had ever thought of asking that question with quite the same angry persistence.

In retrospect, Wilson maintained he was not discussing mere imagination, but something that the French psychologist Pierre Janet called "the reality function." Whenever the reality function is awakened, one feels more alive. Looked at in this light, Romanticism might be regarded as an evolutionary attempt to escape the limitations of the body and the emotions. In short, before one can feel alive, the mind needs to add a dimension of reality to the world of the senses. Wilson concluded that if there is such a thing as the "great secret" of human existence, this is it.

Rollo May

Rollo May was an American existential psychologist, trained in psychoanalysis, who is a towering figure in both existential psychology and humanistic psychology. Early in his career he studied with Alfred Adler and was also influenced by the writings of Eric Fromm and Otto Rank, whom he considered seminal figures in existential psychotherapy. Like Colin Wilson, Rollo May was intrigued by the concept of the outsider, also applying the term to mystics. In *The Courage to Create*, May (1994) wrote that creativity and originality are associated with persons who do not fit into their culture, but this does not necessarily mean that creativity is the product of their neurosis. Hence, May took issue with Adler's notion of "organ inferiority" as being the stimulus for creativity.

May also differentiated between creativity as a superficial aestheticism and its authentic form—that is, the process of bringing something new into being, between artifice and genuine art. May noted that philosophers have made this distinction throughout the centuries. Plato, for example, demoted superficial artists to the sixth circle of reality because they deal with decoration, a way of simply making life prettier. But in the *Symposium*, Plato described what he called the "true artists," those who give birth to some new reality.

In an introductory chapter to the landmark book *Existence*, May (1958) cited modern art as "the most vivid of all portrayals of the meaning of existentialism" (p. 16). He noted that such painters as Van Gogh, Cezanne, and Picasso were revolting "against the hypocritical academic tradition of the late nineteenth century" in "an attempt to pierce below surfaces to grasp a new relation to the reality of nature, as well as to "endeavor to recover honest, direct aesthetic experience," and in "the desperate attempt to express the immediate underlying meaning of the modern human situation, even though this means portraying despair and emptiness" (pp. 16–17).

In *The Courage to Create*, May (1994) observed that in contemporary times it is a common practice to avoid working up the courage required for authentic intimacy by shifting the issue to the body, making intimacy a matter of simple physical courage. Most people find it easier to be naked physically than to be naked psychologically or spiritually; it is easier to share one's body than to share one's fantasies, hopes, fears, and aspirations. It is the latter that are often felt to be more personal, and their sharing is experienced as making one more vulnerable, shyer about sharing the things that matter most. Too many people short-circuit the more dangerous building of a relationship by leaping immediately into bed, assuming that the body is an object and can be treated mechanically. As one enters more deeply into the relationship, each new depth is marked by some new joy but also by some new anxiety. Kierkegaard, Nietzsche, Camus, and Sartre all wrote that courage is not the absence of despair. Rather, courage is the capacity to move ahead despite despair.

May included several examples of courage in his final book, *The Psychology of Existence*, in which an existential psychotherapist, Joan Monheit (1995) reviews her work with gay and lesbian clients, noting that

> a primary concern for existential psychotherapy is the relationship among freedom, limitation, and choice. For lesbians and gay men, the choice is not in being lesbian or gay, that is a given. Rather, the choice is either to embody one's affectional and erotic desires and allow for all the possibilities of who one is, or to limit oneself by imitating the perceived norms of the culture, thereby constricting expression of not only one's sexuality but many other aspects of the self as well. (pp. 226–227)

May also discussed what he considers to be the most important kind of courage, namely creative courage, the discovery of new forms, new symbols, and new patterns on which a rejuvenated society can be built. It is the artists who present directly and immediately the new forms and symbols—the dramatists, the musicians, the painters, the dancers, the poets, and the mystics. They all portray the new symbols in terms of images—poetic, aural, plastic, or dramatic. Most people dream about symbols, but creative people live out what they have imagined and express them in graphic forms. The symbols simply dreamt about by most human beings are expressed and shared by the artists.

But in the appreciation of the created work—for example, a composition by Mozart or a T.S. Eliot poem—someone is also performing a creative act. When we engage a painting, which we need to do especially with modern art if we are to see it authentically, we are experiencing a new moment of sensibility. Some new vision is triggered in us by our contact with the painting; something unique is born within. Therefore, the appreciation of the music or painting or the novel is also a creative act. So it is that artists provide a "distant early warning" of what is happening to our culture. In contemporary art we see symbols galore of alienation and anxiety. It follows that May considered Michelangelo's writhing, unfinished statues of slaves, struggling in their prisons of stone, to be the most fitting symbol for the human condition.

At the same time, there is form amid discord, beauty amid ugliness, some human love in the midst of hatred—a love that temporarily triumphs over death but always loses out in the long run. This is the way that artists express the spiritual meaning of their culture. By the creative act, however, they can reach beyond their own death. This is why creativity is so important and why there is a need to confront the problem of the relationship between creativity and death. This is why authentic creativity takes so much courage: An active battle with the gods is occurring, the gods of conformity, exploitation, and material success. Through the ages, authentically creative figures have consistently found themselves in such a struggle. Degas once wrote, "A painter paints a picture with the same feeling as that with which a criminal commits a crime" (May, 1975, p. 22). Again, May used the symbol of the outsider to express this struggle. Creativity must be married to the passion of the adult human being, which is a passion to live beyond one's death. This is creative courage, however minor or fortuitous one's creations may be.

To recapitulate, May admonished those who preferred a "short-cut" to intimacy by leaping into bed with one's partner to courageously sharing one's deepest feelings. Likewise, he was critical of artists whose work is "pretty" but superficial, encouraging them to summon the courage to do battle with apathy, conformity, and other societal gods, as well as with death itself.

May (1975) wrote that "Creativity is the stepchild of psychology" (p. 18), a statement that characterizes the historically difficult relationship existent between gifted individuals and society, and between science and creativity research. As his statement indicates, the awkwardness of the relationship is apparent in psychology that studies creative products, and the individuals who embody the process, without definitively grasping creativity itself. A similar awkwardness seems to exist in the life sciences that study live organisms without capturing life itself. Just so, the creative process can be observed and described, but its source remains obscure.

May (1998) linked sexuality and the arts through his concept of the "daimonic," an individual's system of motives, which is composed of a collection of specific motives, each of which is called a *daimon,* a Greek word meaning "little god" or "godlike." (The English word "demon" also derives from "daimon" but has negative connotations.) Daimons include lower needs such as food and sex, as well as higher needs such as love and creativity. A daimon is any motive that can take over the person, a situation May refers to as "daimonic possession."

An example of this "possession" is illustrated by one of Colin Wilson's "misfits," Donatien Alphonie Francois de Sade. Born into French nobility, the Marquis de Sade became obsessed with sex, with pain, with the theater, and with a hatred of religion. These daimons produced no end of legal problems, leading to incarceration in jails and mental hospitals. While incarcerated, de Sade spent much of his time writing; his most popular novel *The Misfortunes of Virtue,* published in 1791, tells the story of Justine. Her many adventures include seeking refuge in a monastery where she is flogged, beaten, and sodomized by the monks. Other of de Sade's works, such as *Dialogues with a Priest* and *120 Days of Sodom,* eventually led to the adaptation of his name, sadism, to describe the derivation of pleasure, especially sexual satisfaction, from inflicting pain and suffering on others.

For May, one of the most important daimons was "Eros." Eros is love (either with or without sex), and in Greek mythology was the name of a minor god, typically pictured as a young man. May conceptualized love as the need people have to "become one" with another person and referred to an ancient Greek story by Aristophanes. People were originally four-legged, four-armed, two-headed creatures. When they became too prideful, the gods split them in two, male and female, and cursed them with the never-ending desire to recover the missing half. Like any daimon, Eros is a positive motive unless it takes over the personality, leading to an obsession. Eros can exist without sexuality, but when they are allied, people can be lifted out of their despondency and enter orbits of ecstasy (May, 1969/2011).

Another important concept for May is "will," the ability to self-organize to achieve one's goals. This concept shows the influence of Otto Rank, who used the word in the same way. But will, too, is a daimon that can potentially take over the person. In this and other writings, May (1991) utilizes both ancient and modern myths and ancient history to provide the depth for which his work is noted. For example, he assumed that Marc Antony had numerous sexual encounters before he met Cleopatra, but once their relationship blossomed Eros, the daimon, entered the picture and along with it, Antony's self-transcendence.

In his most popular book *Love and Will,* May (1969/2011) described the "Neo-Puritans" as all will but no love. They have impressive self-discipline and can make things happen, but they have no wishes, erotic or otherwise, to fulfill. They become perfectionistic, empty, and "dried-up." The archetypal example would be Ebenezer Scrooge from Charles Dickens' novella *A Christmas Carol.*

Another type is found among those May referred as "Infantile." They are all wishes but no will. Filled with dreams and desires, they do not have the self-discipline to make anything of their dreams and desires, and so become dependent and conformist. They love, but their love means little and results in nothing. May suggested that Homer Simpson, the cartoon character, may be a clear example.

Yet another type was termed "Creative." This group has cultivated a balance of these two aspects of our personalities. May wrote that the human task is "to unite love and will." This idea can be found among quite a few theorists. Otto Rank, for example, made the same contrast with death (which includes both a need for others and a fear of life) and life (which includes both the need for autonomy and the fear of loneliness). Other theorists have talked about communion and agency, nurturance and assertiveness, affiliation and achievement, and other polarities that can be creatively balanced.

The Greek concept of daimon included the creativity of poets, artists, and spiritual leaders, and the absorption of the beloved by the lover. In their concept of the daimon, the Greeks constructed a bridge between the divine and the human. It is only when the balance among daimons is disrupted that they could be considered "evil." Jung used the term as well, and wrote that humans, driven by their daimons enter the "untrodden, unreadable regions," where there are no charted ways and no shelter spreads a protecting roof over their heads. Indeed, this is a creative challenge.

May used Greek terms to describe other forms of love; *philia* is love of family, *patria* is love of country, and *agape* is spiritual love. Other writers (e.g., Krippner, 1976) have added *familial* or family love, *storge* or neighborly love, *ludus* or playful love, *pragma* or practical love, and *philautia* or self-love. For the psychologist Robert Sternberg (1997), the key dimensions of any type of love are passion, commitment, and intimacy. *Pragma,* for example, may be high in commitment but low in passion while *ludus* might be low in commitment but high in passion. To cite the title of a popular song, "Love is a Many-Splendored Thing."

May's 1985 book, *My Quest for Beauty,* is unjustly overlooked. Illustrated by his own sketches, paintings, and poems, May reveals his inner life as well as his external voyages to exotic destinations. He discusses the social and personal functions of art and provides additional examples of the "courage to create." Many of these thoughts are expressed in a 1986 interview on "New Thinking Allowed," with moderator Jeffrey Mishlove. In the video interview, Mishlove questions May as to whether some existential philosophers were pushing the idea of rebelling against conventional habits of society, and implies that May seemed to also suggest genuine mysticism involves such "cutting-edge rebellion" against such instincts:

> **May:** It's a rebellion against the herd instinct. Sartre was very important in this movement... Camus wrote the book *The Rebel.* And Paul Tillich, who was my dear and very close friend for some thirty years... understood that joy and freedom come only from the facing of life, the confronting of the difficulties. Sartre, when France was overrun by the Nazis, wrote a drama called *The Flies.* This is a retelling of the ancient Greek story Orestes... Zeus tries to get Orestes not to go back to his hometown and kill his mother, which he was ordered to do to avenge his father. Zeus says, "I made you, so you must obey me." And then Zeus gets quite angry, and he has the stars and planets zooming around to show how powerful he is, and he says, "But do you realize how much despair lies ahead of you if you follow your course?" And Orestes says, "Human life begins on the far side of despair."

Now, I happen to believe that... despair has a constructive side, as well as anxiety having a constructive effect.

Mishlove: Would I be correct in assuming that when you speak of anxiety you don't think of it as a symptom to be removed, but rather as a gateway for exploration into the meaning of life?

May: Well, you've got that exactly right. I think anxiety is associated with creativity. When you're in a situation of anxiety, you can of course run away from it, and that's certainly not constructive; or you can take a few pills to get you over it...

Mishlove: You could meditate.

May: Well, you could meditate. But I think none of those things, including meditation, which I happen to believe in, none of those paths leads you to creative activity... It's as though the world is knocking at your door, and you need to create, you need to make something, you need to do something. I think anxiety, for people who have found their own heart and their own souls... is a stimulus toward creativity, toward courage. It's what makes us human beings. Joy is the zest that you get out of using your talents, your understanding, and the totality of your being, for great aims. Musicians... Mozart and Beethoven and the rest of them, always showed considerable anxiety, because they were in the process of loving beauty, of feeling joy when they heard a beautiful combination of notes. That's the kind of feeling that goes with creativity. That is why I say, "the courage to create." Creation does not come out of simply what you're born with. It must be united with your courage, both of which cause anxiety but also great joy.

A. S. Maslow

Abraham S. Maslow was an American psychologist who played a seminal role in the creation of both humanistic and transpersonal psychology. Rather than viewing people as a "bag of symptoms," he focused on their positive qualities. Maslow is best known for his "hierarchy of human needs," which proposed that these be fulfilled in priority, culminating in self-actualization. Eventually, Maslow (1971) added "self-transcendence" as an even later stage that some people attain. However, he admitted that there were many exceptions to the hierarchy, not only from individual to individual but from culture to culture.

Maslow began his career as a behavioral psychologist, conducting laboratory research with apes, dogs, and rats. This background probably led to his classification of sex as a "physiological" need along with sleep, nutrition (food and water), and shelter. In his theory of human motivation, Maslow (1943, 1954) placed safety, security, and stability at the next level, followed by love and belonging. The final "deficit" need is esteem, where one achieves status and self-acceptance for one's accomplishments.

Unlike the other physiological needs, sex is not necessary for a person's survival. One may become frustrated without sex, but one's life will not be at risk as is the case with food and shelter. Rollo May (1969/2011) made this clear by separating sex from "Eros" in his discussion of love. The culmination of sex is the orgasm, but the culmination of Eros is penetration, the moment when lovers transcend themselves.

Once deficit needs have been met, higher order needs come into play. Cognitive needs result in stimulation and exploration, while aesthetic needs include harmony, order, and beauty. "Self-actualization" is the final level, in which one's full potential is realized and creativity can be manifested. In Maslow's words:

> This is precisely what the great artist does. He can bring together clashing colors, forms that fight each other, dissonances of all kinds, into a unity. And this is also what the great theorist does when he puts puzzling and inconsistent facts together so that we can see that they really belong together. And so also for the great statesman, the great therapist, the great philosopher, the great parent, the great inventor. They are all integrators, able to bring separates and even opposites together into unity. (Maslow, 1968, p. 140)

Taking issue with the psychoanalytic perspective of sublimation, Maslow (1962) proposed that:

> Self-actualized creativeness is "emitted" like radioactivity, and hits all of life, regardless of the problems, just as [a] cheerful person "emits" cheerfulness without purpose or design or even consciousness. It is emitted like sunshine; it spreads all over the place; it makes some things grow (which are growable) and is wasted on rocks and other ungrowable things. (p. 145)

Maslow (1962) surveyed several "self-actualized" creative people, finding that they had many traits in common. He reported:

> All of my subjects were relatively more spontaneous and expressive than average people. They were more "natural" and less controlled and inhibited in their behavior which seemed to flow out more easily and freely and with less blocking and self-criticism. This ability to express ideas and impulses without strangulation and without fear of ridicule turned out to be an essential aspect of self-actualized creativity. (pp. 137–138)

Further:

> The creativity of my subjects seemed to be an epiphenomenon of their greater wholeness and integration, which is what self-acceptance implies. The civil war within the average person between forces of the inner depths and the forces of defense and control seems to have been resolved in my subjects and they are less split. Consequently, more of themselves is available for use, for enjoyment and for creative purpose. They waste less of their time and energy protecting themselves against themselves. (p. 141)

Although Maslow does not refer to Reich, there is a parallel between his use of the term "energy" and Reich's ideas of a "creative energy," which those who have trained themselves allow themselves to recognize. For both, this is the wellspring of creativity and art. When Maslow (1962) states that the creative person merges "forms that fight each other, dissonances of all kinds, into a unity" (p.140), he describes a union of opposites like Jungian concepts. Maslow (1954) continued, "A musician must make music, an artist must paint, a poet must write, if he is to be ultimately at peace with himself. What a man can be, he must be" (p. 46). This is reminiscent of the description of "destiny" discussed by Rollo May (1982) in his book *Freedom and Destiny*.

Maslow (1962) subsequently conceptualized two forms of creativity: "special talent creativity" that is found in the arts, and creativity that can be found in everyday life. In discussing the latter, Maslow (1962) noted, "I learned from her and others like her that a first-rate soup is more creative than a second-rate painting" (p. 136). His self-actualized people "seem to have a uniformly good appetite for food; they seem to sleep well; they seem to enjoy their sexual lives without unnecessary inhibition and so on" (Maslow, 1954, p. 156).

This group was more prone to have what Maslow called "peak experiences," those times of awe and ecstasy that often represent sudden insights into life as a powerful unity transcending time, space, and the self (VandenBos, 2007, p. 680). Maslow found peak experiences in a variety of instances: love based on "being" rather than on "deficit"; the parental experience; the mystic, oceanic, or nature experience; aesthetic perceptions, creative moments, therapeutic or intellectual insights; the orgasmic experience; certain forms of athletic fulfillment; and other "moments of highest happiness and fulfillment" (Maslow, 1954, p. 73). Maslow's informants cited their

> feelings of limitless horizons opening up to the vision, the feeling of being simultaneously more powerful and also more helpless than one ever was before, the feeling of great ecstasy and wonder and awe, the loss of placing in time and space with, finally, the conviction that something extremely important and valuable had happened (p. 164)

These peak experiences were noted to have occurred during sexual union, as well as through intense enjoyment of music or art. It is important to observe that this type of sexuality goes beyond the "survival needs" originally described by Maslow in his celebrated hierarchy.

Later, Maslow (in Krippner, 1976) described the "plateau experience" as reported by those people who went beyond self-actualization to "self-transcendence." He and his colleagues developed transpersonal psychology as a result of these reports, focusing on the study of concerns and experiences that transcend personal identity, attained through meditation, prayer, psychedelics, or occurring spontaneously. Maslow (1968) observed that "we already know something of these integration techniques—of insight, of intellect in the broader sense, of love, of creativeness, of humor and tragedy, of play, of art" (p. 11).

Implications

The personal and social transformation that often results has important implications for development and for psychotherapy. Eastern thought contains far more connections between transpersonal states, sexuality, and the arts than does Western psychology; Alan Watts (1963) has cited Hindu dance, painting, poetry, and sculpture as examples of how sexuality and the arts are effortlessly blended. This blending is also apparent when one examines the work of transpersonal psychologist Jenny Wade (2000) and her interviews of 86 participants from the United States, a group that was ethnically diverse and represented a variety of religious and sexual orientations. Wade's participants were selected because of their alleged "transformational sexual experiences," those that involved some type of "cosmic energy" or "kundalini" and that resulted in spiritual insights and personal transformation. She advocates a greater sharing of these experiences, especially with one's psychotherapist, because of their potential value in personal change.

Wade's participants reported what she called "an astonishing array of experiences" (p.119), notably the expansion of customary time and space boundaries, sharing of "kundalini" energy with one's partner, identification with other animals and other aspects of nature, and the incorporation of spiritual entities (which Jungians might refer to as "archetypes"). This is reminiscent of Watts' observation regarding the blending of sexuality and the arts in various Eastern traditions. The ancient *Kamasutra* text, probably the first sex manual, lent itself to many sculptures, most notably the 6th century productions in the Vaishnavism caves. There are earlier examples of erotic art in Hindu, Jain, and Buddhist temples; especially notable are the 64 Yogini temples of Khajuraho. Typically carved from sandstone, the artwork depicts acrobatic coupling of both humans and deities, sometimes of the same sex and some even with animals and plants (Rawson, 1977).

During the Edo and Meiji dynasties in Japan, some of the artwork portrayed "beautiful youth," a "third gender" of young men equally desired by both men and women (Uhlenbeck & Winkel, 2005). The clay pots of ancient Peru typically featured spouts in the form of a penis. Peruvian erotic art included other aspects of nature, such as a coupling on an ear of maize. Not only were sex and art, as well as humans and nature, linked in these products, but they often served other purposes such as sex education in India and birth control instructions in Peru. Rather than featuring deities, one large Japanese chamber depicted sex among commoners who were the most frequent visitors (Mathieu, 2003).

Colin Wilson and Abraham Maslow emphasized the role that transcendence has played in human evolution. Psychiatrist Ruth Richards (2018) has taken a similar point of view, writing that beauty can at times assume "a transcendent importance," going beyond sexual selection" and resonating "with realms of higher meaning" (p. 375). The ornithologist Richard Prum (2017) has pointed out that Darwin, in his 1871 tome *The Descent of Man*, saw beauty as a second strand in evolutionary science, addressing natural selection within a species rather than between species. For example, in discussing the male Arbus pheasant, Darwin (1871/1952) wrote that its "most refined beauty may serve as a sexual charm, and for no other purpose" (p. 474). Prum (2017) underscored the female's role in mate selection and how beauty denotes good health, resulting in a dependable relationship (Krippner, 2004). This second strand (beauty) complements the first strand (function) but is not identical to it. The second strand is grounded in aesthetics, not functionality. For example, the wing structure of the club-winged manakin was mediated for singing, not for flight; the latter would have been more functional. Notable among humans are the highly styled penis shields of Papua New Guinea, typically the only garment worn by males.

"Aesthetic selection" also explains males' preference for females with breast tissue, relatively narrow waists, and fat deposits on the buttocks. Although they also are functional when it comes to childbirth and childrearing, they have evolved to serve as "ornaments" in ways that cannot be explained by natural selection alone. For example, permanent breast tissue is unique to human females. It is counterintuitive that women do not prefer excessively "masculine" facial features, which denote protection and support for them and their families. Instead, these studies reveal a preference for "intermediate" or even "feminine' facial features and lean rather than muscle-bound physiques.

Prum's (2017) perspective is controversial but presents vital insights into several evolutionary phenomena. It can explain why sex occurs outside of a female's fertile period and how reproduction became uncoupled from sex. Having sex during the fertile period is functional; having sex outside of the fertile period is not functional but is aesthetic. This "second evolutionary strand" validates Richards' emphasis on the link between aesthetics and transcendence, and their role in evolution.

Conclusion

This chapter has searched through the biographies and publications of noted existential psychologists and philosophers, observing that tangible links can be identified between the arts and sexuality. Indeed, for some psychologists of the early 20th century, sex was believed to be deeply rooted in considerable sub-conscious behavior, and it comes as no surprise that expression of this link can be found in literature and visual artwork, music and sculpture, dance and the media. Existential psychologists are uniquely positioned to carry out further explorations of this topic because they are open to aesthetics, phenomenology, and intentionality in their exploration of the human condition.

References

Ansbacher, H.L., & Ansbacher, R.R. (Eds.).(1964). *The individual psychology of Alfred Adler.* Harper Torchbooks.

Arieti, S. (1976). *Creativity: The magic synthesis.* Basic Books.

Bean, O. (2000). *Me and the orgone: One man's sexual revolution.* American College of Orgonomy Press. (Original work published 1978)

Bouchard, B. (2017, October 3). Has Duchamp's final work harbored a secret for five decades? *Art World.* https://news.artnet.com/art-world/duchamp-etant-donnes-secret-serkan-ozkaya-1103216

Brandon-Friedman, R.A. (2021). Sexual identity. In H.L. Armstrong (Ed.) *Sex and sexuality: Understanding biology, psychology and culture* (pp. 657–659). ABC-CLIO.

Buss, D.M. (2003). *The evolution of desire: Strategies of human mating.* Basic Books.

Darwin, C. (1952). *The descent of man.* In R. M. Hutchins (Ed.), *Great books of the Western world* (Vol. 49). Encyclopedia Britannica. (Original work published 1871)

Freud, S. (1952). Civilization and its discontents. In R.M. Hutchins (Ed.), *The major works of Sigmund Freud* (pp. 767–802). Encyclopedia Britannica. (Original work published 1930)

Freud, S. (1966). *Leonardo da Vinci and a memory of his childhood.* Bartelby. (Original work published 1910)

Freud, S. (2010). *An autobiographic study.* W.W. Norton. (Original work published 1927)

Greenacre, P. (1958). *Swift and Carroll: A psychoanalytic study.* International Universities Press.

Grew, R. (2007). The immortal self: Surrealist alter-egos. *Quest, 5* [E-journal].

Jung, C. G. (2016). *On psychological and visionary art: Notes from C. G. Jung's lecture on Gérard de Nerval's "Aurélia"* (C. E. Stephenson, Ed.). Princeton University Press.

Jung, C.G. (1966a). *The process of psychotherapy: Collected works* (Vol. 13). Princeton University Press.

Jung, C.G. (1966b). *Spirit, man, and literature: Collected works* (Vol. 15). Princeton University Press.

Jung, C.G. (1971). *Psychological types: Collected works* (Vol. 6). Princeton University Press.

Jung, C.G. (1989). *Analytic psychology: Notes of the seminar given in 1925.* Princeton University Press. (Original work published 1925)

Jung, C.G. (1992). Psychology of the unconscious: A study of the transformation of the symbols of the libido. *Collected works* (Vol. 8). Princeton University Press.

Jung, C.G. (2009). *The Red Book: Leber Novus.* (S. Shamdasani, M. Kyburz, & J. Peck, Eds.) W.W. Norton.

Kim, E., Zeppenfeld, V., & Cohen, D. (2013). Sublimation, culture, and creativity. *Journal of Personality and Social Psychology, 105,* 639–666.

Krippner, S. (1976). The plateau experience: A. H. Maslow and others. In T. X. Barber (Ed.), *Advances in altered states of consciousness and human potentialities* (Vol. 1, pp. 651-664). Psychological Dimensions.

Krippner, S. (2004). Love is good for your health. *Arte-Terapia: Reflexões, 6*, 2–6.

Krippner, S., & Easton, H. (1970). The essential theme in Jungian psychology. *Journal of Contemporary Psychotherapy, 3*, 19–26. https://doi.org/10.1007/BF02110168

Kris, E. (1952). *Psychoanalytic explorations in art.* International Universities Press.

Kubie, L. (1958) *Neurotic distortion of the creative process.* Noonday Press.

Lacan, J. (1992). *The ethics of psychoanalysis: Seminars, 1858–1860 (Book 17).* W.W. Norton & Co.

Lebel, R. (1959). *Marcel Duchamp.* Grove Press.

Lehmiller, J.J. (2014). *The psychology of human sexuality.* WileyBlackwell.

Mahon, A. H. (2005). *Eroticism and art.* Oxford University Press.

Maslow, A. H. (1943). A theory of human motivation. *Psychological Review, 50*, 270–346. https://doi.org/10.1037/h0054346

Maslow, A. H. (1954). *Motivation and personality.* Harper & Row.

Maslow, A. H. (1962). *Toward a psychology of being* (2nd ed.). Van Nostrand Reinhold.

Maslow, A. H. (1968). *Toward a psychology of being.* D. Van Nostrand Company.

Maslow, A. H. (1971). *The further reaches of human nature.* Viking.

Mathieu, P. (2003). *Sex pots: Eroticism in Ceramics.* A&C Black Visual Arts.

May, R. (1958). The origins and significance of the existential movement in psychology. In R. May, E. Angel, & H.F. Ellenberger (Eds.), *Existence: A new dimension in psychiatry and psychology* (pp. 3–36). Basic Books.

May, R. (1975). *The courage to create.* W.W. Norton.

May, R. (1982). *From freedom to destiny.* W.W. Norton.

May, R. (1985). *My quest for beauty.* W.W. Norton.

May, R. (1991). *The cry for myth.* W.W. Norton.

May, R. (1994). *The courage to create* (rev. ed.). W.W. Norton.

May, R. (1998). *Power and innocence.* W.W. Norton.

May, R. (2011). *Love and will.* W.W. Norton. (Original work published 1969)

Miller, H. (1971). *Tropic of Cancer.* Grove. (Original work published 1934)

Monheit, J. (1995). A gay and lesbian perspective: The case of Marcia. In K.J. Schneider & R. May, *The psychology of existence: An integrative, clinical perspective* (pp. 226–233). McGraw-Hill.

Mood, J. J., & Rilke, R. M. (1994). *Rilke on love and other difficulties: Translations and considerations.* W.W. Norton & Company.

Nin, A. (1978). *Death of Venus.* Delta.

Noland, K. (1971). Oral history with Kenneth Noland, 9 October–21 December 1971. *Archives of American Art, Smithsonian Institution.* Washington, DC.

Prum, R.O. (2017). *The evolution of beauty.* Doubleday.

Rank, O. (1989). *Art and artist.* Norton. (Original work published 1932)

Rawson, P.S. (1977). *The erotic art of India.* Universe Books.

Reich, W. (1942a). *The function of the orgasm.* Farrar, Straus, and Giroux. (Original work published 1927)

Reich, W. (1942b). *The mass psychology of fascism* (3rd ed.). Farrar, Straus, and Giroux.

Reich, W. (1948). *Listen, little man!* Orgone Institute Press.

Reich, W. (1951). *The invasion of compulsory sex–morality* (3rd ed.). Farrar, Straus, and Giroux.

Reich, W. (1973). *Character analysis* (3rd ed.). Farrar, Straus, and Giroux. (Original work published 1949)

Reich, W. (1984). *Children of the future*. Farrar, Straus, and Giroux.

Reich, W. (2012). *Where's the truth? Letters and journals, 1948–1957.* (M.B. Higgins, Ed.) *Farrar, Straus and Giroux.*

Richards, R. (1990). Everyday creativity, eminent creativity, and health. *Creativity & Research Journal, 3*, 300–326. https://doi.org/10.1080/10400419009534363

Richards, R. (2018). *Everyday creativity: Dynamic new paths for self and society.* Palgrave/Macmillan.

Sartre, J.-P. (2000). *Existentialism and human emotions.* Citadel Press. (Original work published 1847)

Schultz, W.T. (2008, May 14). Sex and art. Must the poet be in love? *Psychology Today.* https://www.psychologytoday.com/us/blog/genius-and-madness/200805/sex-and-art

Schwarz, G. (2019). Intimate contact: Images of suffering in the work of Carolee. https://www.anothergaze.com/intimate-contact-images-suffering-work-carolee-schneemann-war-feminism-atrocity/

Skov, M., & Nadal, M. (2020). A farewell to art: Aesthetics as a topic in psychology and neuroscience. *Perspectives on Psychological Science, 15*, 630-642. https://doi.org/10.1177/1745691619897963

Spinelli, E. (2013). Being sexual: Human sexuality revisited. *Existential Analysis: Journal of the Society for Existential Analysis, 24*, 297–317.

Stanley, C. (2009). *On "The outsider cycle": A guide for students.* Paupers Press.

Stein, M. (2013). *Principle of individuation: Toward the development of human consciousness.* Chiron.

Sternberg, R. J. (1997). Construct validation of a triangular love scale. *European Journal of Social Psychology, 27*, 313–335. https://doi.org/10.1002/(SICI)1099-0992(199705)27:3<313::AID-EJSP824>3.0.CO;2-4

Taylor, E. (2009). *The neo-Freudians. The mystery of personality: A history of psychodynamic theories.* Springer.

Thompson, P.B. (2014). *Return to conception: Wilhelm Reich's later work as a product of European cultural modernism* [Unpublished Master's thesis]. University of Maine, Maine, USA.

Tompkins, C. (1996). *Duchamp: A biography.* Henry Holt.

Turner, C. (2011). *Adventure in orgasmaton: How the sexual revolution came to America.* Straus Farrar, Straus & Giroux.

Uhlenbeck, O., & Winkel, M. (2005). *Japanese erotic fantasies: Sexual imagery in the Edo Period.* Hotei Publishing.

VandenBos, G.R. (Ed.). (2007). *APA dictionary of psychology.* American Psychological Association.

Wade, J. (2000). Mapping the courses of heavenly bodies: The varieties of transcendent sexual experience. *Journal of Transpersonal Psychology, 32*, 103–122.

Watts, A. W. (1963). *The two hands of God: The myths of polarity.* Brazillier.

Weissman, P. (1968). *Creativity in theater: A psychoanalytic study.* International Universities Press.

Wilson, C. (1956). *The outsider.* Gollancz.

Wilson, C. (1963). *Origins of the sexual impulse.* G. P. Putnam's Sons.

Wilson, C. (1981). *The quest for Wilhelm Reich: A critical biography.* Anchor Press/Doubleday.

Wilson, C. (1988). *The misfits: A study of sexual outsiders*. Grafton. (Original work published 1961)
Wilson, C. (2004). *Dreaming to some purpose: An autobiography*. Random House.

Chapter 5

Growth through Regret: Existential Freedom, Sexuality, and Responsibility

Sara K. Bridges & L. Chandler Batchelor

Abstract

Consensual, yet regrettable, sexual experiences can be a source of preoccupation and shame for many people. While it is possible to regret the outcomes of a sexual experience but not regret the decision to engage in the sexual experience, often regret directly associated with outcomes expands to include the initial consensual decision. In this chapter we propose that by reframing regrettable sexual experiences in a more positive light, these regrettable experiences need not cause suffering and may even be used to increase self-awareness and fuel personal growth. Existential freedom both frees us from feeling like sex "should be" experienced a certain way while also demanding that we take responsibility for all consequences and ultimately for our own sexual satisfaction; therefore, regret has great utility in its ability to inform future decisions rather than simply something to keep us mired in the past. Vignettes are provided throughout to illustrate regrettable sexual experiences and what meaning one might derive from those experiences, with alternative, growth-oriented meanings suggested.

***

Sexuality is considered by many to be a vital aspect of personal well-being and a key component of self-expression (World Health Organization [WHO], 2006). Both the choice to engage in sex and the choice of sexual partner inform us of who we are. Yet rarely do we encounter people who would honestly express: "I live a fully authentic sexual life, filled with pleasure, personal awareness, and freedom from the constraints and pressures of the external word." Instead, sexuality is often wrapped in mystery, insecurity, and doubt. Further, many people have had sexual experiences that they would prefer to forget, to cut off from those experiences that inform identity. When sex happens without consent, the wish to forget makes sense. Yet, there are other times when we would prefer to forget a sexual experience—not because we lacked agency, but rather because of feelings of regret experienced after the fact. This chapter focuses on experiences that were consensual but regrettable.

Sexual choices can be fraught with judgments, both external and internal. Again and again, Western culture catches people between messages of sex positivity and pleasure and messages of modesty and caution. Finding a balance that allows space for positivity, while not requiring every sexual experience to be earth-shattering or even good, moves us toward existential freedom, authenticity, and personal sexual responsibility.

Consent to sexual activities can be a "grey zone," which leaves plenty of room for feelings of regret to take root (Johnson et al., 2021). Even with the recognition that not every sexual encounter necessarily starts with a clear felt sense of yes or no, many may still feel beholden to the external mandate that we should know and express what we want sexually at all times or risk entering into a non-consensual encounter. Consent is a process that happens at multiple points in any sexual encounter, and a "yes" to starting in no way indicates a yes to all possibilities. However, even when sexual encounters are clearly consensual to all parties, feelings of regret may arise due to a multitude of reasons. These can range from consenting because of non-sexual reasons (i.e., didn't want to hurt someone's feelings, went "so far" that it would be "mean" to stop now, or the desire to gain position or privilege) to having the encounter be less satisfying than we would have liked. Rather than seeing these instances of sexual regret as a continued source of shame and suffering, the authors posit in this chapter that a growth-oriented approach to regrettable sexual experiences can be used to re-envision regret as a step toward self-awareness and authenticity.

Sex Positivity

There are many cultural meanings attached to sex that circulate today—some older, some newer, and many contradictory. A historic, moralistic idea is that sex is bad, dirty, and sinful. Though not as widely believed as it once was, this idea is still very prevalent in certain communities, especially highly religious ones. Commonly, these ideas are called "sex negativity." Sex-negative societies often view sex as risky, encourage sexual abstinence, and tend to also hold intersecting sexist, racist, and homophobic ideas. Shame is attached to certain sex acts, such as sex with a same-gendered partner, having sex with more than one partner, having sex that involves voluntary submission or physical pain, or not having sex within the context of a committed relationship. In contrast, sex positivity encourages the embrace of diverse sexual practices and a wide range of personal meanings that sex can hold for an individual (Burnes et al., 2017; Williams et al., 2013).

Through sex-positive culture, Western society appears to be sexually liberated; however, rigid ideas of what constitutes "good" sex still exist (Pertot, 2007). These ideas about sex would not traditionally be thought of as sex-negative, yet their prescriptive nature goes against the ethos of sex positivity. For example, popular media has put forth the idea that good sex necessarily should involve enthusiastic consent, should be passionate and long-lasting, and should have orgasm as the ultimate goal. Some messages masquerading as sex positivity, such as "sex is fundamental to being human" carry the sex-negative reverse implication that to choose not to have sex is inhuman. In many ways, "sex positivity" has become twisted to mean "in favor of specific sexual attitudes" rather than its original meaning of "feeling empowered to engage in whatever consensual sex acts bring you pleasure, without shame" or the equally legitimate "feeling empowered to not engage in sexual activities, without shame."

Sex positivity emphasizes individual choice, bodily autonomy, and the freedom to engage in any safe, consensual sexual practice that is desired; nevertheless, Sloan (2015) warns that the proliferation of sex positive rhetoric runs the risk of privileging sexual expressions of intimacy over equally legitimate non-sexual expressions of intimacy. A truly sex-positive approach affirms both the choice to engage in certain physical activities and the choice to refrain from them.

Sloan's (2015) study of asexual individuals who engage in bondage and discipline, domination and submission, and sadism and masochism (BDSM) challenges the idea that certain behaviors are innately sexual, arguing instead that behaviors are ascribed sexual connotations by actors within a social context. Thus, what is sexual, what is non-sexual, and the significance of certain acts can emerge organically through practice if we are open to taking back the responsibility of self-definition from one-size-fits-all social scripts.

These internalized ideas of what sexual experiences *should* be are what often give rise to regret. Take, for example, the story of Marisa and Katie. The two women have been friends for many years, but one day their interactions turn flirty. That night, just before leaving to go home, Marisa gives Katie a quick kiss. Katie kisses back, but after pulling away an awkwardness hangs in the air. Marisa goes home a little embarrassed, but none the worse for wear. The next day, Katie asks Marisa to come over to talk. Expecting Katie to be shy and awkward about what happened the night before, Marisa is surprised to find Katie angry. At first, Katie accuses Marisa of "taking advantage" of her. When Marisa points out that Katie had kissed her back and had been flirting with her the whole day leading up to the kiss, Katie turns her anger inward and feels guilty for leading Marisa on and "unintentionally seducing" her.

In this example, Katie is attaching a lot of weight and meaning to the kiss she shared with Marisa. Marisa, on the other hand, saw the awkward kiss simply as a sign that she and her friend were perhaps romantically incompatible. Though the awkwardness of the kiss meant that there would likely be no more kisses between them in the future, it was still something special shared with a friend. Though both women experienced the kiss as awkward, only one of them felt shame over the act.

Katie had internalized the message that because the kiss was awkward it must have been "bad" and must have involved coercion on someone's part. Katie had also internalized the cultural belief of the relationship escalator—that relationships which become romantic cannot reverse back to being platonic.

Therefore, the kiss also carried the additional threat of ruining her long friendship with Marisa. It is not that these beliefs are inherently incorrect or harmful; many people subscribe to the idea of the relationship escalator, for example, and genuinely prefer that their relationships proceed in one clear direction at a steady pace. Rather, Marisa's problem arises from the fact that she has internalized these beliefs unconsciously and is not aware that other meanings are available to apply to her situation.

After talking through the situation with Marisa, Katie was able to let go of her regret by reconceptualizing the kiss as a novel, one-off experience with a friend that need not define her in overly restrictive ways. Rather than giving in to what she had internalized a kiss must mean, she was able to attach a new meaning to the kiss that wasn't shameful and opened up new ways of being in the world. Sex positivity gives us agency to put our own meanings onto sexual experiences.

Existential Freedom

If we look at freedom existentially, not as the right to have a clear say in a desired outcome but rather the freedom to make a choice, this calls the nature of regret, as it is typically understood, into question. For some, regret can be a consequence of a choice that was made, the determination that an undesirable outcome indicates a wrong choice. Yet, to embrace true existential freedom, outcome must be untethered from choice. In any choice, perhaps the most that can be hoped for is to make the best decision possible at the time, to consider the external and internal factors and then make a decision. Some decisions are clear and apparent (e.g., to have coffee in the morning), while others are much more complicated (e.g., where to attend college, a mid-life career change, whether or not to have children). But all go through a matter of choosing.

When faced with an unwelcome outcome of a choice, it is common for people to go back to the original decision and regret the choice that was made. It's as though what happens after the decision is made retroactively labels the decision itself as good or bad. No matter how much time, effort, thought, or careful consideration the choice entailed, having a negative outcome necessarily means that the choice was wrong (i.e., regrettable). This way of evoking 20/20 hindsight is especially true with sexual regret. When experiencing regret following a consensual sexual experience, we commonly regret agreeing to have sex or initiating sex in the first place rather than regretting aspects of the sexual encounter or simply regretting "how things turned out." Regretting a choice also robs a person of the freedom that came with that choice. We must sit in the full knowledge that, while perhaps unhappy with the outcome, the choice made was still an expression of the freedom to choose and was the best decision that could have been made at the time with the information available.

Yet, what about the unwelcome outcome? Does having the freedom to choose to negate the impact of a negative outcome or eliminate feelings of regret? Or is it possible to break down any sexual encounter into many small decisions, small choices along the way that could leave us content with our decision making and choices even if the outcome is less than ideal? McCabe and Killackey (2004) used the theory of planned behavior to understand the small choices that factor into young women's sexual decision making. According to the theory of planned behavior, behaviors can be predicted by intentions, which can in turn be predicted by attitudes, perceived norms, and perceived behavioral control. While McCabe and Killackey found that peer and parental norms predicted their participants' intentions, these intentions did not predict actual behavior. They suggest these findings indicate that young women's sexual decision making is perhaps more influenced by "heat-of-the-moment" situational factors rather than the logical decision making typically described by the theory of planned behavior. Other research has, in fact, demonstrated that situational factors, such as arousal states, are crucial to understanding the factors that play into the decision to pursue a sexual encounter (Ariely & Loewenstein, 2006). While this research is helpful in thinking about what goes into the decision to have sex, it neglects the evaluative process that occurs after a decision to have sex has already been made. Perhaps an example would help here:

Sherry and Tyrone are in a fairly new relationship and have been spending a lot of time together. After having sex one evening at Tyrone's apartment, Tyrone kissed her and then rolled over in bed and picked up his video game controller to play a game. Staring at Tyrone's back, Sherry thought to herself, "I am such an idiot. I never should have had sex with him. What was I thinking?" and continued to lie in bed feeling abandoned, neglected, and irritated with herself for her choice. Eventually, Sherry got out of bed, got dressed, and announced that she was going home because she had to work in the morning. Tyrone paused his game, got up to give her a hug, and said he hoped she slept well. Feeling pleased with how the evening went, Tyrone went back to his game and Sherry drove home spitting mad.

In this example, Sherry felt regret in reaction to Tyrone's behavior after having sex rather than in reaction to the sexual encounter itself. She regretted her initial decision because her emotional need for connection after intimacy was not met, and she believed that his behavior was an indication of how Tyrone felt about relationships in general or worse, about her, in particular. Naturally, this interpretation of events led to Sherry feeling abandoned and neglected. Yet, had Sherry chosen to interpret Tyrone's behavior differently, these feelings may have been less intense or avoided entirely. Sherry had an expectation about how a couple should act following a sexual encounter, and when that expectation was not met, she immediately felt regret about having sex with Tyrone and left rather than communicating her needs and desires to him. In Sherry's worldview, she shouldn't have to ask for Tyrone to connect with her after sex; it should be the natural way that the situation unfolded, and he should have wanted to connect with her. Moreover, she had a very clear definition of what connection looked like and felt hurt that her needs were not being met, even though she had not expressed those needs to him. This hurt led to a shame cascade where she regretted having sex with him, called herself an idiot, and questioned her own judgment. However, if she had made the choice to tell Tyrone that she would like a little more together time before he turned his attention to his video game, she would be taking responsibility for her needs, wants and choices. By taking time to understand that her regret was originating from a specific, unmet need (not connecting after sex) rather than a more comprehensive experience (the entire sexual interaction), a new interpretation of her regret can emerge. Taking responsibility by asking for what she needs could remove some of the self-blame and shame from the situation and allow Tyrone to meet her now-spoken needs. The choice to be authentic and vulnerable by expressing what we want (and don't want) from a sexual interaction is not easy, yet it is still a choice.

Regret, Authenticity, and Growth

Traditionally, existential regret has been conceptualized as an intense, unpleasant feeling that has a focus on the past, an orientation toward meaning making, and attempts to answer the question, "How do I reconcile this choice I made with who I am?" While this is perhaps an accurate way to describe regret, this framing tends to invite shame rather than growth. Nevertheless, it is important to understand how regret is typically experienced before reconceptualizing it.

According to existentialist thought, we are tasked with taking responsibility for our own destinies and living a life that feels in sync with our values and sense of self (Lucas, 2005). However, inevitably, we all fail to take responsibility for ourselves from time to time. These are the instances that may give birth to feeling regret, that uncomfortable sensation of shame that can stick with us like a persistent mental itch. There are a wide range of sexual experiences that may give rise to feelings of regret. For example, across several studies, college student participants cited multiple situations that led to sexual regret, including sexual decisions that were not in line with their morals, the involvement of alcohol in the sexual encounter, realization that they didn't want the same thing as their partner, lack of condom use, and a desire to not engage in sex before marriage (Johnson et al., 2021; Oswalt et al., 2005). Certain individual characteristics have also been associated with increased likelihood of experiencing sexual regret, such as a greater number of sexual partners, greater willingness to engage in casual sex, higher sexual disgust sensitivity, internalization of a sexual double standard, and the belief that alcohol consumption is a normal part of college life (Osberg & Boyer, 2016; Oswalt et al., 2005; Stob, 2020).

Sexual experiences, in fact, are the most common source of regret in the United States (Morrison and Roese, 2011), and research suggests that certain groups may be more likely to experience sexual regret. Galperin and colleagues (2013) suggest that women tend to experience more sexual regret than men, which may be due to the evolutionary pressures on women to be more sexually selective; however, other studies have found no significant gender differences in the prevalence of sexual regrets (Oswalt et al., 2005). Membership in certain religious communities may be associated with higher rates of regrettable sexual experiences; however,

Longest and Uecker (2018) found that among adolescents a high level of individual religiosity, or internalized religious beliefs, was a better predictor of sexual regret than mere participation in religious activities. On college campuses, Johnson and colleagues (2021) found that those involved in Greek life and athletics may be more likely to experience sexual regret, largely due to having cultures that encourage in-group loyalty and secrecy combined with competitiveness, aggressiveness, and high rates of sexual exploitation.

Sexual regret is a common phenomenon, but what is it? According to Lucas (2005), existentialists see regret as stemming from a combination of existential anxiety and guilt. The American Psychological Association (APA; 2020) defines existential anxiety as "the angst associated with one's freedom as a human being to make choices; with one's responsibility for the consequences of those choices; and with the sense that one's existence is devoid of absolute meaning and purpose." Existential anxiety arises from the knowledge that the past is immutable. Choices made cannot be changed. Given the importance of sexuality to sense of self and well-being, the consequences of sexual choices can feel especially weighty. Nevertheless, existential anxiety is a normal, even healthy human experience. The first step in making meaningful choices, after all, is the awareness and acknowledgment that no one has the answers for how we should live our life. Some anxiety surrounding such an open field of possibilities for our life direction—and the consequent void of possibilities for our past—is natural.

Guilt is distinct from existential anxiety. Specifically, guilt arises when past choices do not align with values or sense of self (Lucas, 2005). This often results from taking the path that feels easiest over the path with more personal integrity or opportunity for achievement. Research by Towers and colleagues (2016) supports this idea that acting in bad faith results in more intense regret. When it comes to sexual choices, this may manifest as going along with a date's sexual advances because it is easier to say nothing than to "ruin the mood" by saying no. Another example might be acquiescing to a partner's request for sex to avoid getting into another argument about it. In other words, guilt results from shying away from making a firm choice, taking for granted that not asserting ourselves is a choice in and of itself. Guilt results from realizing that, rather than acting in accordance with our values, we instead let others essentially make our choices for us. To most existentialists then, regret results from the knowledge that we must live with the consequences of past decisions, combined with the belief that past decisions were not made in accordance with our values.

While it is important to make conscious, authentic choices for ourselves, it is equally important to acknowledge situations in which we have no choice or in which our choices are very limited. For example, in cases of rape or assault, choice is denied altogether. Such terrible circumstances have been described as a "thrown condition" (Lucas, 2005). We have no power to choose many of the circumstances life throws at us; the key for the existentialist is to find where our choices lie and then choose consciously. It is also important not to confuse a mistake with a choice made in bad faith. For example, we may choose to sleep with someone who seems great, only to find out later that they have been unfaithful. We may again feel a sense of existential anxiety for choosing such a partner; but, ultimately, humans are not omniscient, and we make the best choices we can with the information we have.

In theory, thrown conditions and mistakes can be separated from choices that were made in bad faith, but this can be difficult in practice when it comes to sexual experiences. Johnson and colleagues (2021) recognize a "grey zone" of sexual experience, in which consent to sexual activity exists on a continuum from clear examples of sexual victimization to clearly consensual sexual experiences. At what point does pressure to have sex become coercion? At what point does intoxication become incapacitation? These blurry boundaries make it difficult to determine with certainty when feelings of regret are coming from angst over thrown conditions and when regret arises from the knowledge that we should have chosen differently.

When viewed in this way, regret can tend to keep us mired in the past, ashamed by our past decisions but incapable of going back in time to change them. When doing something that feels out of character, we are left trying to reconcile prior actions with the person we want ourselves to be. As clinicians, the authors have seen several clients whose regrets have gotten them stuck in this way. Take, for example, a client we will call Luiz. Luiz, a twenty-one-year-old undergraduate in his junior year, presented for counseling at the university counseling center after the termination of his relationship with his long-term, long-distance high school girlfriend. After the breakup, Luiz had begun engaging in several casual sexual encounters, but he now expressed regret over these hookups. He explained that he really was not the kind of person to have casual sex, and he did not know why he continued going to parties and hooking up. While casual sex usually seemed like a good idea to him in the moment, looking back on his behavior filled him with shame and disgust.

Some exploration in counseling revealed that Luiz had worried that he had been "missing out" on the college experience after spending the last two years faithful to his long-distance girlfriend. He wanted to experience the fun that his friends had been having hooking up at parties. He had also internalized some of the negative aspects of *machismo* culture that insisted that men should be sexually assertive. Luiz's engagement in casual sex came from a real need for connection and intimacy, but he had chosen to meet that need by relying on internalized beliefs of how a man should be sexual rather than taking responsibility for meeting that need on his own terms, in a way that felt true to his authentic self. Thus, Luiz felt stuck with the knowledge that he could not undo the way he had behaved and the way it made him feel about himself.

Traditional interpretations of existentialism posit that regret arises from inauthentic actions, acting in bad faith, even in "betrayal" of the self (Lucas, 2005). At the same time, we often remain in a state of inauthenticity for a reason: It is comfortable. Cole (2016) contends that authenticity is not inherently better than inauthenticity; rather, each has its benefits and drawbacks. Remaining in a state of inauthenticity allows one to avoid the uncertainty and existential anxiety of accepting responsibility for our direction in life, yet allowing others to make decisions for us often gives rise to looking backward with regret. Living in a state of authenticity necessitates facing existential anxiety head-on, but from this position regrets that arise can be harnessed as a valuable vehicle of growth. Rather than past-focused, meaning-oriented, and attempting to answer the question, "How can I reconcile this decision with who I am?" we posit that regret can be reframed as more present-focused, action-oriented, and attempting to answer the question, "What does this decision say about the person I want to become?"

Returning to the example of Sherry and Tyrone, Sherry's feelings of regret resulted from her misplaced negative evaluation of her decision to have sex with Tyrone rather than her awareness that her needs for connection after intimacy were not met. She may have wondered why she continued in a relationship in which her needs were not met. She may have struggled to attach any meaning to sex that felt detached to her in retrospect. This feeling of disgust keeps her stuck in the past, trying to make sense of her "idiotic" decision.

The underappreciated positive consequence of regret, whether it arises from personal agency or from situations where agency is denied, is clarification of what is important. Galperin and colleagues (2013) posit that regret can enhance decision-making quality by discouraging us from acting similarly in the future. Thus, regret can be seen as bestowing important self-knowledge, a critical step in the journey toward living with greater intentionality and authenticity. Regret can be a big emotion with a lot of psychic energy behind it. One can choose to use that energy to mire oneself in the past, or one can use that energy to carry oneself forward with intention. In the example of Sherry and Tyrone, Sherry could allow her regret to highlight the dissatisfaction she's feeling in her relationship and encourage her to take a more active role in getting her needs met.

Of course, giving voice to our needs does not always mean that others will agree to satisfy them, and this may lead to disappointment (regret arising from a "thrown condition," out of personal control); however, this is qualitatively different from the regret we feel for failing to give voice to our needs at all (regret arising from "acting in bad faith," which is not only within one's control but is one's existential responsibility). Rather than focusing on trying to make sense of past decisions, regret can point our attention toward a need to re-evaluate and change direction, whether that takes the form of realizing that we need to act more authentically and honestly (in situations where we have agency) or taking steps to change the situation we find ourselves in (in situations where we lack agency).

Personal Responsibility

Taking responsibility for our needs and wants in an authentic and genuine way is often the well-intentioned directive of friends, family members, and mental health professionals (among others). Common advice stresses the importance of living authentically, knowing what we want, speaking clearly about those wants, and negotiating wants with others. The concern here for many is that what begins as a romantic and intimate experience morphs into a transactional interaction. Taken to its logical extreme, heterosexual relationships can even be analyzed from an economics perspective using social exchange theory, in which women offer sex in exchange for social resources offered by men (Baumeister & Vohs, 2004). While expressing wants and needs seems like a positive approach to open communication and improved relationship quality, the risk of overidentifying with our needs and turning the intimate relationship into a "business" form of transactional relationship is also present. In a transactional relationship, the focus is more on self-benefits than couple mutuality; while there is an appropriate amount of "give and take" in healthy intimate relationships, a business-like "give and take" approach to sexuality is ill-advised.

Another difficulty with taking authentic responsibility for wants and needs is the assumption that wants and needs are a static presence that remain consistent over time. From day to day, situation to situation, and over time, sexual wants and needs may change, and it is quite feasible that a person will not necessarily know what these needs are at any given moment. The challenge then is to enter into a consensual "maybe" that encourages dialogue, exploration, and vulnerability for both partners in a sexual encounter. In this scenario, partners need to be able to tolerate hearing "no" as well as "yes" and stay tuned in to the other, a position made much more possible when each partner takes responsibility for their own wants and needs and has a capacity to cope with disappointment.

Personal responsibility for positive sexual interactions can also be hindered by the social mandate that discussing sexuality in a personal, subjective way should be reserved for the most intimate of relationships. This mandate creates a reduction in the opportunities for practice in revealing one's sexual desires to another person and, thus, relegates these conversations to the most vulnerable of situations. Moreover, sexual conversations can be difficult or even taboo for many sex is something that it is okay to do, but not to talk about based on family of origin modeling, lack of positive sexual education, and a dearth of acceptable terminology.

Yet another roadblock to personal sexual responsibility is the "natural mystery" of sex. If sex is "good" in movies, fictional novels, and popular culture in general, the common message is that talking during sex in general is not needed, each partner will "naturally" know what the other person needs and desires; the magic of sexual chemistry will take over, rendering communication unnecessary. If fact, some would go so far as to say that needing to tell someone their wants and desires necessarily means that they are not compatible sexually. This kind of approach to sexual communication, unfortunately, may have its roots in the well-intentioned positions of early sexual pioneers (e.g., Kinsey et al., 1948) who argued that sexuality was no different than other natural body processes (i.e., digestion or respiration). By making this argument, many pathways to studying sexuality as a biological process were opened; however, the necessity of communicating about these processes for the benefit of pleasure and satisfaction was not.

How then can authentic personal responsibility be enacted in sexual interactions? How can we use regret to inform our future choices and head toward personal and relational fulfillment? It's possible the answer to these questions rests in the understanding that existential freedom and personal meaning making exist even in the "natural" aspects of sexuality. Needs, wants, likes, and dislikes are all meanings that are available to the individual to know and understand in the formation of an authentic, responsible relationship with the self. Beyond mere knowledge of these meanings, each individual has the choice whether or not to communicate these meanings.

Yet, it is the possibility of discovering these aspects of the self *while in relation with others* that is necessary for entering into consensual, non-regrettable intimate relationships over time. Understanding the meaning-making or construal processes of the self and the other(s) and, perhaps more important, allowing the other(s) to see the central meaning-making processes of the self, allows for the formation of role relationships (Epting & Leitner, 1992). Entering into a relationship where needs and wants can be spoken and understood by the other(s) can be deeply satisfying and also terrifying. The risk of having personal sexual meanings rejected or invalidated by a loving other can feel catastrophic. Thus, the challenge and dance of engaging versus retreating from being known is a core aspect of living authentically and struggling with the possibility of regret. Yet, the regret now could be more about a guide to living more authentically and responsibly rather than simply dissatisfaction with the outcome of a choice.

Conclusion

Cole (2016) warns that favoring authenticity over inauthenticity is a subjective value judgment, and such a stance should not be lightly foisted upon a friend, a client, or even ourselves. He highlights the use of inauthenticity in holding onto past, preferred selves. Living inauthentically can be reassuring; accepting ultimate responsibility for oneself can be terrifying, especially with regard to sexual experiences, which often come laden with feelings of vulnerability and inflexible cultural beliefs. At the same time, living inauthentically can often lead to painful regrets. Regrettable sexual experiences may result from adhering too rigidly to societal scripts for how sex and relationships are "supposed to be" and denying our own agency to create meaning that is more consistent with our values and more coherent with our core selves. Likewise, regrets may arise when we fail to voice our relational wants and needs, effectively ceding our agency and letting others take responsibility for our own happiness.

Stepping into authenticity, as frightening as it may be, holds the real possibility of transforming feelings of regret into opportunities for growth. In order to grow through regrets, we must be brave and authentic, or else "one becomes stuck, continually laboring in the past of what 'could have been'" (Cole, 2016, p. 298). By being courageously authentic, by taking on the responsibility for our own happiness, we can transform the painful thorn of regret into something that spurs us onward into a life worth living.

References

American Psychological Association. (2020). *Existential anxiety.* APA Dictionary of Psychology. https://dictionary.apa.org/existential-anxiety

Ariely, D., & Loewenstein, G. (2006). The heat of the moment: The effect of sexual arousal on sexual decision making. *Journal of Behavioral Decision Making, 19,* 87–98. https://doi.org/10.1002/bdm.501

Baumeister, R. F., & Vohs, K. D. (2004). Sexual economics: Sex as female resource for social exchange in heterosexual interactions. *Personality and Social Psychology Review, 8*(4), 339–363. https://doi.org/10.1207/s15327957pspr080

Burnes, T. R., Singh, A. A., & Witherspoon, R. G. (2017). Sex positivity and counseling psychology: An introduction to the major contribution. *The Counseling Psychologist, 45*(4), 470–486. doi: 10.1177/0011000017710216

Cole, G. (2016). Existential dissonance: A dimension of inauthenticity. *The Humanistic Psychologist, 44*(3), 296–302. http://dx.doi.org/10.1037/hum0000035

Epting, F. R., & Leitner, L. M. (1992). Humanistic psychology and personal construct theory. *The Humanistic Psychologist, 20*(2–3), 243–259. https://doi-org.ezproxy.memphis.edu/10.1080/08873267.1992.9986793

Galperin, A., Haselton, M. G., Frederick, D. A., Poore, J., von Hippel, W., Buss, D. M., & Gonzaga, G. C. (2013). Sexual regret: Evidence for evolved sex differences. *Archives of Sexual Behavior, 42,* 1145–1161. https://doi.org/10.1007/s10508-012-0019-3

Johnson, N. L., Corbett-Hone, M., Gutekunst, M. H. C., & Wolf, J. A. (2021). The grey zone of collegiate sexual regret: Questionable consent and sexual victimization. *Culture, Health & Sexuality, 23*(2), 159–175. https://doi.org/10.1080/13691058.2019.1696985

Kinsey, A. C., Pomeroy, W. B., & Martin, C. E. (1948). *Sexual behavior in the human male.* W. B. Saunders Co.

Longest, K. C., & Uecker, J. E. (2018). Moral communities and sex: The religious influence on young adult sexual behavior and regret. *Sociological Perspectives, 61*(3), 361–382. https://doi.org/10.1177/0731121417730015

Lucas, M. N. (2005). Existential regret: A crossroads of existential anxiety and existential guilt. *Existential Analysis, 16*(2), 336–346.

McCabe, M. P., & Killackey, E. J. (2004). Sexual decision making in young women. *Sexual and Relationship Therapy, 19*(1), 15–27. https://doi.org/10.1080/14681990410001640808

Morrison, M., & Roese, N. J. (2011). Regrets of the typical American: Findings from a nationally representative sample. *Social Psychological and Personality Science, 2*(6), 576–583. https://doi.org/10.1177/1948550611401756

Osberg, T. M., & Boyer, A. (2016). Dangerous beliefs: College alcohol beliefs are associated with increased risk of regretted sexual encounters. *Substance Use & Misuse, 51*(12), 1555–1565. https://doi.org/10.1080/10826084.2016.1188953

Oswalt, S. B., Cameron, K. A., & Koob, J. J. (2005). Sexual regret in college students. *Archives of Sexual Behavior, 34*(6), 663–669. https://doi.org/10.1007/s10508-005-7920-y

Pertot, S. (2007). *When your sex drives don't match: Discover your libido types to create a mutually satisfying sex life.* Marlowe & Company.

Sloan, L. J. (2015). Ace of (BDSM) clubs: Building asexual relationships through BDSM practice. *Sexualities, 18*(5/6), 548–563. https://doi.org/10.1177/1363460714550907

Stob, B. (2020). Predictors of casual sex regret in university students. *Michigan Sociological Review, 34,* 130–159. https://www.jstor.org/stable/48638066

Towers, A., Williams, M. N., Hill, S. R., Philipp, M. C., Flett, R. (2016). What makes for the most intense regrets? Comparing the effects of several theoretical predictors of regret intensity. *Frontiers in Psychology, 7,* 1–8. https://doi.org/10.3389/fpsyg.2016.01941

Williams, J. D., Prior, E., & Wegner, J. (2013). Resolving social problems associated with sexuality: Can a "sex-positive" approach help? *Social Work, 58,* 273–276. https://www.jstor.org/stable/23719251

World Health Organization. (2006). *The World Health Report 2006: Working together for health.* http://www.who.int/iris/handle/10665/43432

Chapter 6

Eros and Shame: A Theoretical Autoethnography on Group Work and Masculinity

Micah Ingle

Abstract

In this chapter, I explore how affect theory can inform a novel perspective on subjectivity and group therapy. After providing an overview of affect theory, individualism in psychology, and the potential amelioratory value of group therapy, I will illustrate affect theory concepts through autoethnography by relating experiences I have had in group therapy and group process-oriented settings. A secondary goal of this chapter is to discuss socially normative codings around masculinity, including illustrations of some of the difficulties of and opportunities for combating individualism and toxic masculine norms in group therapeutic practices. My goal is to trouble some of the givens of normative psychological theory (or allegedly a-theoretical empiricism) around issues of masculine gender and subjectivity, and to pose a tentative counter-framework. I will focus on three themes from my own experience, augmented by insights from affect theory: "the individual and community," "head and heart," and the social dynamics of Eros, or "connection and shame."

***

In the recent science fiction television series *Devs* (Garland, 2020), there is a scene in which a computer engineer shares groundbreaking work with his supervisors: he and his team have become capable of mapping out the next few seconds of a nematode worm's movements and behaviors. This coherence of future prediction quickly destabilizes as the complexity of the worm's possible behaviors—despite it being a relatively simple multi-cellular organism—renders the predictive apparatus (some kind of algorithm-based program) inadequate, and the simulation falters. However, it is viewed as a marked success and catapults the engineer into a promotion.

This scene illustrates important issues I explore in this chapter. First, it points to nonlinear, complex systems, known colloquially as the "butterfly effect"—the notion that a butterfly flapping its wings on one side of the world could conceivably, because of the nature of how multiple systems and their elements interact in unpredictable ways, cause hurricanes on the other side of the world. The nematode resists mapping of future action beyond a few seconds because the variables that go into its behavior are too numerous and unpredictable (i.e., effects of its own internal organization motivating behavior as well as external impacts such as light, warmth, and surrounding movement). It is impressive that within the frame of the series even a few seconds are predicted. Second, it points to a contemporary human desire to know the future, to predict and control, as seen in the scientific method and its modern Western ideological and motivational underpinnings. From a Foucauldian perspective, we might talk about the appeal of this power in terms of *biopower*, or the "government of populations" linked to the modern nation state and its impetus to preserve and amplify its own structures—economic, sociocultural, psychological, and more (Foucault, 2007).

How do these issues relate to Eros, or forms of the "life-binding instinct" (Freud, 1975), affect theory, group work, and autoethnography? My primary goal in this chapter is to point toward an alternative framework from many conventional cultural and psychological models for understanding the self and its relationships, particularly regarding group therapy or other kinds of group work in the context of socialized masculine norms. The choice to use a theory-inflected form of autoethnographic reflection relates to my own cultural "expertise" and situatedness as a participant in different process-oriented therapy groups, including ones dedicated to work with men around topics of masculinity. I include autoethnographic vignettes of experiences that were significant to me and can be utilized to illustrate the conceptual territory explored by affect theory, in service of fleshing out a different understanding of cultural issues such as masculinity, individualism, and connection, or Eros. As Adams, Holman Jones, and Ellis (2015) describe, autoethnography "uses deep and careful self-reflection—typically referred to as 'reflexivity'—to name and interrogate the intersections between self and society, the particular and the general, the personal and the political" (p. 2). I am envisioning here a dialogue between these experiences, their instantiation in broader cultural discourses and practices, and affect theory.

As in the example of the nematode, my basic theoretical orientation here is one of complex systems, wherein multiple and heterogeneous elements of different systems interact in nonlinear and largely unpredictable ways to produce different effects. This understanding of complex systems is refracted through an affect-theoretical lens, using ideas from the philosopher Gilles Deleuze and other theoreticians, such as Jean-Paul Sartre and Felix Guattari, who attempt to understand how bodies interact and transform as an effect of their interactions (Gregg & Seigworth, 2010). And in terms of the desire to predict and control, to enact forms of biopower, I would like to suggest an orientation to group work that focuses less on preordained outcomes associated with positive mental health and more on immanent, here-and-now "experimentations" in living and relational constructions of subjectivity as they relate to male-identifying persons.

Normative Subjectivity

I view psychology as a largely individualistic enterprise, with that culture of individualism ranging in influence from its theories of human nature to its biomedical emphasis on treatment. A number of scholars within critical psychology and adjacent fields have criticized this individualistic conception of the person as inadequate and harmful (Prilleltensky et al., 2013; Bertau & Karsten, 2018; Gergen, 2009; Martin-Baro & Aron, 1994; Parker, 2007; Sampson, 1993; Watkins & Shulman, 2008). What is this "individual" that is being targeted? For Gergen (2009), a social constructionist, the history of Western culture since the 16th century is marked by an increasing "boundedness" of self: "My private world is unavailable to you. What is essential to me is 'in here,' a private space that neither you nor anyone else can enter" (p. 5–6). Gergen (2009) argues that the ideals of bounded selfhood consist of "autonomy, individual reason, personal conscience, liberty, free competition, and self-knowledge" (p. 5). Bertau *Bertau* Karsten (2018), invoking Soviet psychology and Bakhtinian dialogical thinking, argue against the Cartesian dualism inherent in modern understandings of the self, with mutually exclusive "private" and "public" dimensions, and a "monolithic Cartesian ego" or "mastering I" that bifurcates self and other/self and world (p. 9). Sampson (1993), borrowing from the embodied cognitive science of George Lakoff and Mark Johnson as well as dialogical thinking, points out that Western culture idealizes the metaphorical picture of the person as self-contained and strictly demarcated from external bodies, such that feelings, attitudes, beliefs, motivation, will, and more exist within the "skin-encased […] body-as-container" (p. 34). This psychological image of the person delimits the self to a highly specified, bounded, agential, and self-interested body that possesses and is responsible for its capacity to labor. In times of neoliberal capitalism, this specification and intensification of atomized personhood extends even to the ephemeral contents of consciousness: emotion/affect, aesthetic dimensions of experience, personal identity-based branding, and self-narrativizing (see Shaviro, 2013).

Critiquing this portrait of selfhood from within a specific El Salvadoran political context, decolonial liberation psychologist Martin-Baro (1994) argues that individualism in psychology "ignores the reality of social structures and reduces all structural problems to personal problems" (p. 22). Following his lead, Watkins and Shulman (2008) argue that psychology's focus on the individual (or the family) leaves out important issues of "normalized power structures, gender relations, and ongoing cultural trauma" (p. 14). Psychology's image of the individual, for them, is ahistorical and acontextual. Critical psychologists Prilleltensky, Austin, and Fox (2013) state that the capitalist economic status quo in which psychology is embedded privileges a "supreme self" marked by "the promotion of self-interest through self-help" above social systems, with a concurrent belief that "changes ought to come from the former rather than the latter" (p. 17). Marxist critical psychologist Parker (2007) states that psychology universalizes its object of inquiry—this Western individual by whom and on whom much psychological research and practice is conducted. This individualized self is abstracted from its social and economic embeddedness and treated as a "self-managing unit" that serves at the pleasure—or displeasure, it hardly matters—of a capitalist economic system (Parker, 2007, p. 37).

As Sloan (1996) notes, modern Western subjectivities are defined by a "narcissistic style" that lends to their being "[un]prepared for participation in the democratization of social spheres currently dominated primarily by social steering media such as the police, the commercial news, advertising, educational and personality testing, social welfare bureaucracies, private banks, [and] quality circles" (p. 122). This is not to suggest an essentialist inadequacy or incapacity, but merely a deficit of socialization in forms of collective life and consequent "psychodynamic barriers" that interfere with "capacities for communication and empathy" (Sloan, 1996, p. 121). As Gilbert (2014) argues: "the individualist tradition mistrusts all collectivities, and it cannot actually imagine the collective as anything other than a state of absolute disorder or of meta-individuality" (p. 70).

To summarize, I believe it is important to consider how those of us living in Western societies, as well as Western-based psychotherapists, have been enculturated into models of atomistic selfhood, as well as self-centered self–other relations, which can cause problems for many, and which are also difficult to view critically or to oppose in practice. Addressing masculinity in particular, it can be argued that male-identifying persons sometimes bear the brunt of these socially codified varieties of rugged individualism as they face social pressures and discourses emphasizing the *self-made* (personally agential) man, the *dominating* man, and other personality attributes associated with contemporary Western masculinity (Connell, 2005). In the next section, I will discuss affect theory's potential to provide an alternative mapping of what it means to be a (male-identifying) person, with these various critiques in mind.

Affect Theory

If we are to rethink the issue of atomistic individualism and the bounded masculine subject, masculinity theorists require, in the words of Hickey-Moody (2019), "theoretical frameworks that are responsive to these material and emotional conditions of contemporary life, and they must approach these considerations as a political project" (p. 46). Recently in the critical humanities and social sciences there has been an "affective turn" (Clough, 2008). Clough describes this turn as proposing "a substantive shift in that it returned critical theory and cultural criticism to bodily matter which had been treated in terms of various constructionisms under the influence of post-structuralism and deconstruction" (p. 1). Affect theory has in the past couple of decades developed numerous strands of scholarship, perhaps most prominently a Spinoza/Deleuze-derived "posthuman" variation and a more human-focused strand following the psychologist Tomkins (see Gregg & Seigworth, 2010, for a more comprehensive overview). I will focus in this chapter on the Spinoza/Deleuze-derived strand of affect theory.

In order to understand affect theory, it will be helpful to provide a brief overview of the kinds of philosophical thinking from which many affect theorists draw—specifically, the 17th century Enlightenment philosopher Baruch Spinoza and the 20th century French philosophical duo Gilles Deleuze and Felix Guattari. Additionally, I will touch on how affect theory can reorient our understanding of the aforementioned "bounded subjectivity" as well as conventional notions of masculine gender.

Affective Capacities

It may be helpful to first state that many of the ideas in affect theory, especially those to do with Deleuze and Guattari's reading of Spinoza, involve a certain amount of speculative play, a playful deployment of concepts that are oriented toward *use* rather than attempting to fulfill the scientistic validity criteria of a correspondence theory of truth—a framing that Guattari's (Guattari et al.,1995) later solo-authored work continues to emphasize. This is a contentious issue, as some scholars (e.g., Levi-Bryant, 2008) argue for the logical coherence of Deleuze's thought and decry its more creative, aesthetic, playful deployments, without an exhaustive familiarity with his philosophical corpus. Nevertheless, as a psychologist and psychological practitioner, my primary interest is the ways in which these concepts can be mobilized toward certain transformative ends—a mobilization I believe fits with the spirit of Deleuze and Guattari's love for creative experimentation and addressing psychosocial problems.

To lay the philosophical groundwork undergirding affect theory, we can say that, ontologically, Spinoza is concerned with understanding objects and beings according to a different system of classification than conventional scientific thinking, which invokes categories such as "genus" and "species" in a table-like format—a mode of thought Deleuze and Guattari (1987) label as arborescent. *Arborescent* here links in thought to the image of a tree, with its hierarchical structure of roots, trunk, and branches. In contrast, it is not the hierarchical, scientific characteristics of an organism or set of organisms with which Deleuze is concerned, but with an organism's potential to affect and be affected. Spinoza classifies natural objects according to their "capacity for being affected, by the affections of which they are capable, the excitations to which they react, those by which they are unaffected, and those which exceed their capacity and make them ill or cause them to die" (Deleuze, 1988, p. 45). This necessarily includes an organism's ecological embeddedness and relatedness, because for Deleuze, individuation is always an "involution"—a "becoming" that is always moved and affected by its external relations. It is important to note for a psychological application that Deleuze and Guattari are not arguing for a radical exteriorization of individuation, the likes of which some social constructionists may be accused. For Deleuze and Guattari (1987), individuation is precisely this "involution" or "in-folding" of an organism's involvement in a "pack" as well as a territory, as connected with many ecological forces (p. 241). Parr (2005) argues these forces to be as diverse as "geography, biology, meteorology, astronomy, ecology, and culture" (p. 12). To give a full account of Deleuze's notion of "the fold" would require a philosophical exegesis of his broader ontological works and is beyond the scope of this paper; but it can be understood without losing *too much* subtlety as the means by which subjectivities come into being through dynamic, reciprocal interplay with ecological forces—picture a Möbius strip with its "externality" and "internality" in constant dynamically reciprocal movement. This is not merely a metaphor for them but an attempt to point conceptually to material forces in the world that go into the constitution of any body, following Spinoza.

In addition, this folding inward of the outside is not externally deterministic but produces various possible modes of self-relation (e.g., as outlined by Deleuze's contemporary Michel Foucault and his work on ethics or aesthetics of subjectivity; see Smith, 2015). It is not just radical exteriority (the beyond-human world) but radical interiority (an interiority always interconnected, always in negotiation with the "bodies" discussed above) as it finds itself at the nexus of many different relations. How do we account, as an example, for different modes of self-construal throughout differing historical and contemporary societies? Again, these thinkers would argue that embodied subjectivity is always formed, *in*formed, in ongoing *relationship* with its milieu—its ecological, technological, economic, and social environments, to name a few. Within this mode of thought, outside and inside are in total relation, though this is not necessarily a harmony but may proceed through "tensions, points of excess, the development of a tipping point or form of emergence, forms of becoming that coexist at best uneasily [...] these points of instability are the sites around which individuality may emerge" (Grosz, 2012, p. 39). These insights about the ecological embeddedness of subjectivities can rewrite/reconstruct, or "deterritorialize" and "reterritorialize" in Deleuzian terminology, bounded and atomistic notions of subjectivity. Here we begin to see hints of a psychological subject that is neither externally determined nor internally isolated but is a multilayered set of processes of continual creative negotiation between the two. Biology, chemistry, physics, culture, technology, education, geography, and more can be seen as merging in these processes against the common divides we make between the "natural" and "cultural" worlds, for example, or between the natural sciences and the humanities.

The boundaries between people become—when conceived of at the *molecular* as opposed to the *molar* level—porous and negotiable and always in transition according to different affective thresholds within a world of multiple beings (or "becomings") and their relations. *Molecular* refers to processes of micro-perception and ecological engagement at the level of bodily affect, contraposed against the *molar*, which is concerned with stable, arborescent entities that are "hierarchical systems with centers of significance [an untranslated French term] and subjectification, central automata like organized memories. In the corresponding models, an element only receives information from a higher unit, and only receives a subjective affection along preestablished paths" (Deleuze & Guattari, 1987, p. 16). The difference may be thought of, roughly, as the distinction between transcendent/top-down and bottom-up, or what Deleuze terms "rhizomatic," processes of thinking and enacting gender—the organized figure of man or woman versus the figure of a yet-to-be-known, partially undifferentiated body composed of multiple flows of affect that also exceed its boundaries. Deleuze uses the figure of the rhizome to counter this transcendental, "arborescent" understanding of the self, and of philosophical knowledge as well. A rhizome is a subterranean plant structure (e.g., a tuber) that connects to other structures through lateralization and nonlinearity, as opposed to the hierarchy of a tree. This is the model of thought that Deleuze & Guattari choose as in some ways an exemplar of their subjective and ecological political project.

Affective Genderings

What this means for a Spinozist–Deleuzian account of gender is the necessity of a deterritorializing "becoming-molecular" process, by which arborescent or transcendent structurings of gendered identity become destabilized and reorganized through particular affective relations with other bodies. What is a body in this framework? What is an affect? For Deleuze, a body is "any whole composed of parts, where these parts stand in some definite relation to one another and has a capacity for being affected by other bodies" (Parr, 2005, p. 35). Under this definition, a body can be anything from a human body to "a body of work, a social body or collectivity, a linguistic corpus, a political party, or even an idea" (p. 35). A body here is not understood only as materially or organically composed but as consisting of both dynamic internal relations related to "relative motion and rest, speed and slowness," and external relations in terms of actions and reactions oriented toward a milieu. The simplest way to understand "affect" for Spinoza and Deleuze is to think of it as a passage or a transition in a process of becoming between organisms. It is conceived as prior to language or conceptualization, although it does contribute to the particular forms that symbolically inflected experiences (i.e., emotions) may take. Affect can become emotion through this process of being mediated, interpreted, and symbolized semiotically (Massumi, 1995).

As an illustration, Deleuze and Guattari (1987) describe the different affects of a tick as involving its attraction to light, its sensitivity toward the proximal bodies of mammals, and its digging into skin and feeding (p. 257). They continue to say that in terms of affect, "a racehorse is more different from a workhorse than a workhorse is from an ox" (p. 257), signaling this approach to understanding based in affective relations as opposed to hierarchical knowledge. What of the affects and potential affective relations of, for example, a male body? Creating a full list is impossible, given the complexity of a human (male) body and our inability to understand, *a priori*, its capacities. However, a male body is capable of a number of affective responses and relations: to tense up and act protectively, to soften and become receptive, to mourn and grieve, to be in open awe, to become furious and bristle, to create and express. The list is an inadequate accounting of the exhaustive set of possibilities, but I hope that it begins to suggest a complex mapping of desire outside of arborescent prescriptions.

To summarize, affect theory as an ontology derived from Spinoza privileges bodily, affective *encounters* rather than *interiorities*. According to Seyfert (2012), echoing Spinoza and Deleuze, bodies are endlessly mutually constituted by their "capability to affect or to be affected, [...] their power to conjoin other bodies or to split up" (p. 32). Gregg and Seigworth (2010) state that "affect is born in in-between-ness [and] can be understood then as a gradient of bodily capacity—a supple incrementalism of ever-modulating force-relations—that rises and falls [...] along various rhythms and modalities of encounter" (p. 2). Affect theory is less concerned with what is inside people (except insofar as individual bodies themselves are composed of multiple bodies—e.g., cells, organs, macrobacteria) and more interested in what happens between people—or rather, between bodies and other bodies, both human and nonhuman; affect theory attempts to avoid the overemphasis in psychology and social science on processes of subjectification that occur "within 'the faculties of the soul,' interpersonal relations or intra-familial complexes" (Guattari, Bains, & Pefanis, 1995, p. 9). Affect theory is concerned with bodily encounters that happen at all levels of existence, from the interpersonal and linguistic to the sensorial and material. This emphasis on ecological encounters offers a strong critique of individualism in psychology, as it focuses on "forces" that both constitute and extend beyond individual bodies and subjectivities. For Guattari, Pindar, and Sutton (2000), "interiority" is established at the "crossroads" between these different human and nonhuman forces (p. 36).

Individualism and Group Work

Several theorists and clinicians have pointed to group therapy, and group work, as a potential antidote to this isolated, alienated individualism that I have criticized. I suggest that group therapy, or group work conceived more broadly, is a site where an ecologically sensitive and loving commons can be cultivated, in contrast to individualistic enactments of human subjectivity. Kemp (2010) believes that collective and group forms of therapy arose precisely as a natural historical balm to the individualized alienation of modernity, a "truncation of relatedness" that may be healed through group therapy's exposure of "our communality through collective attention" (p. 289). Barwick and Weegmann (2018) quote one of group (psychoanalytic) therapy's originators, Trigant Burrow, as arguing that "western culture had taken a 'wrong turn.' In progressing towards greater individualism, a hyper-individualized consciousness had evolved which had 'sever[ed] the natural bond between elements of the societal body'" (p. 6).

From a Sartrean perspective, group therapy or group work provides an opportunity for a re-formulation of subjectivity, in the context of communal group life, away from the "serial alterity" of isolated alienation (Cannon, 2005, p. 135). This connects with psychoanalyst Felix Guattari's use of two ideas, building from Sartre: subjugated groups and group-subjects. Watson (2009) discusses Guattari's understanding of subjugated groups as those that disown and defer their desire, preferring the ritualized seriality of hierarchical systems to which they can passively attach themselves—for example, transcendent moral systems and social normativity. Subjugated groups constituted by modern, alienated subjects prefer "Sartre's 'practico-inert'" (Watson, 2009, p. 27). Cannon (2005) uses the example of a bus to describe the practico-inert:

> Sartre uses people queuing up to a bus as an example of the series. The bus is the practico-inert object. It is not merely a physical object. It is imbued with human meaning and purpose, that is, the meaning of transportation from one place to another. This is the exigency of the bus. [...] The practico-inert refers back to the human praxis, which inscribed its meanings in matter. The difference between value and exigency is that value refers to the power of freedom to create novelty (even amid previously seemingly static structures), while exigency refers to the acceptance of the future as closed—as that 'which cannot be transcended.' (p. 135)

In practical terms, this refers to a constant deferral of desire toward "outside" systems that are not "here," in and belonging to the group. Subjugated groups that orient to the practico-inert are marked by "passive activity" and "impotence" (Cannon, 2005, p. 135).

In contrast, Watson (2009) describes group-subjects as "brave, efficacious, and self-directed, boldly taking the floor to speak" (p. 28). They are said to face the possibility of their death, providing less reassurance against anxiety than subjugated groups, while orienting toward collective responsibility and the ineffable as the source of a potential disruptive creativity. They are able to overcome "serial alterity" by constantly working to form "a common or group praxis," a set of life-affirming values and commitments (to each other, to worldly projects) constructed from within (Cannon, 2005, p. 136). Additionally, rather than being themselves alienated, group-subjects are always orienting toward other groups. It is, in fact, the precondition of their existence: "a good group does not take itself to be unique [...] but instead plugs into an outside that confronts the group with its own possibilities of non-sense, death, and dispersal 'precisely as a result of its opening up to other groups'" (Guattari, Deleuze, & Hodges, 2015, p. 7). Often, at least in conventional therapy groups, the substance of this work is in exploring and discussing "interpersonal/intrapsychic conflicts that an individual brings from the outside world" (Cannon, 2005, p. 142).

Relatedly, it is certainly possible for group therapy to maintain its commitments to the kinds of liberal (and neoliberal) individualism found in psychology. As Arfken (2018) argues, in order to resist neoliberalism we must resist the psychologization of empowerment, lest empowerment becomes a neoliberal term indexing an increase in individualized freedom to better adapt to and navigate the existing socioeconomic and cultural order. Guattari's answer to this problem was not merely to practice a classical form of group therapy, that is, gestalt or psychoanalytic (or modern cognitive-behavioral therapy), which may remain focused on the individual—taking turns—utilizing the resources of the group to heal from individual neuroses. Instead, Guattari proposes transversal processes in group work as a means to cultivate the genuine freedom of group-subjects. Rejecting the classical psychoanalytic mapping of desire in terms of transference and countertransference, Guattari believed that groups must work to refigure themselves against the reifying hierarchies of psychiatric and other types of social institutions. Like psychoanalysts, Guattari operated from the assumption of the existence of the unconscious; unlike psychoanalysts, he believed that the unconscious was "directly related to a whole social field, both economic and political, rather than the mythical and familial grid traditionally deployed by psychoanalysis" (Guattari, Deleuze, & Hodges, 2015, p. 8). Guattari's project, as a clinician and a political militant, was to find ways to unleash the libidinal energy of the unconscious from its attachment to familial and other socially adaptive forms of capture in order to promote human freedom and communalism, without reducing what he and Deleuze call "singularities" to simply their environs. The promotion of transversal processes is one way that Guattari opted to work, defying the dyadic and triadic/familial emphases of psychoanalysis.

This "transversality" is grounded in Deleuze and Guattari's (1983) Spinoza-inspired understanding of bodies as organisms composed of bodies co-constituted in relation to other bodies. As argued by Brown and Stenner (2001), this Spinozism has something to offer to a "post-cognitive" understanding of affective bodies in relation. According to Guattari, Bains, and Pefanis (1995):

> We know that in certain social and semiological contexts, subjectivity becomes individualised; persons, taken as responsible for themselves, situate themselves within relations of alterity governed by familial habits, local customs, juridical laws, etc. In other conditions, subjectivity is collective - which does not, however, mean that it becomes exclusively social. The term 'collective' should be understood in the sense of a multiplicity that deploys itself as much beyond the individual, on the side of the socius, as before the person, on the side of preverbal intensities, indicating a logic of affects rather than a logic of delimited sets. (p. 9)

Guattari's work, then, concerns itself with the previously discussed "deterritorializing" of individual selves, working toward collective and revolutionary forms of life, grounded in "new utterances of desire" where, contrary to liberal (psychological) individualism, "political economy and libidinal economy are one and the same" (Guattari, Deleuze, & Hodges, 2015, pp. 16–17). Guattari brought the practice of transversality (a form of socio-therapy or "institutional psychotherapy") to his work at the French psychiatric clinic La Borde, where he employed a variety of techniques. Among these were: "group interpretation," with an emphasis on avoiding preconceptions as to the meaning of symptoms or psychic structures (Guattari, Deleuze, & Hodges, 2015, p. 108), and practices of transversal opening whereby "there is maximum communication among different levels and, above all, in different meanings" between people and between different institutional levels (i.e., psychiatrists, nurses, patients, etc.; Guattari, Deleuze, & Hodges, 2015, p. 113). Aside from more conventional group meetings, people at La Borde also engaged in radical practices of transversal opening such as encouraging a rotation of shared activities and responsibilities between staff and patients (and other personnel), as well as theatre productions and other artistic, expressive endeavors (Guattari & Lotringer, 2009).

All of this is, again, grounded in the Spinozist understanding of encounters between bodies amplifying or diminishing our capacities to act. The specific goal at La Borde was to refuse institutional hierarchies and produce a "collective mode of expression" whereby individual symptoms, meanings, and desires are revealed and taken up in their communality:

> If a certain degree of transversality becomes solidly established in an institution, a new kind of dialogue can begin in the group: the delusions and all the other unconscious manifestations which have hitherto kept the patient in a kind of solitary confinement can achieve a collective mode of expression. (Guattari, Deleuze, & Hodges, 2015, p. 116)

My interest here is not in establishing a kind of radical institution like La Borde, but rather in identifying certain theoretical and practical themes that point to the potential for group work to avoid simply reifying liberal individualist subjectivities.

Before moving on, it should be noted that group therapy/group work is one potential avenue for the creation of a common or collective mode of subjectivity such as Guattari's group-subjects, and it is rooted in Western cultural and historical modes of subjective formation. Following Hardt and Negri (2009), it is important to consider how strategies for the creation of a common mode must necessarily be contingent, rather than universal. It may not be appropriate or sensible for some cultures to engage in traditional therapeutic or therapeutically inspired practices. The Western psyche, to risk homogenization, has been constructed in particular ways through historical discursive, material, and economic modes of socialization, foregrounding the "private property" of the bounded self. In order to work against this model of subjectivity, it may be valuable to work from the "inside out" by engaging with certain therapeutic techniques—an "altermodern" perspective that respects our embeddedness in contingent historical traditions while calling for a shift from "identity to becoming" (Hardt & Negri, 2009, p. x). For cultures starting from a different historical and subjective position, the application of these psychological methods may be ineffective at best and violently imperialistic at worst (see Watters, 2011).

The Individual and Community

Just now, prior to writing, I was pouring cereal for breakfast. A small piece of chocolate granola bounced out of the bowl, so I grabbed it and put it back, wary of ants. The act satisfied me; I was putting something where it belonged, aiming toward sustainability and coherence of my body and environment. I drew a link in my mind between that act of returning, that recomposition, and this paper. In some sense, my primary goal in this theoretical and autoethnographic analysis is to return things to where I believe they belong. I also hope not simply to represent, but to engage in a production of new thoughts and affects.

My interest in group work is a deep fascination. During my adolescence, I experienced a great deal of social isolation. I like to think that I spent those years developing a rich internal world, but one that felt disconnected from others and the world at large. I have spent the past decade trying to build bridges between these worlds without diminishing either what I discovered "within" myself— which I believe to be a misnomer in some ways, as I was always in relation even in isolation, but old habits die hard—and outside of myself. Group work, particularly process-oriented group therapy, has been the place that has felt the most natural (or offering the highest degree of *capacity*) to me in tying these complex ribbons together, even re-formulating what it means to be a person or to belong to something.

Vignette I
The group facilitator turned to me and said: "You seem like you have a lot going on right now." I tensed my body, or continued to tense, and responded, "I can't feel anything," feeling despondent. They looked at me softly but incisively and said, "You seem to be feeling a lot, to me." As soon as they said it, the tension left my body and I started to weep. In that moment, I was encountering things I had not encountered before. First was the group itself, the group as a whole. If the facilitator had said this to me in another setting, I likely would have kept tense. But in this *space*, which I can only consider in terms of a phenomenal sense of expansiveness, a wide room with plenty of space to move around, it felt appropriate, safe, good, desirable to drop something, and to welcome something else in. Of course, these metaphors of "inside" and "outside" participate in the kind of boundedness that I hope to avoid. I was not a cognitive, interior subject receiving information from an external subject, which passed through cognitive mechanisms of interpretation and parsing. My body was *struck* at an affective level by the affects that the facilitator and the group itself, in its ritualistic holding of

space, embodied and enacted. Their words were sacrificial daggers that had been purified before a ritual. Affective, bodily processes were *reterritorialized*—reformulated in their capacities. Toward the group, toward our interrelating, toward an interpenetrating. I could tell that my weeping was deeply affecting for them as well. I left the group with a new sense of myself, that maybe what I had regularly interpreted as a lack of capacity—social anxiety, maybe some minor form of autism—was actually a strong capacity for expression and relation simply "on hold" for a space in which to emerge and mingle, to involve itself with others.

I frequently wonder, in light of this experience, how many men struggle to find a place for their own rich affective and bodily involvement. Numerous U.S. and U.K. studies suggest that "traditionally" identifying men are less likely to seek psychological assistance in the form of counseling and psychiatric services (Addis & Mahalik, 2003; Berger et al., 2005; Fischer & Good, 1997; Galdas et al., 2005; Good & Wood, 1995). Much of this research focuses on alexithymia, defined as "problems identifying and describing emotions in self and other," which is associated with interpersonal dysfunction and fear of intimacy (Sullivan et al., 2015, p. 196). These personality characteristics relate to "traditional masculinity" and positively correlate with resistance to help-seeking. In an effort to consolidate this research, a recent meta-analysis of 37 different studies on the relationship between "traditional masculinity" and psychological help-seeking concluded that conformity to traditional masculine gender roles plays a part in higher rates of suicide among men than women, and goes so far as to suggest that "reframing a more fluid masculinity to integrate depression may boost help-seeking" (Seidler et al., 2016, p. 106). On the relationship between traditional masculinity and individualism, one meta-analysis of nearly 20,000 U.S. participants found a significant positive correlation between adherence to "self-reliance" (among other masculine-related norms) and increased psychological distress (Wong et al., 2017, p. 81).

The healing and empowering aspects of group work are, I believe, in its facilitation of greater communal engagement, but not one-to-one, atom to atom. Rather, as Guattari suggests in his concept of the transversal, there is an opening of capacity that can occur as bodies interact and come to mutually co-constitute and re-constitute each other. Of course, our *mode* of engagement matters. I believe process-oriented group work can achieve such success here because it grounds itself so immanently in what is happening right here, right now. Bodily defenses that maintain a sense of separateness can become relaxed, curiously finding themselves not needing or desiring to maintain themselves in the same configuration of the bounded self that is so ubiquitous in Western liberal societies. The *effect* can be a reterritorialization of top-down gendered identities; I was certainly not enacting the kind of masculinity I had been socialized to model growing up in rural East Texas. I also was not consciously rejecting anything or trying to transcend to something else, but responding to immanent, embodied, and affective invitations toward novel ways of interrelating.

Before moving on, I want to emphasize that I am not primarily interested in these possibilities for the exclusive recuperation or social adaptation of the individual. Echoing Watkins, Lipsitz, and Bradshaw (2019), I believe we are in serious need of new "commons," new modes of collective being that can allow us, as in Guattari's appropriation of Sartre, to form liberated, self-affirming and life-affirming "group-subjects" beyond the domain of the atomized, though perhaps less emotionally frustrated, individual. The lesson for me in this story is less about my personal catharsis, facilitated through the efforts of the group, and more about what groups of people can become together to carry liberatory force against many of the ills that face us psychically, socially, economically, and existentially. The fact that it may provide healing is an effect of its power, but I believe not the end goal in terms of the reterritorialization of the liberal individual, except insofar as it opens up our capacities for deeper engagement and action in determining our own future together.

Head and Heart

During my graduate work at the University of West Georgia, I have often felt torn between two poles. The psychology department—referred to affectionately as "Melson" (Hall) by students—is rooted in traditions of experiential humanistic psychology as well as transpersonal and contemplative approaches to human science. More recently, it has incorporated a "critical" dimension, with a broad interest in sociocultural issues and methodologies, from looking at social discourses to analyzing the effects of social systems and institutions on the constitution of the psychological subject. Classes I have taken, for example, range from exploring the thought of cyberneticist Gregory Bateson contraposed with psychoanalyst Felix Guattari, to a methods course on Discourse Analysis, or Discursive Psychology.

Although I am nearing the completion of my PhD from this program (aptly titled "Consciousness and Society"), I began my journey here as a Master's student in 2014 and took part in clinical training from an integrative humanistic, psychoanalytic, and gestalt framework. Many of my classes had an experiential component. For instance, "Group Counseling & Psychotherapy" utilized part of the course to explore the ideas of Irvin Yalom and others on group therapy, while the rest of the course was an experiential sampling of process-oriented group work. This modeling was not a "mock" scenario but involved students as actual participants in group work, with our professor as the facilitator. Outside of class, my peers and I frequently explored an experiential, existential mode of being with one another, aiming at vulnerability and openness. We felt that we were doing something significant, sacred even, as these encounters with others and ourselves encouraged shifts in the horizon of our being (and certainly what we thought clinical work, and life itself, was all about).

A great deal of my Master's degree was devoted to these experiential adventures, which I cherish. On the other hand, there is a segment of the department that is, if not openly scornful of experiential work, at least far more concerned with academic and intellectual inquiry. I valued these pursuits as well, leading me to enroll in the doctoral program upon completing my Masters. Straddling these worlds was and is not easy, however. Many seem to privilege one or the other—head or heart. I have always felt (and thought) that, rather than needing to be at odds, the two are powerful when complementary. I imagine something like an alchemical marriage, comingling their strengths, buttressing their weaknesses or points of oversight in contributing to the overall project of living.

Vignette II
This intuition came to a head after a weekend of group process-oriented work in which I participated. It had been a rough few days. There was conflict with people I cared for and who cared for me. I still remember the piercing, unyielding glare of a friend who felt I was betraying our common politics and, ultimately, our friendship. I felt broken by their judgment. Apart from that conflict, I also felt that I had made a home for myself in the community, in these groups. I spoke with conviction about personal beliefs and views. I felt accepted, validated, appreciated. I felt that I was given an avenue to express my own validation, appreciation, and love for others in ways that had not felt open to me before.

After the weekend concluded, I went with several people to a nearby beach and waded out into the ocean. I remember the scene with crystalline clarity, as clear as the water—jeans rolled up, leather jacket tied across my waist, feet bare in the shifting sand. I was still reeling from the effects of the conflict with my friend, still trying to piece myself back together, but I also felt a sense of continuity and belonging, like I was on the *right track*. An image came to me on the beach of my purpose, and it looked like that alchemical marriage of head and heart. My past isolation and headiness seemed to have found a friend in this newfound capacity to relate with others and to engage with others affectively in a deep and meaningful way. On the beach, I recalled a passage from Wolfe's (1994) *Book of the New Sun*:

> What struck me on the beach and it struck me indeed, so that I staggered as at a blow—was that if the Eternal Principle had rested in that curved thorn I had carried about my neck across so many leagues, and if it now rested in the new thorn (perhaps the same thorn) I had only now put there, then it might rest in anything, and in fact probably did rest in everything, in every thorn on every bush, in every drop of water in the sea. The thorn was a sacred Claw because all thorns were sacred Claws; the sand in my boots was sacred sand because it came from a beach of sacred sand. The cenobites treasured up the relics of the sannyasins because the sannyasins had approached the Pancreator. But everything had approached and even touched the Pancreator, because everything had dropped from his hand. Everything was a relic. All the world was a relic. I drew off my boots, that

had traveled with me so far, and threw them into the waves that I might not walk shod on holy ground. (p. XXXI)

As feminist philosopher Braidotti (2000) notes, the "enfleshed Deleuzian subject... is a folding-in of external influences and, simultaneously, an unfolding outwards of affects" (p. 159). Looking back, I feel that I was deterritorialized and reterritorialized by the encounters of the weekend, both the painful and exultant experiences—a "becoming-molecular" process. Certain aspects of my gendered socialization were destabilized, and other modes of affective being and relating were explored. What I had considered a mute force in many instances—the affective capacities and relations in which I participate—was discovered to reside on "holy ground," once I recognized its purposeful relationship with the mind in the greater context of my life.

It is tempting once more, for myself and perhaps for the reader, to interpret this vignette as an example of personal empowerment, liberation, or healing movements toward a crude variety of self-actualization (versus an embedded and ecologically sensitive variety, which I view as worth pursuing). That is a very real temptation for me, but I also insist that the value in these experiences cannot and should not be delinked from their status as a series of encounters, with "collective modes of subjectivity" arising through immanent interrelations. It was not just me that changed—that both *enabled the changing* and was *produced as an ongoing new set of possibilities for relational being*—but a "we." Particularly, I believe, for men, this work offers an important aspect of healing from alexithymia as well as the opportunity to cultivate greater community and purpose in efforts to heal many of society's ills (see Hickey-Moody, 2019 for an exploration of how toxic forms of masculinity may contribute to social problems), writing new embodied and affective scripts away from the mind–body dualism of Western life and psychological understanding.

Eros and Shame

The final theme of the chapter I would like to address, Eros (or connection—that which binds—following Freud's understanding of Eros) and shame, is perhaps the most difficult for me to discuss. I keep circling around this theme in my work and in my own life: a desire to belong, to be intimate with others, and yet an affective and relational sense of difficulty as alluded to earlier, as well as a sense of shame around this. When I have felt most alive, most connected, most purposeful, it has been in the context of this kind of group work, exploring and deterritorializing some of what Sloan (1996) describes as the psychodynamic barriers associated with individualism. These barriers seem to be particularly challenging for men, as alluded to earlier, and as embodied in some of the mythic images of modern, Western masculinity, with their themes of stoicism, self-reliance, and more (see Connell, 2005). In my own work in these group spaces, I have noticed this quite strongly as well: both a yearning desire for connection and a sense of boundedness or withdrawal, which I believe to be associated largely with an affective sense of shamefulness. A deep sense of ambivalence seems to be at the core here, as noted by the affect theorist Tomkins (Sedgwick & Frank, 1995): "In shame I wish to continue to look and to be looked at, but I also do not wish to do so" (p. 137). He goes on to say that "while shame is dominant it is experienced as an enforced renunciation of the object" (p. 138). What object is being renounced here? I would suggest it is intimacy, even love. Why? I would tentatively suggest, despite the dangers of over-generalization: because many men in Western cultures have difficulty experiencing themselves as *good enough for love*—perhaps most particularly *receiving* love.

Vignette III

I was not sure how I felt about this man, this group facilitator. I had a hard time trusting them. I sat next to them, apprehensive, expectant. Over the course of our hours together, I became impressed, likening them in my mind to a drunken martial arts master, subtly weaving in and out of the way of the group's process, a small adjustment or suggestion here, a clarification there. I shared this with them at one point: my initial skepticism along with my burgeoning respect. They offered me a hug. I waited until the end of our session together. I was nervous about how it would feel—and would I be "available" for the kind of connection I desired? Would they? In my life, I have found that moments of real meeting—real openness and love—can be rare, though I cherish them when they emerge. When I hugged them, I felt my body soften into theirs. The masculine boundedness I regularly held on to, projected outward as an affective guardedness (or toughness), seemed less important here. I did not try to go beyond it, transcend it, change it, move it, undo it. It fell apart within the context of our work together—including the whole group—and the mutuality we seemed to experience. The hug lasted a good amount of time, and I felt myself tearing up. I offered a genuine smile afterward, grateful.

I am aware that quite often in ordinary life I feel a sense of breath-holding anticipation around moments of potential meeting. Anticipating difficulty around the meeting of different rhythms, different levels of bodily-affective availability and comfort with intimacy, I cut myself short, or I extend a bit, feel, sense, and then return. It seems to me that the rhythms of daily life in modernity contribute to this unease, this play of Eros, this connect–withdraw dynamic, renouncing our objects out of shameful concerns. I believe masculine norms play a significant role here, as well. How grateful I am to be able to meet, though—to share in love. This moment, and others like it, announce the presence of alternative possibilities for me, though I am far from finished with battles around shame.

These moments are, I believe, not merely referencing some "internal desire" on my part or on the part of another. They are *enabled* or *facilitated*. The context of group work enables certain kinds of relation, and subjective reformulation, to occur. Of course, it takes more than an enabling environment; it takes meeting that openness, receptively and actively forming the kinds of "group-subjects" that

Sartre and Guattari advocate. This is, I would argue, a collective group mission, achieved through interpenetrating *transversal* processes of deterritorialization and reterritorialization rather than one that can be accomplished through the willfulness of a commanding interior subject alone.

Conclusion

In this chapter, I have provided outlines of what I view as normative modes of individualized (particularly masculine) subjectivity, affect theory, the potential for group work to address individualism, and finished with three autoethnographic vignettes of my experiences with group work. I hope that my efforts here contribute, not necessarily to an exact theoretical clarification of certain ideas (or methods of practice), but to an openness and creative thinking around issues of what compromises the person and how we may beneficially reconceptualize ourselves in relation to others—particularly the masculine-identifying among us. I would like to conclude with a passage from Hardt & Negri (2009), which follows from their Spinozist–Deleuzian political vision:

> When we band together, when we form a social body that is more powerful than any of our individual bodies alone, we are constructing a new and common subjectivity. Our point of departure [...] is that love is a process of the production of the common and the production of subjectivity. This process is not merely a *means* to producing material goods and other necessities but also in itself an *end*. (p. 180)

References

Adams, T. E., Holman Jones, S. L., & Ellis, C. (2015). *Autoethnography*. Oxford University Press.

Addis, M. E., & Mahalik, J. R. (2003). Men, masculinity, and the contexts of help seeking. *American Psychologist, 58*(1), 5–14. https://doi.org/10.1037/0003-066X.58.1.5

Arfken, M. (2018). From resisting neoliberalism to neoliberalizing resistance. *Theory & Psychology, 28*(5), 684–693. https://doi.org/10.1177/0959354318800

Barwick, N., & Weegmann, M. (2018). *Group therapy: A group-analytic approach*. Routledge.

Berger, J. M., Levant, R. F., McMillan, K. K., Kelleher, W., & Sellers, A. (2005). Impact of gender role conflict, traditional masculine ideology, alexithymia, and age on men's attitudes towards psychological help seeking. *Psychology of Men and Masculinity, 6*(1), 73–78. https://doi.org/10.1037/1524-9220.6.1.73

Bertau, M.-C., & Karsten, A. (2018). Reconsidering interiorization: Self moving across language spacetimes. *New Ideas in Psychology, 49*, 7–17. https://doi.org/10.1016/j.newideapsych.2017.12.001

Braidotti, R. (2000). Teratologies. In Colebrook, C., & Buchanan, I. (Eds.), *Deleuze and feminist theory* (pp. 156–172). Edinburgh University Press.

Brown, S. D., & Stenner, P. (2001). Being affected: Spinoza and the psychology of emotion. *International Journal of Group Tensions, 30*(1), 81–105. https://doi.org/10.1023/A:1026658201222

Bryant, L. R. (2008). *Difference and givenness: Deleuze's transcendental empiricism and the ontology of immanence.* Northwestern University Press.

Cannon, B. (2005). Group therapy as revolutionary praxis: A Sartrean view. *Sartre Studies International, 11,* 133–152. https://www.jstor.org/stable/23512964

Clough, P. T. (2008). The affective turn: Political economy, biomedia, and bodies. *Theory, Culture & Society, 25*(1), 1–22. https://doi.org/10.1177/0263276407085

Connell, R. (2005). *Masculinities* (2nd ed.). Polity.

Deleuze, G. (1988). *Spinoza: Practical philosophy.* City Lights Publishers.

Deleuze, G., & Guattari, F. (1983). *Anti-Oedipus.* University of Minnesota Press.

Deleuze, G., & Guattari, F. (1987). *A thousand plateaus: Capitalism and schizophrenia.* University of Minnesota Press.

Fischer, A. R., & Good, G. E. (1997). Men and psychotherapy: An investigation of alexithymia, intimacy, and masculine gender roles. *Psychotherapy, 34*(2), 160–169. https://doi.org/10.1037/h0087646

Foucault, M. (2007). *Security, territory, population: Lectures at the Collège de France, 1977–1978.* (M. Senellart, F. Ewald, A. Fontana, & A. Davidson, Eds.) Palgrave Macmillan.

Foucault, M. (2009). *Security, territory, population: Lectures at the Collège de France 1977-1978* (M. Senellart, Ed., G. Burchell, Trans.). Palgrave Macmillan. (Original work published 2004)

Frank, A., & Sedgwick, E. K. (Eds.). (1995). *Shame and its sisters: A Silvan Tomkins reader.* Duke University Press.

Freud, S. (1975). *Beyond the pleasure principle.* W.W. Norton.

Galdas, P. M., Cheater, F., & Marshall, P. (2005). Men and health help seeking behaviour: Literature review. *Journal of Advanced Nursing, 49*(6), 616–623. https://doi.org/10.1111/j.1365-2648.2004.03331.x

Garland, A. (Director). (2020, March 5). Season 1, episode 1, *Devs.* FX on Hulu.

Gergen, K. J. (2009). *Relational being: Beyond self and community.* Oxford University Press.

Gilbert, J. (2014). *Common ground: Democracy and collectivity in an age of individualism.* Pluto Press.

Good, G. E., & Wood, P. K. (1995). Male gender role conflict, depression, and help seeking: Do college men face double jeopardy? *Journal of Counselling and Development, 74*(1), 70–75. https://doi.org/10.1002/j.1556-6676.1995.tb01825.x

Gregg, M., & Seigworth, G. J. (2010). *The affect theory reader.* Duke University Press.

Grosz, E. (2012). Identity and individuation: Some feminist reflections. In A. Boever, A. Murray, J. Roffe, & A. Woodward (Eds.), *Gilbert Simondon: Being and technology* (pp. 37–56). Edinburgh University Press.

Guattari, F., Bains, P., & Pefanis, J. (1995). *Chaosmosis: An ethico-aesthetic paradigm.* Indiana University Press.

Guattari, F., Deleuze, G., & Hodges, A. (2015). *Psychoanalysis and transversality: Texts and interviews 1955–1971.* Semiotext(e).

Guattari, F., & Lotringer, S. (2009). *Chaosophy: Texts and interviews 1972–1977.* Semiotext(e).

Guattari, F., Pindar, I., Sutton, P. (2000). *The three ecologies.* Athlone Press.

Hardt, M., & Negri, A. (2009). *Commonwealth.* Harvard University Press.

Hickey-Moody, A. (2019). *Deleuze and masculinity*. Palgrave Macmillan.

Kemp, R. (2010). The emergence of group and community therapies: A metabletic enquiry. *Existential Analysis, 21*(2), 282–294.

Martín-Baró, I., & Aron, A. (1994). *Writings for a liberation psychology*. Harvard University Press.

Massumi, B. (1995). The autonomy of affect. *Cultural Critique, 31*, 83–109. https://doi.org/10.2307/1354446

Parr, A. (2005). *The Deleuze dictionary*. Edinburg University Press.

Parker, I. (2007). *Revolution in psychology: Alienation to emancipation*. Pluto Press.

Prilleltensky, I., Austin, S., & Fox, D. (2013). *Critical psychology: An introduction*. Sage.

Sampson, E. E. (1993). *Celebrating the other: A dialogic account of human nature*. Harvester Wheatsheaf.

Seidler, Z. E., Dawes, A. J., Rice, S. M., Oliffe, J. L., & Dhillon, H. M. (2016). The role of masculinity in men's help-seeking for depression: A systematic review. *Clinical Psychology Review, 49*, 106–118. https://doi.org/10.1016/j.cpr.2016.09.002

Seyfert, R. (2012). Beyond personal feelings and collective emotions: Toward a theory of social affect. *Theory, Culture and Society, 29*(6), 27–46. https://doi.org/10.1177/0263276412438591

Shaviro, S. (2013). Accelerationist aesthetics: Necessary inefficiency in times of real subsumption. *e-flux, 46*.

Skott-Myhre, H. A. (2008). *Youth and subculture as creative force: Creating new spaces for radical youth work*. University of Toronto Press.

Sloan, T. S. (1996). *Damaged life: The crisis of the modern psyche*. Routledge.

Smith, D. (2015). Foucault on ethics and subjectivity: 'Care of the self' and 'Aesthetics of existence'. *Foucault Studies, 19*, 135–150. https://doi.org/10.22439/fs.v0i19.4819

Sullivan, L., Camic, P. M., & Brown, J. S. (2015). Masculinity, alexithymia, and fear of intimacy as predictors of UK men's attitudes towards seeking professional psychological help. *British Journal of Health Psychology, 20*(1), 194–211. https://doi.org/10.1111/bjhp.12089

Watkins, M., Lipsitz, G., & Bradshaw, G. A. (2019). *Mutual accompaniment and the creation of the commons*. Yale University Press.

Watkins, M., & Shulman, H. (2008). *Toward psychologies of liberation*. Palgrave Macmillan.

Watson, J. (2009). *Guattari's diagrammatic thought: Writing between Lacan and Deleuze*. Continuum International Publishing Group.

Watters, E. (2011). *Crazy like us*. Robinson.

Wolfe, G. (1994). *Sword & citadel: The second half of the book of the new sun*. ORB/Tom Doherty Associates.

Wong, Y. J., Ho, M.-H. R., Wang, S.-Y., & Miller, I. S. K. (2017). Meta-analyses of the relationship between conformity to masculine norms and mental health-related outcomes. *Journal of Counseling Psychology, 64*(1), 80–93. https://doi.org/10.1037/cou0000176

Chapter 7

Sexuality, Sex, or "Love"?: An Existential Approach[2]

Digby Tantam

Abstract

Sexual activity for primates is never just about procreation although it remains essential for procreation, with the sole exception of laboratory procedures of in vitro fertilization and cloning. But apes have also made use of the pleasures and satiation provided by sex for other social benefits, such as peace making. It has only been in the last 80 years that one primate species, man, has been able to be sexually active, confident that even heterosexual intercourse between post-pubertal men and women who are having regular menses will not result in a pregnancy. These are the years of greatest sexual activity, too. So, I consider these two aims of sexual activity independently in this chapter. I start with some definitions because sex, sexuality (and, of course, the related term "gender") are used differently by different people and in different contexts.

Sexual intercourse is culturally regulated. Procreative sex is of particular concern to authorities within societies and families who wish to maintain optimal families, secure hereditary obligations, optimize childcare, and minimize jealous conflicts. Non-procreative sex affects societies differently, although even those who practice it may still be affected by the expectation that non-procreative sex might often be the modern-day way of "falling in love," a path that converges with the others that lead to procreation and family formation. Acculturation determines much of our sexual behaviour, but not to the complete exclusion of biology. Culture and biology are diverging, with some critics of heteronormativity even arguing that the physical differences between men and women are a cultural product and not biological at all. Sexual desire is also a joint production of culture and biology. Existential theorists have made a particular contribution to

---

[2] I am, as always, grateful to Emmy van Deurzen for ongoing discussion about existential ideas and about psychotherapy but particularly grateful for her detailed comments on this chapter. Her knowledge of existential ideas and her ability to champion a woman's perspective are invaluable. Any inelegance that remains is entirely attributable to myself, as are any errors or omissions.

understanding sexual desire, especially in its role of overcoming individuality. I summarize the positions of Kierkegaard, Sartre, and de Beauvoir on the desirability of letting another person "in" sexually, whether through penetration of one's body or one's values and projects, or both. I argue that desire, and gratifying that desire, is one of the principal routes to loving another person (I do not consider that it may also be a route to hating them, although it may be). And I consider some of the existential thinking on love, with a particular emphasis on Kierkegaard's favorite philosopher, Socrates, or rather the views on erotic love of Socrates as reported by Plato in the Symposium. They provide a justification for considering that sexuality and erotic desire provide us with many challenges when we try to live well but can be the source of not just love for one other person but of loving kindness for many more.

***

The word "sexuality" is used over 20 times more frequently in Anglophone books published in 2019 than it was in those published in 1960, when the rise in frequency began (Google Books Ngram Viewer, 2022). Perhaps, as people say, Anglophone culture has become sexually obsessed. But there are many other possible explanations. One may be that the more we write or speak about sexuality, the more there is to say and the less we can consign to established knowledge—or so it seems to me. Even the words associated with sexuality are widening in their denotations. This is because their cultural underpinnings are being stretched as biology and culture move apart. Sexuality once referred simply to biological sex, as in the sexuality of plants, according to the Oxford English Dictionary, but it now refers to sexual identity, specifically an identity that is personally and culturally constructed around the preferred object of sexual orientation.

"Sex" too has become semantically unmoored from its former biological signifier, the division of animals into two forms, one male and one female (see Table 1) for the purpose of reproduction combined with controlled mutation. The basis of reproduction is the same in all eukaryotes: that a male gamete fuses with a female gamete to create a new organism (though parthenogenesis may occur in a small number of species, including insects, fish, and reptiles–but not humans). Human beings take it for granted that they can recognize another human being who is an egg carrier and one who is a sperm carrier, basing this on appearance and behavior. But these are no longer unquestioned (Dickens, 2018; Karkazis, 2019).

The recognition of a member of the "opposite sex" is a step on the path to procreation. Culture has in the past reinforced binary genders corresponding to the biological sexes, possibly as an extension of the social control of procreation that is found in most societies (Burfoot et al., 2021).

Procreation may be the most biologically, socially, and psychologically profound consequence of having sex. For women, it entails the biological burden of pregnancy, and, as they are customarily expected to be the main careers of children, the more prolonged burdens of infant and childcare. This is one of the many reasons that women have considered themselves disempowered or trapped, according to Simone de Beauvoir and many other commentators. Since women are customarily expected to be the main carers of children, this is one of many in-built disadvantages of being a woman that de Beauvoir itemized in *Second Sex*, published in 1949. I shall be using the word "sex" in the sense that de Beauvoir did, but in the third sense shown in Table 1, "an activity involving the deliberate, pleasurable stimulation of at least one body, typically in the genital area."

People have sex far more often than they procreate. Many people can, and do, have this kind of "recreational" sex with no risk of procreation at all. Recreational sex, once considered reprehensible by many of the religious and professional authorities who seek to regulate sex, has become unfettered. But with freedom comes uncertainty and anxiety–another explanation perhaps for why sexuality appears so often in Google books. It has become harder to know what to do about sexual stirrings when there is no clearly defined procedure for dealing with them. The freedom to have regular hookups and, therefore, sex with different partners in college has not improved the well-being of college students beyond the satisfaction that they may have in a relationship. In fact, women who choose multiple partners are less sexually satisfied (Armstrong et al., 2012).

Culture versus Biology

Sexual desire makes itself known after the maturation of the adrenal glands (adrenarche) initiates a growth spurt, and the hypothalamus triggers an increased secretion of sex hormones. Sexual attraction to particular individuals upends previous social groupings, activates a slew of new rules and role performances, and leaves most adolescents faced with new mysteries that might never get answered. For example, how does their sexuality compare with other people? Are they attractive to other people? Will they ever find a life partner who will love them?

One reason that it is difficult to theorize about sexuality is that it remains ineluctably private, and this is as true of desire as any other aspect of sexuality. Like other sensations, the quality of desire is difficult to convey, even to the extent that it is difficult to compare the intensity of one person's desire with another. This would matter less if many societies do not just control the sexual activity of their members but try to control their desire, too. Foucault (1997) argues that the early Christian fathers succeeded in imposing the regulation of desire through the device of confession. This paralleled a deep suspicion of sexual desire that ran counter to the easy-going, voluptuous attitudes of classical times.

St. Paul's views on sex are set out in the Christian New Testament (most explicitly in the first letter to the Corinthians). They are amplified by those of the repentant fornicator, St. Augustine of Hippo (2011). Both of them thought that sex was a troubling necessity, to be restricted to marital relations. These views are often contrasted with the easy-going attitude to homosexual desire portrayed in Plato's (2005) *Symposium*. What is not always noted about this philosophical *tête-à-tête* over dinner is that Socrates, while not condemning love, makes clear that it should not be about sex. In the Symposium, Alcibiades talks about trying to seduce Socrates and failing. Socrates' views about sex are clear from his endorsement of the parable of his sophist teacher, Prodicus, as reported in Xenophon's memoirs (Xenophon & Waterfield, 1990). In this parable, Herakles finds himself caught between the blandishments of a voluptuous young woman, "Vice," urging him to come home with her, and another young woman (at least in Durer's engraving) who is sterner, fully dressed, and carrying a stick. Her name is "Excellence" or "Perfection of a skill." Presumably the skill that Xenophon and Socrates had in mind, as mercenary soldiers, was to fight wars. And indeed, Alcibiades argues that gay partners make great soldiers if they fight alongside each other and support each other in battle. Perhaps this is why the custom of adolescent boys having an older male lover during their teenage years is encouraged in other militaristic societies, such as some tribes in New Guinea (Bleibtrea-Ehrenbeg, 1990) and in contemporary Afghanistan.

Sex, including sexual intercourse, is put to many uses in primate societies, of which those of bonobos (*Pan paniscus*) are probably the closest to human societies. But the main aim, so far as evolutionary biology is concerned must be reproduction. Even bonobos, who are notoriously sexually active and regularly have non-penetrative sex, may not have turned sex into a recreation as humans have, probably using sex as a means of conflict reduction or social cohesion. Procreation is not always welcome but has until recently always been a risk of sexual intercourse. It is only in the last 60 years or so that a cisgender woman can take steps to make the chance of reproduction after the ejaculation of sperm into her vagina unlikely even if she is fertile.

Disordered reproduction creates social disorder. The accumulation of property is just one feature of social organization that relies on orderly reproduction. It is difficult for the social agencies that maintain social order to frame their social "rules" to preserve this order, though. Most societies welcome the desire to have sex that leads to children so long as those children are contained within an economically and emotionally viable social unit, which in many cultures means that the unit will be centered around a father and a mother. The Christian Church has sometimes been grudging about even this, though. The Venerable Bede, otherwise pragmatic, praised women who died as virgins, reporting them to be "incorruptible," meaning that their bodies did not rot after burial (Bede & Sherley-Price, 2010).

Desire that led to intercourse other than intromission into the vagina of one's wife has been considered socially disruptive, and to be controlled. Anal sex, oral sex, solo sex, sex with animals, same-sex sex, sex with children, sex with dead people, sex during menstruation, sex that does not lead to ejaculation–all of these have been proscribed, and many still are, along with adultery, rape, sadistic sex, and fornication. Societies and religions privilege desire that is limited to bonded partnerships who take responsibility for the children of that partnership. There are other traditional arrangements, but these are dying out because the special economic circumstances that normalized them are dying out. Polygamy cemented political alliances between powerful men but now runs against modern conceptions of civil society. Polyandry enabled women to bring up children in environmentally marginal environments, ensuring that landholdings would not be sub-divided from generation to generation but is dying out in those families who have fled to India, where fertile land is more readily available (Childs, 2021).

The dissociation of reproduction and sex may have removed the basis of the religious or familial authority over sexual desire, at least in the West where male control over women is condemned. This is not to say that there are no reasons for desire to be controlled at least on a personal level, if not a social one, but they no longer have the force of the eternal punishment that previous generations of Christians might have experienced; the religious bias against all sexual desire and toward chastity is no longer dominant even in most Christian environments. Secular moralists are, if anything more condemning of non-consensual sex than are some priests who winked at the abuse of children. But more and more adults now consent to practices that would have earned severe penances from those same priests in times past. Whether this has resulted in changes in personal sexual desires is not possible to say because our predecessors kept them private, just was we still do.

This is not to say that we live in a secularized world in which sexual desires are conflict free. Even if we regard ourselves as non-religious there are emotional dispositions that we acquire within our families and communities that still regulate our sex lives. We do not want to feel jealous, or for others to make us jealous in retaliation, and so continue to be faithful to a chosen partner even if we no longer believe that we will be damned in the afterlife if we do not. Disgust and shame rule out many sexual practices for the majority, even though a vocal minority enjoy them and even though depictions of these practices are readily available in the public domain on porn sites, thereby becoming increasingly common. Continence remains a virtue for many of us, just as it did for Socrates and for St. Augustine (2009).

"The Battle of the Sexes": How Biological Sex Interacts with Sexual Being

Biology has influenced psychological thinking about sex, focusing on procreative sex and on human sexual dimorphism. Evolutionary psychologists supposed that this dimorphism necessitated cismen and ciswomen having different "mating strategies" that are so deeply engrained that they continue to be acted out in online environments (Bhogal et al., 2021). There is no doubting the different biology of almost all natal males and females. Intersex conditions in which chromosomal sex is inconsistent with phenotypic sex, or in which the phenotype is not classifiable as either male or female, do occur but only in 18 live births per 1000 (Sax, 2002).

The gametes of female mammals are rich in cytoplasm, develop during infancy, and remain dormant until puberty. There is a limited stock of ova, and the frequency of their release tapers off after the onset of the menopause. Post puberty they are released from the ovary into the uterus (in placental mammals), where fertilization may take place. If so, the fertilized embryo remains and grows in the uterus. The mother provides the nutrition during this period of growth, copes with the physical changes induced by pregnancy and the risks of birth, and then often provides the bulk of infant care. Males produce their gametes, which consist of little more than DNA and thus can be copiously produced with little drain on nutrition. Seminal fluid containing sperm is produced daily from puberty potentially until the end of life, although the sperm may not be viable well before that. Males are biologically required for successful procreation by providing viable sperm—more than one though, as spermatozoa cooperate with other spermatozoa produced by the same male in penetrating the outer layers of the egg. Sperm from another male may also compete, and many animals open the battle of the sexes with anatomical arrangements of their penises that can damage the vagina to prevent other males mating with the female.

Evolutionary theories turn on two presumptions based on this uneven distribution of the demands of parenthood. One is the theory that men seek to impregnate as many women as possible; its corollary is that women have a "fundamental motive" (Cook et al., 2021).

Evolutionary models have been criticized on the basis that they rely heavily on generalization to humans from other animals, whose behavior may be little understood. Another critique is that evolution is served better by pair bonding, providing a family that can better ensure the welfare of the human infant during its unusually prolonged period of immaturity (Dyble et al., 2015). Experimental studies do suggest that men value novelty in sex more than women (Hughes et al., 2021) but this Arnocky and his colleagues (2021) suggest following a meta-analysis, only applies to men who consider themselves to have high "mate value" and accounts for only a small determination of their behavior.

Feminists criticize evolutionary psychology theories because they seem to deny women's enjoyment of sex for sex's sake (Tavris, 2022). Sex is not primarily about procreation, Tavris argues, and all of the rules and role expectations that are based on the sex for procreation assumptions have become ways of denying women (and by extension other genders) their sexual freedom.

The Secret Life of Sex

One way in which most humans have sexual freedom is in their imaginations, but it is harder to investigate this than it is to consider attitudes or behavior.

Sexual desires may be concealed even from sexual partners, let alone from friends or researchers. Most of our knowledge about other people's desire is limited. Fictional accounts may be bowdlerized or exaggerated. Psychotherapy clients may be more revealing, but no doubt hold much back. Priests may hear more—indeed Foucault (1997) argued that they were training to root out desires in the confessional and not just sinful actions—but they are not telling. All of these sources do agree this can be far more elaborate and unexpected than might appear from our manifest sexual activity. Surveys (Mercer et al., 2013) indicate that sexual activity remains conservative in the UK. Frequency of sexual acts has, if anything, fallen off slightly. There is more acceptance of same-sex activity although only women seem to have had more sex with other women (I am using the terms "men" and "women" that are used in the surveys, and I assume that it refers to cisgender individuals). More respondents have had anal sex and more oral sex, but there is little change in the number of partners during one's lifetime (once an earlier age of first sex is taken into account) and unchanged attitudes against non-exclusivity in marriage.

A majority of men and women between 18 and 60 have watched porn (Herbenick et al., 2020). What these users search for in the galleries of images and videos stored on porn sites gives a previously unparalleled indication of desire in a virtual world, and, thus, of imagined sex. One of the major porn sites, Pornhub (with 130 million visitors per day and 11 petabytes of stored data), surveys the categories that get the most hits from their users. The top category in the 2021 survey was "hentai," followed by "romance," "group sex," "fitness," and "swapping." As the anonymous commentators on the site note, these are categories that were also popular in mainstream media supporting Merleau-Ponty's (1945/1962) presumption that sexual being suffuses and is infused by all other aspects of experience.

Is Sexual Behavior Simply the Product of the Interaction of Biology and Culture?

Sexual behavior has been studied by anthropologists, criminologists, sociologists, theologians (Marion, 2007), medical practitioners, biologists, and pharmacologists as well as many others, including the statisticians employed by Pornhub. Many of these studies focus on sex acts, sexual encounters, and episodes of physiological arousal. But, as noted above, imagined sex is an important component of sexual experience, too. It provides a world of sexual expression that is unbound by actuality and free of biology so long as the desire is there to explore. Cultural prohibitions need not apply either. It is a world created out of one's own desires, a world of sexual being that one enters because one is a sexual being, and not for other reasons.

What is it Like to Be in a Sexual World?

It is a world of desire of a particular kind, of erotic desire but also of its opposite, disgust–that is, sexual disgust. I shall argue that it is also a world of love (and hate).

The experience of being in a world has been particularly considered by existential philosophers and psychotherapists. It is their approach that I shall consider in the remainder of this chapter. Existential philosophy recognizes two foundations: the phenomenology taught by Brentano and the ontology of Heidegger. Rather than define these terms, I shall demonstrate them in their application to how it is to desire and to love as I discuss them in this chapter.

There have been other existential approaches to this subject. Koestenbaum (1974) defines existential sexuality as the sex life one has chosen authentically and says of it that "our freedom is total" (p. 10). Ferrarello (2019a) has also written about existential sexuality and about phenomenological approaches to erotic and other kinds of love. That is not what I have in mind. I do not think that the existential approach entails judging whether or not another person is acting authentically or if they are right to assume that they are free to act as they wish.

Ferrarello has also provided an existential account of sexual being and intimacy expanded as a phenomenological account in a book published in the same year (Ferrarello, 2019b). She notes the complexity of the topic redefines the study of human sexuality as a study of love and considers how "instincts and drives develop into desires and relational bonds to finally become political subjects" (p. 5). The approach is reminiscent of Freud's influential reconstruction of the sexual development of children based on the memories of his adult patients. But, for me, her account does not give me a sense of what it is like to be sexual. For that, we need to turn to the French existentialists and phenomenologists—including Gabriel Marcel who coined the term "existentialism"—that introduced a phenomenology of the body.

Merleau-Ponty (1945/1962), in his usual combination of common sense and dense, intellectually rigorous reasoning, summarized the main points of a phenomenology of sexual being, or "the body in its sexual being," in chapter 6 of his *Phenomenology of Perception*. He argues that sexual being requires that particular bodily systems have developed and is manifest in a world of other human beings with whom there is "inter-communication" (or intersubjectivity or, as I term it, a world of interbrain connection) but cannot be defined by particularities of the body, of behavior, or of social relations. Sexuality is one aspect of existence and is marked by particular feelings ("affectivity") that we recognize when they arise in our bodies in relation to other bodies. Merleau-Ponty seems also to say that sexual affects may become so intense that our bodies can switch into a bodily state (sleep is an example that he gives of a bodily state, and also functional aphonia) of sexual being. He refers briefly to the Sartrean idea of the gaze (Sartre and Merleau-Ponty were collaborating on opposition to the German occupation of France when writing *Being and Nothingness* (2003) and the *Phenomenology of Perception* 1962), respectively). He also considers that the sexual being might itself become a world that the owner of the body might scrutinize phenomenologically, leading to a "transcendence" (Merleau-Ponty's term) of sexual being into meaning.

I will come back the transcendence of sexual being, but first I will consider the world that the body in its sexual being creates. I shall ignore for the moment the negative experiences—Merleau-Ponty calls these pains—that sexual being may create, such as disgust, aloneness, jealousy, and so on. Instead, I will focus on the pleasures, which I will group under the general heading of sexual desire, or simply desire. I shall follow Merleau-Ponty in his treatment of desire as more like a state and less like a wish for a particular something or someone.

The Desire World

Sartre in his *Sketch for a Theory of the Emotions* (1971) considered how emotions can transform our world, including the facts of the world, our *facticity*. He proposed the thought experiment of trying to reach to pick a bunch of grapes, finding ourselves too short, and concluding that they are too green to eat. Frustration of a desire, Sartre argues, has magically transformed our world. Sartre calls this process "magical" because he sees it as a kind of "bad faith," as he would later call it. But it need not be (Hartmann, 2017).

But can desire itself magically transform the world for us? Is this one escape from facticity? Sartre assumed that such transformations are self-serving, but there is plenty of evidence that is not always the case. Posttraumatic Stress Disorder is an example of the emotional transformation of the world into one of fear or pain. There is considerable evidence that desire can, so long as it lasts, also transform the world.

Socrates reported by Plato (2005) in *The Symposium* refers to a certain Diotima, who tells him how he should view desire. It should start, she says, from the contemplation of beautiful bodies, but it should not stop there because there is something beautiful in all bodies. Beauty and ugliness are not dichotomous. From seeing beauty in bodies, Diotima advises that the next step is to see beauty in actions, and then in society. It is not unmixed with badness or ugliness but, I would say, seeing it vividly, even if momentarily, leaves behind the same afterglow as feeling the intensity of sexual desire and finding satisfaction. However, it is not sexual any longer but an awareness that goodness (or excellence to use the word that is so beloved by Athenian philosophers) survives.

Glamour

Glamor etymologically derives from "grammar," referring to the use of books of spells and perhaps also to the transformative experience of being able to read and write. Walter Scott introduced the term into mainstream English from the Scots to mean a spell that transforms experience.

Glamor is strongly tied to desire, and being filled with desire creates a glamor. I shall call this world transformed by desire, the desire world. Scruton (1986) while critical of phenomenology, makes the same case for the transformation of facticity as Husserl and Sartre but uses a different nomenclature to mine. What I call "desire," he calls "arousal" and restricts "desire" to what I call the "desire world."

Fiction provides many examples of how a person may be taken over by a desire world. Barthes and Howard (1979) brilliantly extract many of them with an emphasis on Goethe's *The Sorrows of Young Werther*, which the philosopher John Armstrong (2003) considers having introduced the "dominant vision of love today" (p. 1). There are powerful fictional accounts by women of female desire worlds, too (Barthes is somewhat biased towards a male view). *Lust* (Jelinek & Hulse, 1992) won the Nobel prize. *Wetlands* was the world's best-selling novel for a month in 2008 despite its focus on the mucilaginous aspects of sex.

Existential Approaches to the Desire World

The desire world is one in which attraction becomes elaborated into potential rapture that takes over ordinary living. Armstrong (2003) considers two literary examples. One is Stendhal's autobiographical *Love*, in which Stendhal describes the power of imagination to embellish, which Stendhal likens to a twig in a limestone cave that gets gradually coated and thickened by calcification. Stendhal calls this "crystallization." The other is Turgenev's *Spring Torrents*, in which the hero, Sanin, becomes infatuated by an Italian girl, Gemma, fights a duel apparently on her behalf, and gets engaged to her. He has some business dealings with another married woman, Maria Nikolaevna, and within days has gone to Paris with her and her husband, abandoning Gemma. Turgenev himself lived in a ménage à trois with the pianist and opera singer Pauline Viadot and her husband. It is a common theme: the callous lover who arouses the desires of the purported loved one, only to abandon the other and leave their desires hanging.

Kierkegaard (1999) describes this very well in his novella about A's seduction of Cordelia. There is the same irradiation of A's everyday world by the image of Cordelia, so that as he goes to her home and her bed A writes in his diary, "Who I am is irrelevant; everything finite and temporal is forgotten; only the eternal remains; the power of erotic love, its longing, its bliss." But on the following day, A writes in his diary (or rather, Kierkegaard writes for him): "But now it is finished, and I never want to see her again. For when a girl has given away everything, she is weak...Now all resistance is impossible, and to love is beautiful only if resistance is present, as soon as it ceases, to love is weakness and habit" (pp. 198–199).

Updike, in his introduction to this edition of *Diary of a Seducer* (Kierkegaard, 1999), stresses what other commentators have noted: the parallels between the seduction of Cordelia and what Kierkegaard imagined might have been the experience of Regine Olsen, to whom he had become engaged and then broken that promise to her and her family. Kierkegaard imagined her as having been destroyed by this experience. One might argue that this assumption was an indication of the delusional nature of his desire world, which failed to include the "real" Regine. The real Regine married another suitor quite soon after the end of her engagement, moved to Patagonia with him when he was appointed Danish ambassador there, and lived to a ripe age, looking back on her now famous engagement to Kierkegaard fondly.

Kierkegaard's naivety is not the unusual feature of his account. Many philosophers of love have had limited personal experience of long-term sexual relationships. One thinks of Kant, Schopenhauer, Hume, or Nietszche. What is different in A's account is that desire gives way several times in the narrative to something darker.

Kierkegaard (1992) wrote *Either/Or,* which contains *Diary of a Seducer* under one of his more usual pseudonyms, Victor Eremita (hermit winner). The diary is presented as a manuscript that Eremita found in a locked drawer in a secondhand desk interspersed with copies of letters that the seduced Cordelia wrote to A and that Eremita has inserted between diary entries. Eremita writes in his introduction that "Behind the world in which we live...lies another world, and the two have about the same relation to each other as do the stage proper and the stage one sometimes sees behind it in the theatre (p. 7). It is, Eremita says, a world of mist, suffused with anxiety.

Robert Stoller (1970a, 1970b, 1991, Stoller & Herdt, 1985), a psychiatrist specializing in sexuality and gender issues, wrote a series of publications about desire in which he proposed that desire was often mixed with other emotions, often negative ones, which it transformed into a more intense, sometimes desperate, desire world. He described one of his cases, a man who was brought up by his aunts who insisted in dressing him as a girl rather than a boy when he was in middle childhood. Later in life, he could only orgasm if he was cross-dressed as a woman, but his sexual excitement was enhanced by his feelings of triumph that he had escaped his aunt's prohibitions and become the man that he really was.

Readers familiar with Sartre's *Sketch for a Theory of the Emotions* will be reminded of Sartre's account of the "magical transformations" of situations by emotion. I extended both Stoller's and Sartre's ideas to include the transformative effect of desire in a chapter on "Addiction" in a book written many years ago (Tantum, 2002). I further argued that desire can be intensified when it transforms another emotion, and that this strengthened emotion can imbue a previously neutral aspect of the experience. So a photograph, a dress, a watch, a gesture, a journey—indeed any aspect peculiar to that experience—can re-evoke longing (Tantam, 2003). I assumed that this process might be mediated by the oldest cortex, the rhinencephalon, and so I termed it the flavor of emotion. Merleau-Ponty (1945/1962) had put forward a similar hypothesis about desire, which he called sexuality, writing in the *Phenomenology of Perception* that it was a "scent."

The flavor of desire and other pleasurable emotions brings joy to life, but the joy may be fleeting. It is typically destroyed by deliberate repetition (Kierkegaard, 2009). It is probably best to consider these moments as gifts, in the case of erotic desire as gifts from the beloved. In those exceptional moments of falling in love, moments of delight or joy such as I have mentioned may be prolonged, creating a world of desire. There is a risk that in this world, the desirer's focus will be on the gifts that they can give to the beloved. This then leads to a blindness to the actuality of the object of desire and a concentration on how to maintain the world of desire by possessing the desired person.

Kierkegaard (2009), writing as Victor Eremita, notes the effect of this on its anti-hero, A. Desire and other pleasures, "living aesthetically" as Kierkegaard terms it, is the main goal of A's life. Kierkegaard acknowledges that this might be driven by a wish to gather up and transform "darker" feelings. But the effect is to create remoteness from everyday life, which often lacks an erotic glamor, and to live in what Eremita calls a world of "mist" that has to be maintained by rekindling desire over and over again.

Both Merleau-Ponty (1945/1962) and Kierkegaard (2009) gave accounts of what they called sexuality, which they thought perfused every human experience. Merleau-Ponty's argument for this was based on a man, Schneider, who had experienced multiple penetrating wounds to his skull following an explosion when he was serving as a soldier in the first world war (for more details, see Jensen, 2009).

This very general use of sexuality includes sexual desire but is much more than that, and closer to a Kierkegaardian "aesthetic" or emotionally colored world (Merleau-Ponty uses the metaphor "perfumed") that over-stretches the term sexuality. Merleau-Ponty's careful analysis of the motor consequences of Schneider's injuries does fit with modern neurological accounts of Schneider's occipital lesions if they involved lesions of the cerebellar vermis and might accord with some theories of the cerebellum's role in socialization (see the review of the effects of cerebellar lesions in Tantam (2012). Mice with cerebellar lesions become cut off socially and emotionally, as Schneider apparently was (although he had multiple lesions in other brain areas, too). This fits with Merleau-Ponty's hypothesis that sexuality serves as a means of connection to other people in general. But this proposal is obviously false if we apply it to the world of desire for another person. For that person may not correspond in any but superficial ways to the real person, just as Regine Olsen in Kierkegaard's mind does not seem to have corresponded to the Regine Olsen that spoke so fondly of him (Garff, 2005) years after his death.

Other People and Desire

While Merleau-Ponty considers that the sexual life of the body is entangled with that of other bodies, he only hints at the significance of the meaning that other people make of the sexual beings disclosed to them. Sexual being is one aspect of being, and the existential position is that, as Heidegger put it, we are beings in a world. This is among other features in a world of people, embodied people with whom our bodies are engaged. But it is also a world of agents, and we gradually recognize ourselves as agents among them. As we grasp these facts, we "Dasein." *Dasein* means existence in everyday German, but it appealed to Heidegger because it is etymologically derived from "being there" or "situated being," and so conveyed his view, contrary to that of Freud, that people were not born with the capacity to be human in any but a biological sense and that this capacity required interaction with a world.

We exist in a world of bodies, but we gradually discover that we also exist in a world of ideas and agents, a world of thought. Any of these have the potential to impose themselves on our desire world.

Unloving Desire

Desire mixed with negative emotion may feel good to the desirer but it carries costs. One is the potential addiction, or at least repetition, that is required to ameliorate the negative emotion. The other is the discrepancy between the image of the person desired and the actual person. This can lead to grief when it becomes apparent that the object of the desire is unobtainable, as usually happens when the infatuation is one-sided as in a "crush." Or, worse, the desirer may compel the object of their desire to conform to their imagination, giving up their own world for the world of the desirer. If that compulsion fails, the object of desire may become an object of hate or rage.

The same stimuli that can arouse desire can also arouse disgust. So these two emotions may intertwine. Desire for someone makes them attractive, but disgust makes them repulsive, leading to sexual confusion for the desiree and, if sexual relations do occur, for the person desired. Sartre's work is shot through with feelings of shame, and disgust. The famous *Nausea* that he discusses in his novel with that title is the nausea that arises from disgust (Legeard, 2002) with the world as it presents itself to us. Sartre (1943/2003) considers nausea in several places in *Being and Nothingness* but not always in relation to sexual desire. But he ends this, his best-known book, with a detailed discussion of the viscous (translated as the slimy, in my edition), holes, masculine and feminine, and the risk that the viscous poses to the full potential of a person, the "for-itself." The viscous also figures in his account of the relationship of Marcelle and Mathieu in his novel *The Age of Reason*, published two years after *Being and Nothingness*. The character of Mathieu is based on himself, and Sartre/ Mathieu cogitates during the course of the book about all of the disgusting viscosity that can potentially be found in sex, including that of his production. All of it disgusts him.

It does seem as if there is a repugnant misogyny in this. In *Being and Nothingness* Sartre (1943/2003) writes: "Slime is the revenge of the In-itself. A sickly sweet, feminine revenge that will be symbolized on another level by the quality "sugary." Sartre then considers "holes," passes onto sexuality and of this writes, "the obscenity of the female sex is that of everything which 'gapes open'" (p. 613). There are people, Sartre was perhaps of that number, who are disgusted by sex. A proportion of people who count themselves as asexual are like this (Brown et al., 2021), but this is not how most people experience sex.

The argument at the end of *Being and Nothingness* (1943/2003) is purportedly an existential one. It is difficult to follow, but it seems that Sartre is arguing that if disgust (of the slime) dominates a person's actions, or if the need to fill the hole does, then choice is dominated by facticity and is not free. The solution seems to come down to mixing the slime with other flavors that cover it up, allowing the disgust to be turned into something palatable, just as foetida can lose its disgusting flavor when mixed into lentil soup.

It is a more important argument than it might seem because the world of desire relies on the suspension of the In-itself, the prosaic everyday world in favor of a kind of dream. The dream is that the other is perfect for us. Anything that reminds us that this is not true–a mass of pubic hair, a sharp nail scoring a tender part, a word out of place–can abolish desire if we are not careful.

But this raises a bigger problem about the nature of love. If love means loving another as one loves oneself, then why is the fumbling of the loved person not overlooked as one overlooks fumblings in oneself?

Being Desired

De Beauvoir's novel *The Mandarins* won the Prix Goncourt following its publication in 1954. It is dedicated to her lover at the time, Nelson Algren, the left-wing author known for his tough guy image and championship of the dispossessed. His novel *The Man with the Golden Arm*, won the US National Book Award in 1950. De Beauvoir and Algren had a passionate affair that is incorporated in *The Mandarins* (although de Beauvoir denied that the novel is a roman à clef, it has been taken by many people as being about Algren, Camus, Sartre, and herself in fictionalized form. She is Anne and he is Lewis). Toward the end of the book, and the end of the account of the affair, Anne writes: "I closed my eyes. A man's body was once more weighing on me, heavy with all its confidence and all its desires. It was Lewis. No, he hadn't changed, nor had I, nor had our love. I had left, but I had come back; I had found my place again and I was released from myself" (de Beauvoir, 1999, p. 540).

None of de Beauvoir's writing, whether fictional or polemic, is without a philosophical undertone. No doubt her feelings about Algren led her to reflect on the woman in love in her most famous book, *The Second Sex*, and see her as trapped by her voluntary enslavement to a man (de Beauvoir, 1949, p. 653). De Beauvoir sees this as a political and social problem that gives men power and opportunity and denies it to women. It is difficult, however, to suppose that Anne/de Beauvoir saw herself as enslaved to Lewis, but perhaps she was considering the struggle for a woman to be for-herself rather than in-herself. Elsewhere in *The Second Sex* she considers how hard it is for a woman to transcend being an object. So perhaps she was simply giving voice to the relief in not having to continue this struggle and to be "released from myself."

But there is another kind of entrapment at work that results from being the object of another's world of desire. As mentioned above, both men and women (there were no study participants who identified with another gender) gave "the person really desired me" as a reason for having sex (it was the 19th most commonly given reason out of 267). It is rewarding, especially since the desire for the body of a person who has always looked down on their own body is thrilling and reassuring at the same time (Bogaret & Brotto, 2014).

This motive for sex is discussed in the *Second Sex* but attributed to women and not men. De Beauvoir considers men to be motivated by their desire for the other's body, and unconcerned with the other's desire for theirs. Although the sharp divisions that de Beauvoir makes have become more blurred than they were, particularly as she considers only men and women in heterosexual relationships, it remains true that being desired continues to be an especially strong motive for heterosexual women today (Bogaret & Brotto, 2014). In fact, it is so desirable to be desired that the threat of having that desire taken away may be coercive. In particular, it may be a factor in explaining why so many women have sex despite not wanting to—11% of those under 20, while another 49% have mixed feelings (Weitzman & Mallory, 2019).

There are also conflicts about what values should apply to love. Sartre and de Beauvoir thought that freedom was the fundamental value, and that this meant freedom to have concurrent sexual partners as long as their love for each other was essential and for keeps (de Beauvoir, 1992). This conflicts with other views that being faithful to a life partner is the proper expression of love (and is also out of sync with the current majority of UK participants in the survey of sexual attitudes, noted above). Sartre thought that sex made freedom problematic because love as described by other philosophers involved mergence not just in the act of sex but also much more widely. Sartre and de Beauvoir refer back to Hegel who raised this issue and concluded that a sado-masochistic relationship inevitably resulted, although he went on to argue that becoming self-conscious, and aware that the other was self-conscious and therefore separate, too, was the final result. De Beauvoir moved beyond this proposing that love, particularly maternal love brought out generosity that could find pleasure in the independent good fortune of another. Sartre does not seem to have been so sure until late in life (Boule, 2010–2011). Perhaps de Beauvoir was thinking of what Spinoza wrote about love (Spinoza 2000): "We endeavour to affirm, concerning ourselves and everything we love, everything we conceive to affect pleasurably ourselves or the loved object. Contrariwise, we endeavour to negate everything, which we conceive to affect painfully ourselves or the loved object" (Proposition XXV). But Spinoza's formulation makes the lover subservient to the loved one. Exactly the lack of freedom that de Beauvoir was trying escape from.

Recreational Sex

In the Prodicus parable mentioned previously, both Vice and Excellence are personified as women. Freud wrote about this split in men's view of women on male sexuality (Freud, 1912) later termed the Madonna–whore complex (Hartmann, 2009). Patriarchal men are still inclined to see women as being either a virtuous Madonna or the whore, as the Ancient Greeks apparently did Garcia et al., 2012). Desire for sex is, according to this stereotype, exclusively experienced by the women you bed and not by the women you wed, to quote the catchphrase that some men still use.

Garcia and colleagues (2012) reviewed the literature on hookups, sexual encounters intended to lead to pleasure only, and not dates that would be considered "courting" that might end in a committed relationship. They provide a brief history of the growth of hookup culture and refer to a book series on "The Happy Hookup," explicitly directed to "single girls." Their review is a comprehensive overview of many aspects of the changing expression of sex and sexuality (they are careful to consider both gay and straight hookups) and worth a look.

In addition, they review the evolutionary theories of sexuality that posit a drive for men to have as much sex as they can manage with as many partners as possible, and for women—because of the much greater reproductive effort that is required of them—to reduce the number of partners and encounters. This would fit in with another long-standing assumption about desire: that it is easily elicited in men, but that women spend much of their effort inhibiting male desire and require an outstanding male performance to elicit it in themselves. Garcia et al. (2012) find that hookup behavior does not support this model. Maybe this is because sex and reproduction have become uncoupled.

Moreover, they also reviewed social explanations for desire, most prominently that women and men's desire is controlled by a social script that dictates that good girls are not promiscuous and save themselves for marriage. Garcia et al. (2012) note that desire rarely forms part of a woman's sexual education, but do not find support that men and women operate from different scripts. Surveys show hookups are infrequently about casual sex in either gender. Both men and women hope that a hookup will become something more permanent (they exclude "friends with benefits" or relationships in which casual sex is accepted by both participants). But nearly half of women regret the hookup the day after, and only just over a quarter of men do so.

Surveys of what women want from sex that is not restricted to dating disclose a wide range of reasons–267 of them in one study (Meston & Buss, 2007). There was little difference in the top 50 reasons for men and the top 50 for women. Men gave more reasons that mentioned physical features in their partner; women mentioned having sex for the partner's sake ("I wanted to say I've missed you" and "I wanted to keep my partner satisfied"). Both men and women were turned on by being desired, and wanting to feel loved was also a reason for sex in both men and women (other genders were not included in the study). This study perhaps makes too much of reasons, though. Sex often occurs in a fog of desire, anxiety, and sometimes inebriation, with not much reasoning at the time.

Male sexual desire is easy to detect as it is signaled by a stiffening and then an erection of the penis. Male sexual satiation is also overt. Orgasm is also easy to detect as it results in an ejaculate in men who do not have a prostate problem. Female sexual desire is more subtly expressed. There is probably no ejaculate (although many men would like there to be) if most physiologists are to be believed, although urinary incontinence triggered by an increase of intrapelvic pressure may mimic ejaculation. Other aspects of female sexual function such as the presence or absence of a G spot remain a mystery even to experts. Not surprisingly, men find satisfying women sexually sufficiently puzzling to read manuals about it. Women find it possible to simulate desire and even orgasm. Many anecdotal reports confirm that many women find cunnilingus a good preparation for vaginal sex, but many fewer heterosexual men provide this to their heterosexual partners than lesbian partners provide it to theirs. More sexually assertive women experience more orgasms than less sexually assertive women (Lentz & Zaikman, 2021). Maybe this is because sexually assertive women are more willing to ask for what they want, though bodily self-confidence may also lead to feeling more easily sexually aroused.

We should not assume that what women want from sex is to orgasm, or that this is the acme of sexual pleasure for women as it is for men. This does seem to be what most men want from sex. In fact, some men believe that they have a right to orgasmic sex. The 'Incel' movement seems to be based on the notion that society, or perhaps just women, owes each of them orgasmic sex. But do women give such priority to their own orgasms? It is difficult to answer this question without provoking indignation from those who think that women deserve as much sexual pleasure, and sexual freedom, as men. This is undeniable, but, even so, whether or not women put giving sexual pleasure before receiving it is an open question. Some evidence suggests that only a minority of women do (Brede et al., 2020). Women's clothes, make-up, perfume, and behavior are all expected to be arousing to men, and transgender women are expected to adopt the same practices.

There are societies that still consider a woman's sexual pleasure is a dangerous destabilizing force—to the extent that girls' genitals are mutilated to remove those areas that are most pleasurable when stimulated, usually just the clitoris but sometimes also the labia minora. Many other societies consider that the embryological remnant membrane that stretches across the vagina of many young women (the hymen) belongs not to the young woman to perforate as she wills but to a future partner who decides when it is to be perforated.

This idea of the dangers of female desire may be linked to the assumption that men breaking sexual boundaries have done so because their desires have been inflamed by a woman (or a gay man) and that women potentially have power over men that needs to be controlled and suppressed. This is a consistent theme running throughout the history of patriarchal societies of Europe and the Middle East since the Neolithic period. Pain and suffering have typically been the societal prescriptions to suppress desire, and these have directed at women and gay men disproportionately often (Berkowitz, 2012).

Love and Sex

Sexual being is often discussed as if it is about other people and not the author themselves, much as Kierkegaard presented kissing in the *Diary of a Seducer* (Kierkegaard, 1999). While Kierkegaard may have had little or no experience of sex that he was willing to disclose, he was willing to talk about his personal experience in many other fields, and particularly his religious experience. In fact, he pioneered a kind of philosophy in which deep and honest inquiry into personal experience could provide universal truth. This approach led to the phenomenological method used by many existential philosophers that allows them to set aside the "natural attitude," as Husserl called it, revealing more of how our minds create that world. One analogy might be, if we limit ourselves to perception, a photograph of a studio with the actors and the scenery that we would normally see with the natural attitude, but that would also take in the lights and the cameras around the scene that create that image. Heidegger used this as a starting point for how we can stand aside from our immersion in a taken-for-granted world to consider what our actual situation is as beings that are changing as time passes and that will die (Heidegger called this the ontological perspective). Sartre also contrasted three modes of consciousness: being in-itself and being-for-itself, to which he later added being-for-others. The being-in-itself is all of the past: it is the being of objects that are just so, and in being-in-itself we make ourselves into an object. Sartre considers this a form of bad faith, as it limits what we can do, or think, or feel. The being-for-others is also a reduced way of being, which is the effect that others have on us, inhibiting and controlling our actions, particularly through shame. We can resist this, but rarely do. These personal factors he called "facticity.

Being-for-itself is, like Heidegger's ontological perspective, meta-stable and quickly collapses into being-for-others, and so needs to be constantly renewed. There is a strong implication that being-for-itself is "better" than other kinds of being, just as the ontological or authentic perspective seems better for Heidegger than the ontic perspective. It is difficult to imagine what it would be like to live with someone who is completely free of the influence of other people or who is "authentic" through and through. Falling into the everyday social influence but also being able to rise from it seems the "best" way of living, if a value can be applied to other's people's existence.

Sartre (1952/1963) thought that facticity could be "nihilated" or set aside by imagination that could make our future projects free of the influence of facticity, just as an author might create a character that is free of the author's personality and the author's time and place. He wrote biographies of Genet, who escaped his life as a thief by becoming an intellectual, and Flaubert (Sartre, 1971), who was considered by his surgeon father to be the family idiot but reinvented himself as one of the great French novelists. Creating a new world into which other people can be drawn is the quintessential expression of freedom. It is also one of the steps toward a loving relationship. It transcends the ordinary because it is brand new "project," to use Sartre's term for the future.

What is the Meaning of Being in a World of Desire?

It might seem that the pleasure of the early moments of a new relationship do not need any kind of analysis. Expectations and hopes are high. There may be moments of intense pleasure, preceded by equally intense desire. It is a disruptive time, often entailing pain and loss and fear as well as pleasure...and worry. We worry that it will "turn out all right" without clearly knowing what "all right" would be. It is a *bouleversement*, what Jaspers (1919) called a "limit situation."

The most common term for this state is "falling in love." Love might precede desire, coincide with it, or follow from it later. When the onset of desire and love coincide, it is proverbially a thunderbolt (*"coup de foudre"*). Scruton (1986) describes it as a moment: "it is the glance of sexual interest that precipitates the movement of the soul, whereby two people come to stand outside the multitude in which they are presently moving, bound by a knowledge that cannot be expressed in words and offering to each other a silent communication that ignores everything but themselves."

Falling in love is, for many, what gives desire meaning. For many, it is also what gives life itself meaning.

Erotic Love

According to Google's Ngram, the word "love" occurred 2.7 times in every 10,000 words published in all books written in English and published in 2019. This was about twice as often as the word "food" and four times as often as the word "sex." It was used with similar frequency in 1810, too, and every year thereafter although with a dip around the 1980s.

The English word "love" covers all types of love and the objects of love that are differentiated in other languages. Some authors have made systematic lists of these, differentiating erotic love, the kind that I shall be considering, from love of children, of antiques, of God, of motherland, of driving fast...and every other thing, object or person that we can say that one loves in English.

The existentialist philosopher Robert Solomon edited a book of readings with his wife, Kathleen Higgins, also a professor of philosophy, in which they showcased an impressive range of views about "erotic love" from the Western tradition. Two principal models recur within these writings. The Athenian model of a homoerotic relationship between a male adolescent and an older male citizen that does not recoil from its sexual aspect and a later Christianized model of love with sex downplayed or absent. The Greek model also occurs in other warrior societies (Bleibtreu-Ehrenberg, 1990), although none have elaborated a cultural tradition by this means as influential as that of the Athenians.

Non-Western cultures' approaches to love are not much considered in the selection of readings by Solomon and Higgins. Fair enough, given the paucity of philosophical treatments of love that they find. There are other biases too. Most of the authors are men despite the obvious attempts of the editors to balance out the genders. They do succeed in the later, more contemporary sections of the book, although at the expense of a certain degree of misandry.

The male authors tend to specify what love is, with little recognition that each couple or polyamorous group might recreate love according to their own terms. There is, in any case, a presumption that true love requires monogamy. This assumption has been called into question by some existential psychotherapists (Barker, 2021) drawing on the work of de Beauvoir and Sartre. De Beauvoir did write about polyamory and also lived it. But not, it seems, happily. Many now think her first novel, *She Came to Stay* (de Beauvoir, 1943/1984), was the inspiration for the treatment of romantic relationships by Sartre in *Being and Nothingness* (Fullbrook, 1999). But it was also an account of a polyamorous relationship, which itself was a fictionalized account of the sexual relationship between de Beauvoir, who was bisexual, her lover Sartre, and two sisters, Olga and Wanda Kosakiewicz. In the novel, Olga and Wanda were combined in the character of Xaviere, who is at the end of the book murdered by Françoise, the de Beauvoir character. In reality, Olga believed in the love triangle. She switched from medicine to the theatre, and Sartre tried to help her career along. Olga married another, male, lover of de Beauvoir. Wanda was less caught up, and later had a relationship with Camus, who was at the time a friendly rival of Sartre.

De Beauvoir and Sartre were sure that any kind of loving relationship must increase, not restrict the freedom of all involved. They must, I think, have told themselves that their multiple relationships were the expression of this freedom, but I am not sure whether they considered the freedom of the partners who were left behind. It is arguable whether being loved by de Beauvoir and Sartre did leave Olga and Wanda free at least in their later choice of partners.

Erotic love often has its origins in the beginning of new intimate relationships, which may be why we associate it particularly with adolescence and young adulthood. Erotic love in adolescence may often lead to longer term relationships and to parenthood, but whether it does or not is, I think, incidental to its nature. Love, like desire, may be a defined and therefore recognizable emotion—one may, for example, have a pang of love—but is not confined to that. Like desire, it is a state of being. The similarities between desire and love arise because states of desire often precede and transform into states of love. In that sense Scruton (1986) is right when he calls desire a "motive" for love.

What Turns the World of Desire into a World of Love?

The desire world is not shared. "A" desired Cordelia, as we saw previously, only so long as she was unobtainable to him and not of his world. As soon as he had possessed her and she entered that desire world, his desire vanished and the world of desire with it.

What turns the world of desire into a world of love is when another person (or persons, if one believes polyamorous claims) enters that world—which means that the desirer needs also to enter the world of the desired. This is an affective world. It does not imply shared ideas or beliefs (although big discrepancies in these lead to conflict, and the affective world gets suffused with negativity), but it is a world that our bodies inhabit. This is the basis for love that Plato attributes to Aristophanes in the *Symposium* (2005): that love means reuniting with the other half of our body that Zeus split from us. The expression has continued to the present: We may still refer to our other half, sometimes our better half, when we mean our partner. Ovid refers to this, too, in book four of his *Metamorphoses* (Ovid, 8 CE). This is about the nymph Salmacis, who is granted her wish to never be parted from Hermaphroditus, the man she has fallen for, by Jupiter, who fuses the bodies of Salmacis and Hermaphroditus together.

Max Scheler, a famous phenomenologist and Catholic thinker in his time (although his reputation was harmed by his three marriages to younger and younger women) thought love required a linkage between bodies (Vandenberghe, 2008). He, like other members of the Munich School of phenomenology, attributed this linkage to *Einfühlung* (Scheler, 1954), which the British psychologist Titchener mistranslated as "empathy." Einfühlung is not an act of imagination or even a voluntary act at all; it is a reflex response involving frontotemporal areas and readily downregulated by upstream cortex (see Tantam, 2017). Empathy in Scheler's usage provides a connection with others, but it is only active when the other person is loved. Loving sex, "the act of love," provides a deep understanding of the partner without needing or being able to account for how we have reached that understanding (Zachary & Steinbock, 2018).

It is no surprise that sexual satisfaction and the capacity for empathy are correlated especially in women (Galinsky & Sonenstein, 2011). But empathy also provides an explanation of why it is commonly thought that love is a kind of fusion between two people, for empathy means that what another person feels is felt directly and immediately by oneself.

Edith Stein, Husserl's first paid research assistant and a Catholic convert like Scheler who influenced her (she was later canonized as St. Teresia Benedicta a Cruce) also believed that there was a strong tie between human love and the love of God (Stein, 1916/1964). She wrote in depth about Einfühlung and phenomenology but also wrote about the role of women anticipating later feminist views of women's different voice of caring, compromise, and moral responsibility. This value-driven analysis seems to fit with the disputed findings about the differences in empathic ability between men and women (Baron-Cohen, 2003; for a rebuttal, see Fine, 2010 and Eliot et al., 2021). But there is no reason to suppose that in a couple there cannot still be some differentiation between a caring role, and an achieving role.

The same issues were considered by de Beauvoir in the *Second Sex*, although she saw the caring role as a trap that was sprung particularly on women in Western society. De Beauvoir had also considered the philosophical consequences of being fused with another person in the way suggested by Stein and Scheler, but dismissed it as impossible (Ward, 1999). The most that she thought one person could do would be to create a mutual (reciprocal) undertaking to respect each other's freedom. This freedom precluded de Beauvoir and Sartre from living together, getting married, or being faithful to each other. Both of them carved out an enormous reputation in applied philosophy. Their ideas so overlapped that it is still a matter of contention who was the originator of some of them. They were considered a couple but intellectually free to develop their own ideas. Desire for each other, and that mystical sense of transcendence that lovers attribute to sex, may not have been a long-term factor in their relationship. Sartre, so many people have commented, was not physically attractive and de Beauvoir was.

What they both (de Beauvoir particularly in the *Ethics of Ambiguity*) stressed was that a loving relationship (an essential as opposed to a contingent love, as Sartre put it to de Beauvoir when they were first dating) had to leave both partners free. The implication is that a love that is intimate, that encompasses knowing another person's eating habits, behavior in the bathroom, political views, spiteful side, less than flattering views of one's intelligence or physique must be free to work on these behaviors and ideas as they see fit. Moreover, one must as a lover of that person love them as one loves one's own blind spots and ugly toes. De Beauvoir considers this an ethical duty, perhaps inspired by Kant's categorical imperative. But it is also the liberation and "expansion" that is ascribed to being in a loving relationship. For, and here again both de Beauvoir and Sartre express the same ideas albeit in different ways, it is the avoidance of processing shame or disgust about oneself that is a major cause of unfreedom.

When Sex Ends (If It Does)

Many couples, especially if they have been together for a while, might act toward each other in ways that an observer would not find loving, but if challenged the couple might still say that they are in love. Love becomes a world that one can reach but no longer a world that one is in. The same is true of desire. Couples do not continue indefinitely in the desire world. Desire for each other gets compartmentalized after a time as it just gets in the way of getting on with life. Heidegger writes in *Being and Time* of this "fallenness" into the everyday ontic world, using the same word as is used for falling in love.

This is not to say that desire just burns itself out. It just takes its place alongside the many mutual "projects" (to use the Sartrean term) that widen and deepen love. Existential psychotherapists encourage clients to value those crises, including but not restricted to brushes with death and dying that force us to reconsider whether or not our daily concerns are furthering our projects, that is ,what we consider most important for us to be doing with our lives. Mutually satisfying sex also means putting aside the everyday and encountering another person in their full physical presence. Desire for sexual pleasure, along with the desire to give sexual pleasure, may also be one way that couples are stimulated to re-attain a transcendent closeness, if that is what brought them together. Making love recognizes the otherness of a partner and celebrates it.

Take-away Points

Existentialism is based on phenomenology, which is based on a particular view of the relationship between what a person thinks and feels about, and what it is that they are thinking and feeling about. It requires a shift of attitude that calls into question our usual experience so that we understand the experience more fully. When we look at a familiar room, we are not aware of what we don't see (a mark on the carpet perhaps, or how old the chairs look) because we see what we mean to see: maybe that the armchair is beckoning to be sat on, or there has been an intruder who has left their morning paper on the sideboard. But suppose now we put on a blindfold and explore the room by touch and smell. The same things will be in it, but we will be grasping them and not seeing them. The quality of our experience of the room will be changed. One consequence might be that we will wonder why we only take notice of some of the things in the room when there are so many other objects, and components of objects, that we do not normally sense. We might then go on to reflect that what we notice is the meaning the room has for us, but that there could be many other meanings made out of it.

When it comes to sex and love, the phenomenological method is an invitation to set aside what we know about sex and love because what we know will reflect the meaning we inadvertently place on what we have selected to include in that knowledge. This will make us more open to what other people experience in their desired worlds and worlds of love. Maybe we gain this information through their accounts, through the process of therapy that invites clients to challenge their assumptions, or more directly via our intersubjective contact with others.

Undertaking phenomenological reduction is not a one-off but has to occur repeatedly if we want to increase our awareness of what it is to be a sexual being, and what it is to love. Husserl thought of it as widening horizons, but we might also say that it is a route to greater freedom in the sense that Sartre may have intended. It does not mean freedom to have more partners or to try out more sexual acts.

Love has a special role in contributing to this kind of freedom. It transcends the particularities of desire or sexual expression. Like any state of being—happiness for example—it needs constant renewal, and loving sex has an important contribution to make to that.

Appendix 1: Terminology

Words like sex and sexuality are strong signifiers that readily become unmoored and float over a number of different signifieds.

Sex (A)	The attributes that differentiate two types of individual vertebrates, including humans, into males and females. Often known as sexual dimorphism and may be extended to other characteristics not directly related to procreation.	
		Maleness in mammals is marked by the presence of a single male chromosome (Y) and single female chromosome (XY) in cells and femaleness by two X chromosomes (XX) (Male birds are XX). This is not always reliable because rarely there may be a single X chromosome, X0, two X chromosomes and a Y chromosome, or multiple Y chromosomes (e.g., YY, YYY, XYY or XYY).
		Females carry eggs and may become pregnant and carry the embryos to term a womb. Males produce spermatozoa. Unfertilized eggs have mitochondria, and enough food in their cytoplasm to nourish the fertilized egg through its early divisions until it implants into the womb. Spermatozoa are mainly a nucleus and a flagellum with little cytoplasm. and only last three days even within the moist environment of the female reproductive tract. Their flagellum enables them to swim up the reproductive tract if deposited within it, and several spermatozoa

		may compete to fertilize an egg. The nurturance built into the egg and later the placenta, contrasted with the competitive nature of the spermatozoa, may have given rise to the stereotype that female humans create human "nests" for succour and protection, while human males go out and hunt for food.
		Females have a reproductive tract that can be penetrated and from which babies can emerge; males have an organ designed to penetrate.
		High levels of circulating testosterone (males older than 7) or estrogen (females older than 7 and younger than 60)
Sex (B)	A synonym of gender	Socially recognized sexual forms might include "third sexes" depending on the society: non-binary, cis- (no gender change since birth) ,or trans-(gender change since birth).
Sex (C)	An activity usually involving the deliberate, pleasurable stimulation of at least one body, typically in the genital area.	e.g., having sex, wanting sex

Sexuality (1): as a topic, all that pertains to sex (i.e., all that is "sexual"). Sexuality (2): those aspects of a person's sexuality that are applicable to that person (i.e., their existential sexuality). How, when, and with whom a person has sex are thought to be determined by their sexuality. Heterosexuality is the sexual expression of the majority of the world's population and is the only kind of sexual activity that can lead to procreation without some sort of device being used. All other sexualities have fallen under the taboo of one human society or another at different times. Currently, in Western cultures and cultures dominated by the West, homosexuality, solo sex, anal sex, and oral sex are not taboo. Asexuality is not taboo but may be frowned upon. BDSM (bondage, domination, sadism and masochism) may or may not be taboo depending on the exact nature of the activity and whether or not it is consensual. Incest is taboo but has not always been so in every society. Pedophilia and necrophilia are taboo and have probably always been so, everywhere.

Whoever is involved and however it is performed, sex is likely to be motivated in part or completely by sexual desire (although that desire might be itself motivated by something darker). Rather than considering different sexual activities, I shall, therefore, focus on their common origin in desire.

Appendix 2: The Existential Approach

An online discussion forum of leading existential therapists around the world set themselves the task of defining the existential world view in 2016 And that definition is now included in the constitution of the Federation for Existential Therapists in Europe. It reads:

> Existential Therapy values the interactive, relational and embodied nature of human consciousness and human existence. It considers that human beings are free to effect change in their lives in a responsible, deliberate, ethical and thoughtful manner, by understanding their difficulties and by coming to terms with the possibilities and limitations of the human condition in general and of their own life in particular. It emphasizes the importance of finding meaning and purpose by engaging with life at many levels, physical, social, personal and spiritual. It does not prescribe a particular worldview but examines the tensions and contradictions in a person's way of being. This will include a consideration of existential limits such as death, failure, weakness, guilt, anxiety and despair.

Existential therapists look to philosophy for inspiration, particularly to the phenomenologists and the French existentialists. But understandably their work reaches back to much earlier philosophers, too. Nietzsche and Kierkegaard are often considered to be particular influences, but Kierkegaard was inspired by Plato/Socrates and by more modern philosophers who have influenced the existentialist movement, Heidegger was himself inspired by Aristotle. So classical philosophy has also been influential.

Some existential notions include choice and the freedom to choose can co-exist with limits that restrict possibility; every action represents a choice; as Aristotle argued, our choices shape us and any consequences of those choices are our responsibility; social pressures are ever present but can never extinguish the burden of choosing and the freedom it beings. Existential therapists often consider that the question "Where am I going?" is as important a question as "Where have I come from?"

References

Armstrong, E. A., England, P., & Fogarty, A. C. K. (2012). Accounting for women's orgasm and sexual enjoyment in college hookups and relationships. *American Sociological Review, 77*(3), 435–462. https://doi.org/10.1177/0003122412445802

Armstrong, J. (2003). *Conditions of love: The philosophy of intimacy.* Penguin.

Arnocky, S., Desrochers, J., Rotella, A., Albert, G., Hodges-Simeon, C., Locke, A., . . . Kelly, B. (2021). Men's mate value correlates with a less restricted sociosexual orientation: A meta-analysis. *Archives of Sexual Behavior, 50*(8), 3663–3673. https://doi.org/10.1007/s10508-021-01937-6

Augustine, of Hippo, Saint. (2009). *The confessions of Saint Augustine.* Hodder & Stoughton.

Augustine, of Hippo, Saint. (2011). *Confessions.* Hendrickson Publishers Marketing.

Barker, M.-J. (2021). Open non-monogamies: Drawing on de Beauvoir and Sartre to inform sexual work with romantic relationships. In M. Milton (Ed.), *Sexuality: Existential perspectives* (pp. 198–216). PCCS books.

Baron-Cohen, S. (2003). *The essential difference: Male and female brains and the truth about autism.* Basic Books.

Barthes, R., & Howard, R. (1979). A lover's discourse: Fragments. Cape.

Bede, t. V. S. (2010). *History of the English church and people* (L. Sherley-Price, Ed.). Folio Society.

Berkowitz, E. (2012). *Sex and punishment.* Counterpoint Publishing.

Bhogal, M. S., Tudor, C., & Hira, S. (2021). The role of mating-relevant factors in the perpetration of digital dating abuse. *Journal of Interpersonal Violence, 37*(15–16), NP13707–NP13728. https://doi.org/10.1177/08862605211004103

Bleibtreu-Ehrenberg, G. (1990). Pederasty among primitives: institutionalized initiation and cultic prostitution. *Journal of Homosexuality, 20*(1-2), 13–30. https://doi.org/10.1300/J082v20n01_03

Bogaert, A. F., & Brotto, L. A. (2014). Object of desire self-consciousness theory. *Journal of Sex Marital Therapy, 40(*4), 323–338. https://doi.org/10.1080/0092623X.2012.756841

Boule, J. P. (2010-11). Beauvoir, Sartre, and generous passion. *Simone de Beauvoir Studies, 27,* 24–31. https://www.jstor.org/stable/45237626

Brede, J., Babb, C., Jones, C., Elliott, M., Zanker, C., Tchanturia, K., . . . Mandy, W. (2020). "For me, the anorexia is just a symptom, and the cause is the autism": Investigating restrictive eating disorders in autistic women. *Journal of Autism and Development Disorders, 50*(12), 4280–4296. https://doi.org/10.1007/s10803-020-04479-3

Brown, N. B., Peragine, D., VanderLaan, D. P., Kingstone, A., & Brotto, L. A. (2021). Cognitive processing of sexual cues in asexual individuals and heterosexual women with desire/arousal difficulties. *PLoS ONE, 16*(5), e0251074. https://doi.org/10.1371/journal.pone.0251074

Burfoot, A., & Güngör, D., (2021). The social control of reproduction. In A. Burfoot & D. Güngör (Eds.), *Women and reproductive technologies* (pp. 44–69). Routledge.

Childs, G. (2021). The Tibetan stem family in historical perspective. *The History of the Family, 26(*3), 482–505. https://doi.org/10.1080/1081602X.2021.1940238

Cook, C. L., Krems, J. A., & Kenrick, D. T. (2021). Fundamental motives illuminate a broad range of individual and cultural variations in thought and behavior. *Current Directions in Psychological Science, 30*(3), 242–250. https://doi.org/10.1177/0963721421996690

de Beauvoir, S. (1984). *She came to stay.* Flamingo. (Original work published 1943)

de Beauvoir, S. (1992). *The prime of life.* Marlowe and Co.

de Beauvoir, S. (1999). *The Mandarins:* W.W. Norton.

de Beauvoir, S. (1949). *The second sex.* Random House.

Dickens, B. M. (2018). Management of intersex newborns: Legal and ethical developments. *International Journal of Gynecology and Obstetrics, 143*(2), 255–259. https://doi.org/10.1002/ijgo.12573

Dyble, M., Salali, G. D., Chaudhary, N., Page, A., Smith, D., Thompson, J., ... Migliano, A. B. (2015). Sex equality can explain the unique social structure of hunter–gatherer bands. *Science, 348*(6236), 796–798. doi:10.1126/science.aaa5139

Eliot, L., Ahmed, A., Khan, H., & Patel, J. (2021). Dump the "dimorphism": Comprehensive synthesis of human brain studies reveals few male–female differences beyond size. *Neuroscience and Biobehavioral Reviews, 125*, 667–697. https://doi.org/10.1016/j.neubiorev.2021.02.026

Ferrarello, S. (2019a). Existential sexuality and intimacy. *Journal of Constructivist Psychology, 32(*2), 148–159. https://doi.org/10.1080/10720537.2018.1461716

Ferrarello, S. (2019b). *The phenomenology of sex, love, and intimacy.* Routledge.

Fine, C. (2010). *Delusions of gender.* Icon Books.

Foucault, M. (1997). The battle for chastity. In P. Rabinow (Ed.), *Ethics, subjectivity and truth: The essential works of Foucault, 1954–1984* (Vol. 1, pp. 185–197). Penguin.

Freud, S. (1912). Über die allgemeinste Erniedrigung des iebeslebens [The most prevalent form of degradation in erotic life]. Jahrbuch für Psychoanalytische und Psychopathologische Forschungen, 4, 40–50.

Fullbrook, E. (1999). *She came to stay* and *being and nothingness. Hypatia, 14*(4), 50–69. https://www.jstor.org/stable/3810826

Galinsky, A. M., & Sonenstein, F. L. (2011). The association between developmental assets and sexual enjoyment among emerging adults. *Journal Of Adolescent Health, 48,* 610–615. https://doi.org/10.1016/j.jadohealth.2010.09.008

Garcia, J. R., Reiber, C., Massey, S. G., & Merriwether, A. M. (2012). Sexual hookup culture: A review. *Review of General Psychology, 16*(2), 161–176. https://doi.org/10.1037/a0027911

Garff, J. (2005). *Søren Kierkegaard: A biography.* Princeton University Press.

Google_books_Ngram_viewer. (2022). Sexuality. https://books.google.com/ngrams/graph?content=sexuality&year_start=1960&year_end=2019&corpus=26&smoothing=3

Hartmann, M. (2017). A comedy we believe in: A further look at Sartre's theory of emotions. *European Journal of Philosophy, 25*(1), 144–172. https://doi.org/10.1111/ejop.12160

Hartmann, U. (2009). Sigmund Freud and his impact on our understanding of male sexual dysfunction. *The Journal of Sexual Medicine, 6*(8), 2332–2339. https://doi.org/10.1111/j.1743-6109.2009.01332.x

Herbenick, D., Fu, T. C., Wright, P., Paul, B., Gradus, R., Bauer, J., & Jones, R. (2020). Diverse sexual behaviors and pornography use: Findings from a nationally representative probability survey of Americans aged 18 to 60 years. *Journal of Sexual Medicine, 17(*4), 623–633. https://doi.org/10.1016/j.jsxm.2020.01.013

Hughes, S. M., Aung, T., Harrison, M. A., LaFayette, J. N., & Gallup, G. G., Jr. (2021). Experimental evidence for sex differences in sexual variety preferences: Support for the Coolidge effect in humans. *Archives of Sexual Behavior, 50*(2), 495–509. https://doi.org/10.1007/s10508-020-01730-x

Jaspers, K. (1919). *Psychologie der Weltanschauungen.* Springer.

Jelinek, E., & Hulse, M. (1992). *Lust.* Serpent's Tail.

Jensen, R. T. (2009). Motor intentionality and the case of Schneider. *Phenomenology and the Cognitive Sciences, 8*(3), 371–388. https://doi.org/10.1007/s11097-009-9122-x

Karkazis, K. (2019). The misuses of "biological sex." *The Lancet, 394*(10212), 1898–1899. https://doi.org/10.1016/S0140-6736(19)32764-3

Kierkegaard, S. (1999). *Diary of a seducer* (A. Hannay, Trans.) Pushkin Press.

Kierkegaard, S. (2009). *Repetition and philosophical crumbs* (M. G. Piety, Trans.). Oxford University Press.

Koestenbaum, P. (1974). *Existential sexuality.* Prentice-Hall.

Legeard, E. (2001). *Le Narrataire.* Presses Universitaires de Lille.

Lentz, A. M., & Zaikman, Y. (2021). The big "O": Sociocultural influences on orgasm frequency and sexual satisfaction in women. *Sexuality and Culture, 25*(3), 1096–1123. doi:10.1007/s12119-020-09811-8

Marion, J.-L. (2007). *The erotic phenomenon.* University of Chicago Press.

Mercer, C. H., Tanton, C., Prah, P., Erens, B., Sonnenberg, P., Clifton, S., . . . Johnson, A. M. (2013). Changes in sexual attitudes and lifestyles in Britain through the life course and over time: Findings from the National Surveys of Sexual Attitudes and Lifestyles (Natsal). *The Lancet, 382*(9907), 1781–1794. https://doi.org/10.1016/S0140-6736(13)62035-8

Merleau-Ponty, M. (1962). *Phenomenology of perception.* Routledge. (Original work published 1945)

Meston, C. M., & Buss, D. M. (2007). Why humans have sex. *Archives of Sexual Behavior 36*(4), 477–507. https://doi.org/10.1007/s10508-007-9175-2

Ovid. (8). Metamorphoses. Delaware: Petry in translation.

Plato. (2005). *Symposium.* Penguin.

Sartre, J.-P. (2003). *Being and nothingness: An essay on phenomenological ontology.* Routledge. (Original work published 1943)

Sartre, J.-P. (1963). *Saint Genet : Actor and martyr.* Braziller. (Original work published in 1952)

Sartre, J.-P. (1971). *The family idiot: Gustave Flaubert 1821–1857.* University of Chicago Press.

Sartre, J. P. (1971). *Sketch for a theory of the emotions.* Methuen and Co.

Sax, L. (2002). How common is intersex? A response to Anne Fausto-Sterling. *Journal of Sexual Research, 39*(3), 174–178. https://www.jstor.org/stable/3813612

Scheler, M. (1954). *The nature of sympathy.* Archon.

Scruton, R. (1986). *Sexual desire: A philosophical investigation.* Weidenfeld and Nicolson.

Spinoza, B. d. (2000). *Ethics* (G. H. R. Parkinson, Trans). Oxford University Press.

Stein, E. (1964). The problem of empath (W. Stein, Trans.). The Hague: Martinus Nijhoff. (Original work published 1916)

Stoller, R. J. (1970a). Pornography and perversity. *Archives of General Psychiatry, 22,* 490-499. doi: 10.1001/archpsyc.1970.0174030001000

Stoller, R. J. (1970b). "The transsexual boy: mother's feminized phallus." *British Journal of Medical Psychology, 43*(2), 117-128. https://doi.org/10.1111/j.2044-8341.1970.tb02110.x

Stoller, R. J. (1991). Eros and polis: What is this thing called love? *Journal of the American Psychoanalytic Association., 39,* 1065-1102. https://doi.org/10.1177/0003065191039004

Stoller, R. J. & Herdt, G. H. (1985) Theories of origins of male homosexuality. *Archives of General Psychiatry, 42,* 399–404. https://doi.org/10.1001/archpsyc.1985.01790270089010

Tantam, D. (2002). *Psychotherapy and counselling in practice.* Cambridge University Press.

Tantam, D. (2003). The flavour of emotions. *Psychology and Psychotherapy, 76*(1), 23–45. https://doi.org/10.1348/14760830260569229

Tantam, D. (2012). *Autism spectrum disorders through the life span.* Jessica Kingsley Publishers.

Tantam, D. (2017). *The interbrain.* Jessica Kingsley.

Tavris, C. (2022). Bateman is bunk. Evolution and the sexually adventurous female. *Times Literary Supplement* (22 April 2022), 10–12.

Vandenberghe, F. (2008). Sociology of the heart. *Theory, Culture & Society, 25*(3), 17–51. https://doi.org/10.1177/0263276408090656

Ward, J. (1999). Reciprocity and friendship in Beauvoir's thought. *Hypatia, 14*, 36–49. https://www.jstor.org/stable/3810825

Weitzman, A., & Mallory, A. B. (2019). Racial, socioeconomic, and attitudinal disparities in trajectories of young women's willingness to refuse unwanted sex. *Journal of Adolescent Health, 54*, 746–775. https://doi.org/10.1016/j.jadohealth.2018.12.002

Xenophon. *Conversations of Socrates* (Robin Waterfield, Ed.). Penguin.

Zachary, D., & Steinbock, A. (2018). Max Scheler. In E. Zalta (Ed.), *Stanford Encyclopedia of Philosophy.* https://plato.stanford.edu/entries/scheler/

Index

Editor Biographies

Stephen W. Simpson, PhD is a psychologist and Associate Professor in the School of Psychology and Marriage and Family Therapy at Fuller Theological Seminary. He has published a number of articles and books, including *What Women Wish You Knew about Dating: A Single Guy's Guide to Romantic Relationships, Assaulted by Joy: The Redemption of a Cynic,* and *Single Sex Stories: Tales of Unmarried Sexuality and Faith.*

Melissa Racho, PhD is a licensed psychologist in private practice at The Racho Group in Colorado Springs, CO. Using a dynamically informed, existential framework, she provides individual therapy to adolescents and adults, and conducts psychological evaluations for service members and veterans. Dr. Racho serves on the Rocky Mountain Humanistic Counseling and Psychological Association's Continuing Education and Training Committee. In addition to her work in private practice, she founded the Denver Society for Creative Philanthropy. She loves poetry, writing, and hiking, and lives in the mountains with her two young sons.

Brent Dean Robbins, PhD is Professor of Psychology and Director of the PsyD program in Clinical Psychology at Point Park University in Pittsburgh, PA. He has a doctorate in Clinical Psychology from Duquesne University. He is a former President of the Society for Humanistic Psychology (Division 32 of APA), and has served on the Executive Board of the Society for General Psychology (Division 1) and Society for Theoretical and Philosophical Psychology (Division 24). Dr. Robbins is a Fellow of the American Psychological Association, and recipient of the Carmi Harari Early Career Award (Division 32). He is author of *The Medicalized Body and Anesthetic Culture: The Cadaver, the Memorial Body, and the Recovery of Lived Experience* (2018, Palgrave Macmillan).

Louis Hoffman, PhD is a licensed psychologist in private practice and the Executive Director of the Rocky Mountain Humanistic Counseling and Psychological Association. An avid writer, Dr. Hoffman has edited over 20 books and 100 journal articles and book chapters. He has been recognized as a Fellow of the American Psychological Association and six of its divisions (1, 10, 32, 36, 48, 52) and is a recipient of the Rollo May Award of the Society for Humanistic Psychology. Although Dr. Hoffman left full-time academia to pursue private practice, writing, and nonprofit work, he continues to teach at the University of Denver, University of Colorado at Colorado Springs, and Saybrook University. You can find out more about Dr. Hoffman at www.louis-hoffman.com.

Contributor Biographies

Chandler Batchelor, MA holds a BA in psychology and comparative literature and an MA in health humanities, both from the University of North Carolina at Chapel Hill. She is currently working toward completing a PhD in counseling psychology at the University of Memphis. Her clinical interests include trauma work and identity exploration. Her research interests include asexuality, mental illness identity, and how individuals come to adopt certain identity labels to make sense of themselves and navigate their world. Her work has been published in the *Journal for Sex and Relationship Therapy* and on Emory University's peer-reviewed Neuroethics blog.

Sara K. Bridges, PhD is the Co-Director of Training and an Associate Professor of Counselling Psychology at the University of Memphis. Dr. Bridges is also the Co-Director of the Coherence Psychology Institute and a certified trainer and supervisor of Coherence Therapy. She is a recipient of the distinguished Teaching Award for the University of Memphis and an active scholar of constructivism and sexuality. Dr Bridges has co-edited the five-volume *Studies in the Meaning* series. She is a past president of both the Constructivist Psychology Network and the Society of Humanistic Psychology (Division 32 of the American Psychological Association). Dr. Bridges is also a licensed psychologist in Tennessee and New York, with a distance based private practice.

Kathleen M. Collins, PhD earned her doctorate in clinical psychology from the University of Massachusetts Boston. She has published numerous articles and book chapters related to qualitative methods, psychotherapy process, and mental health concerns of sexual and gender minority individuals. She currently specializes in providing affirmative psychotherapy to sexual and gender minority clients at Psychology Specialists of Maine.

Callum E. Cooper is a chartered psychologist with the British Psychological Society (BPS) and a Fellow of the Higher Education Academy (HEA), holding postgraduate degrees in psychology, social science research methods and education, from the University of Northampton, Sheffield Hallam University and Manchester Metropolitan University. He has a long-time association with the University of Northampton and is based there as a senior lecturer in psychology, delivering classes and conducting research on death and bereavement, positive psychology, human sexual behavior, parapsychology, and research methods.

Micah Ingle, PhD is a part-time instructor in Psychology at the University of West Georgia and Point Park University. His recent work addresses individualism and neoliberalism in the practice of psychology, as well as the ameliorative potential of group work. More broadly, he is interested in liberation psychology, critical masculinities/gender theory, and Continental philosophy—particularly phenomenology, hermeneutics, and poststructuralism. Micah works for Mad in America where he covers research exposing the underside of mainstream psychology and psychiatry. He also currently serves as Communications Chair for both the Society for Theoretical and Philosophical Psychology (APA Division 24) and the Society for Humanistic Psychology (APA Division 32).

Stanley Krippner, PhD has held faculty appointments at Akamai University, Fordham University, Kent State University, New York University, Saybrook University, Sofia University, and the California Institute for Integral Studies. He has received lifetime achievement awards from the Parapsychological Association, the International Association for the Study of Dreams, and the Society for Humanistic Psychology. Krippner is a Fellow of the American Psychological Association, which granted him its 2002 Award for Distinguished Contributions to the International Development of Psychology. He is co-author of the award-winning book *Personal Mythology*, and co-editor of the award-winning book *Varieties of Anomalous Experience* and has published over 1,000 peer-reviewed articles.

Heidi M. Levitt, PhD is a Professor in Psychology at the University of Massachusetts Boston. She is incoming Editor for *Qualitative Psychology* and has been an Associate Editor for the journals *Psychotherapy Research* and *Qualitative Psychology* and is a past president of the Society of Qualitative Inquiry in Psychology. An advocate for pluralistic methodologies, she chaired the development of the SQIP recommendations for reviewing and designing qualitative research and of the qualitative and mixed methods APA journal article reporting standards. Her research programs focus on psychotherapy research, especially on clients' experiences and therapists' intentionality, on LGBTQ+ gender identities and communities, and on healing from stigma-related events. In addition to her research, Dr. Levitt teaches students to conduct experiential therapies and is a licensed psychologist. She adopts an integrative approach to psychotherapy and intervention development rooted in constructivist, humanistic, and feminist-multicultural orientations but drawing on psychodynamic and cognitive–behavioral conceptualizations.

Zenobia Morrill, PhD is an Assistant Professor in the Clinical Psychology Department at William James College. Her research interests include critical and liberation psychology, psychotherapy, qualitative methods, and decoloniality. She also serves as the Senior Research Associate of the Psychology Humanities and Ethics Center at Boston College; Fellow of the American Psychoanalytic

Association; and as a board member of the Society for Theoretical and Philosophical Psychology (STPP) and the Society for Qualitative Inquiry in Psychology (SQIP). She is an Editorial Board member for the Psychology and the Other Book Series and the *Journal of Humanistic Psychology*.

Brent Dean Robbins, PhD is Professor of Psychology and Director of the PsyD program in Clinical Psychology at Point Park University in Pittsburgh, PA. He has a doctorate in clinical psychology from Duquesne University. He is a former president of the Society for Humanistic Psychology (Division 32 of APA) and has served on the Executive Board of the Society for General Psychology (Division 1) and Society for Theoretical and Philosophical Psychology (Division 24). Dr. Robbins is a Fellow of the American Psychological Association, and recipient of the Carmi Harari Early Career Award (Division 32). He is author of *The Medicalized Body and Anesthetic Culture: The Cadaver, the Memorial Body, and the Recovery of Lived Experience* (2018, Palgrave Macmillan).

Steve Speer is a researcher operating out of New York City.

Digby Tantam, PhD, MPH, FRCPsych, BA, is Emeritus Professor of Psychiatry and University of Sheffield, visiting professor of psychology at Middlesex University, and a director of the Existential Academy. He is a group analyst and has published books on autism, neurobiology, psychotherapy, public health and emotional well-being among other topics.

Joel Vos, PhD, CPsychol, FHEA is a psychologist, philosopher, and therapist. He works as a Senior Researcher and Senior Lecturer at the Metanoia Institute in London. He is Director of IMEC International Meaning Events and Community. Dr Vos has published over 160 articles and chapters. His recent books include *The Psychology of COVID-19* (Sage, 2021), *The Economics of Meaning in Life* (University Professors Press, 2020), *Mental Health in Crisis* (Vos, Roberts & Davies, Sage, 2019), and *Meaning in Life: An Evidence-Based Handbook for Practitioners* (Bloomsbury, 2019). His forthcoming books include *Doing research in psychological therapies: A step-by-step guide* (Sage), and *COVID-19 and Beyond: Psychological, Existential and Therapeutic Perspectives on mental health and meaning* (Vos, Russo-Netzer & Schulenberg, University Professors Press). Dr Vos's recent research focuses on clinical trials, systematic reviews, meta-analyses, and building evidence-based conceptual models of humanistic and existential therapies, meaning in life, social movements, critical psychology, and social justice. Read more on his personal website: https://joelvos.com.

www.ingramcontent.com/pod-product-compliance
Lightning Source LLC
Chambersburg PA
CBHW080133270326
41926CB00021B/4459